Experimental Archaeology

Experimental Archaeology

JOHN COLES
Reader in European Prehistory
University of Cambridge

1979

ACADEMIC PRESS
A Subsidiary of Harcourt Brace Jovanovich, Publishers

LONDON   NEW YORK   TORONTO   SYDNEY   SAN FRANCISCO

Academic Press Inc. (London) Ltd
24–28 Oval Road
London NW1

US edition published by
Academic Press Inc.
111 Fifth Avenue,
New York, New York 10003

British Library Cataloguing in Publication Data

Coles, John Morton
    Experimental archaeology
    1. Archaeology–Methodology
    I. Title
    930'.1028   CC75   79-41520

    ISBN Casebound edition 0-12-179750-3

    ISBN Paperback Edition 0-12-179752-X

Printed in Great Britain
by Willmer Brothers Limited
Rock Ferry, Merseyside

For MONA

Preface

THE PAST TEN YEARS have witnessed a rapid growth in the field of experimental archaeology, a discipline which approaches archaeological remains in a questioning way, and attempts to understand what ancient man was doing, how he was doing it, and why he was doing it. In the past decade a large number of experimental projects have been devised and set up and, although many of these still remain as single one-off events, others represent the beginnings of longer-term studies. The enormous *Bibliography of Replicative Experiments in Archaeology* published in 1972 by Graham, Heizer and Hester continues to be a useful source for experiments up to about 1970, and my small book, *Archaeology by Experiment*, published in 1973, attempted a survey of the major studies as well as the establishment of some principles of behaviour for experimental archaeology; most of the latter had their origins in earlier pioneering work. The interest shown in the concept of experiment over the past five years, with many new and imaginative projects initiated, and wider circulation of published works in many languages, has prompted this new book.

It represents an attempt, doubtless incomplete and perhaps controversially so, to pick out the major trends in the development of the subject, to applaud some experiments, to criticize others, and totally to ignore many; omissions should not necessarily be taken as judgment against, and certain aspects, particularly lithic technology, with its own specialist publications, probably suffer the most. The choice of work described has to be selective, and has to represent my own interests in archaeological experiments as an important discipline for retrieving and explaining evidence about past human individuals, economies and societies. For shortcomings and omissions, no apologies are offered, except to suggest that the bibliography in this book, supplemented by the lists published in 1972 and 1973, must together provide a near-complete bibliography of experiments published in western languages. Those many experimenters who do not publish results do not appear, of course, and their work must remain unvalued.

The organization of this book takes a fairly traditional approach. The first chapter essays an historical treatment of experimental archaeology, picking out the pioneering souls who often worked alone or in competition with their fellows, questioning the evidence and devising new approaches. Most recognized the importance of fellow ethnographers who provided unique information about the habits and practices of the last survivors of aboriginal and indigenous peoples in the Old and New Worlds. By this pioneering work the foundations of experimental archaeology were laid; and the concluding section of Chapter 1 attempts to enlarge on these beginnings and to define some of the basic principles of the subject.

The following chapters are, I hope, logical in progression, from voyages of discovery and colonization, and land transport, to the establishment of settled communities working the land and providing the first evidence for major building operations in many parts of the world. Primitive and sophisticated arts and crafts are then outlined, with basic inventions in stone, clay and metal described. It will be obvious to the reader that almost all of man's major accomplishments in handling nature's materials were achieved in prehistoric times before the invention of writing; and experimental archaeology goes some way towards a greater understanding of these processes, and of their implications for human societies. Experimental attempts to live "in the past", and logically thereafter to deal with the dead, form the final chapter of the book; here the recent efforts to establish long-term projects involving people in the experiments as well as materials deserve a full assessment. The conclusions sum up the achievements and the potential of experimental archaeology, and stress the huge opportunities that exist for future work. Perhaps unemphasized is the degree of enjoyment that experiments can bring to archaeology, both the mental and physical exhaustion of the task, the satisfaction of the doing, the excitement of discovery. My own personal involvement in experiments with stone, wood, leather, metals and musical instruments has brought all of these.

Many individuals have helped me in compiling information and illustrations for this book; acknowledgements appear in the text and captions, and to all those mentioned, and to many others, I am grateful. My particular thanks go to Gwil Owen for much photographic work, and to my wife Mona for help at all stages of the compilation and writing. I also wish to single out a few people who have been particularly generous in sharing information; all of these have been, and are, engaged in experimental archaeology as a long-term commitment, and they represent more than any others the dedication and inspiration for the future of the subject: Hans-Ole Hansen (Historical-Archaeological Research Center, Lejre, Denmark); Peter Reynolds (Butser Ancient Farm Project, England); R. Horreus de Haas (Ijsselmeer polder, The

Netherlands); Richard Darrah (West Stow Anglo-Saxon Village, England); and Errett Callahan (Pamunkey Project, Virginia, USA). I hope this book will accurately represent to them my firm belief in the value of the subject and in the varying approaches they have adopted for their projects.

JOHN COLES

June 1979

Contents

1 Introduction

Seeking the evidence and experience of life

ARCHAEOLOGY IS THE STUDY of man's past activities, and it includes the examination and assessment of all his requirements for living. These requirements were many and varied; among them were the selection of the land for hunting and farming, the provision of shelter, tools and weapons and the satisfaction of the spiritual needs of the community. Archaeologists use many techniques in their attempts to understand how ancient man lived, and why he behaved as he did; these methods include a great variety of procedures for the discovery and excavation of sites, for the analysis and arrangement of data, for the dating of various cultural groups, and for help in interpreting all of the evidence. Whether the archaeologist is considered to be a scientist or a humanist, whether archaeology itself is a science or an arts subject, matters little because it is one subject that strikes across artificial boundaries, and which seeks to unite those studies which bear upon the origin and the physical and cultural development of man. Archaeology seeks the evidence and experience of life, in the hope and the knowledge that by so doing mankind will better understand why life is as it is, and why man behaves as he does.

One way in which archaeology can reach back and experience some parts of ancient life is through attempts to reproduce former conditions and circumstances. By trying to make and use some of the weapons and tools of the past we can often gain an insight into the importance of these objects to their original inventors and owners. By building copies of houses, palisades, and fortresses we can appreciate better the scale of ancient enterprise, and the organization of labour required. By constructing and using replicas of boats and wagons we can understand the problems of communication and colonization in early times. And by trying to actually live as our ancestors did, by experiencing the concerns of the past, we may become aware of our prehistory, of past problems concerned with food supplies and shelter, and of the inventive nature of man.

Archaeologists who are concerned with these aspects of human society may direct their energies to the laboratory analysis of material, or the typological arrangement of the artifacts; others may devote more time to the discovery and excavation of ancient settlements or cemeteries. Rather fewer will be concerned with the construction of models, and theories, about the evolution of particular groups, and about how such societies operated within their territories. Yet all of these archaeologists can benefit from participation in the growing field of experimental archaeology, a study designed to look at ancient man as an inventor, a technician, a craftsman, an artist, and a human being. By reproducing his actions archaeologists can better understand not only his technical abilities but also his reasons for choosing one course of action rather than another. This is the kind of information which all archaeologists seek, the meaning behind the surviving relics.

As a subject, archaeology has only a recent history. It is difficult to believe today that only a century ago archaeology had limited recognition as a discipline, and that in a majority of minds the great antiquity and prehistory of man was little more than a disturbing rumour. In the middle of the nineteenth century, several major events had combined to convert a number of scientists and others into the acknowledgement of human evolution and antiquity. Charles Darwin's *On the Origin of the Species* (1859) provided a basis for much subsequent work that indicated man's long biological evolution, and his close relationship with the primates. Geologists had already begun to insist that the physical world could only represent the results of enormously long natural geological processes, and that therefore the earth had a great antiquity; Sir Charles Lyell's *The Geological Evidences of the Antiquity of Man* (1863) set out the new claims firmly and persuasively. In the same decades, the idea that man could have had an existence before written history was being actively discussed. The word prehistory was already in existence; it had been coined by Daniel Wilson in *The Archaeology and Prehistoric Annals of Scotland* (1851). The revolution in thought was furthered by Sir John Lubbock in his book *Pre-Historic Times as Illustrated by Ancient Remains and the Manners and Customs of Modern Savages* (1865); he was one of the first to suggest that modern societies might well provide a guide to extinct communities from the way they lived and worked. It was a time of great curiosity about man, and amazement at the wealth of evidence about him that could be observed. The discoveries of Boucher de Perthes in the Valley of the Somme River in northern France were investigated in 1858–59, and applauded by notable antiquarians and geologists. De Perthes had retrieved many chipped flint tools from the gravel banks and terraces of the river, and these tools were accepted as showing human design and workmanship; as they were found in ancient geological deposits, dating to remote periods when the river was flowing at much higher levels than it was in the nineteenth century, these discoveries also helped to prove the antiquity of man.

All of these events combined to persuade many scientists, antiquarians among them, that the earth was untold thousands of years old, perhaps millions, and that man as a tool-maker had been present for part of this long period. These views, accepted today by a majority of people (but certainly not by all) went against the traditional position which had been based upon biblical countback from the birth of Christ back through the generations to Adam and Eve, and the Creation. The absolute and undisputed record of the earth's history calculated by Archbishop Ussher, and printed in many bibles, placed the Creation in the year 4004 B.C., and subsequent elaborations put the actual moment at 9 a.m. on October 23 in that year! All the new and revolutionary evidence about man's ancestry and his great antiquity went against the biblical ideas of man's perfect creation and his subsequent fall from grace, as well as his short time on earth.

Well before the crucial decades 1850–70, however, antiquarians, governments and bandits had begun to gather from the soil the remains of ancient civilizations. Sometimes for curiosity alone, often for deliberate sale to collectors, the eighteenth and early nineteenth centuries saw the destruction of innumerable monuments and their contained relics and treasures. Some artifacts found their way into private, then public, collections, and they form the basis of many of the national museums throughout the world today. The first efforts to arrange these collections in a coherent pattern were based not only upon technical examination of the objects, but also upon ethnographic evidence obtained by the many explorers active during the nineteenth century. In 1813, the Danish scholar Vedel-Simonsen wrote, "The weapons and implements of the earliest inhabitants of Scandinavia were at first of stone and wood. These folk later learnt the use of copper . . . and only latterly, it would appear, iron." By 1819 the National collection in Copenhagen was arranged in the three-age system, a Stone Age, a Bronze Age and an Iron Age. This system is still perpetuated in the treatment of collections today, and it forms a useful guide and indication of materials and technology.

The two nineteenth-century themes most relevant to the field of experimental archaeology were those of technical curiosity about individual objects, and ethnographic recording of existing communities in many parts of the world. In attempting to recognize, retrieve and study objects of stone, bone, wood and metal, antiquarians and archaeologists conducted experiments on raw materials, techniques of production, and methods of use; a few of these are described below. Of greater value to the development of archaeology as a whole were the multitude of observations on native indigenous societies recorded by explorers, missionaries and early colonists and settlers. Such ethnographic surveys continue today, but there can be few communities now totally untouched and unaltered by twentieth-century developments that purport to improve the way of life of all men and women.

Most nineteenth-century archaeologists realized that the pre-industrial communities represented a vast source of data about material equipment and living habits that could be of use to those who studied extinct societies. Lubbock wrote in *The Origin of Civilization and the Primitive Condition of Man* (1870) that "the weapons and implements now used by the lower races of men throw much light on the signification and use of those discovered in ancient tumuli, or in the drift gravels; . . . a knowledge of modern savages and their modes of life enables us more accurately to picture, and more vividly to conceive, the manners and customs of our ancestors in bygone ages." There can be no doubt about the value of such knowledge as it provides a guide to habits and practices of earlier peoples; however, too rigid comparison and analogies drawn between a surviving pre-industrial group and an extinct community must be recognized as unscientific, untenable and invalid. The use of ethnographic analogy is accepted today as providing a general guide only, or a range of possibilities, but not a definite set of answers about the precise manufacture or use of a tool, or the social organization of a community now extinct and leaving no written record. The ethnographic record itself demonstrates the enormous variation in human practices and processes which existed as much in the past as they do today.

One of the earliest accounts of the lives of pre-industrial indigenous peoples was made by John White, Elizabethan explorer in Virginia; his descriptions, and vivid illustrations, of the villages, ceremonies, and hunting and farming activities of the Indians of Pomeiock have provided a major source of information (Fig. 1), particularly as he was writing in 1600 when cultural contact between Europeans and Indians was still slight. His description of arrowhead manufacture by the Virginian Indians was brief but explicit: "His arrowhead he quickly maketh with a little bone, which he ever weareth at his bracert, of any splint of a stone, or glasse in the form of a heart, and these they glew to the end of their arrowes."

Many other explorers, colonists and missionaries recorded their observations and reactions to the almost unbelievable variety of human activities practised in the continents of Asia, Africa and America, and some were not averse to fabrication in order to fascinate their readers and listeners. The opportunity to observe, however, was in effect both the first and the last chance. Almost as soon as contacts were made between Europeans and indigenous peoples, the losses began, both deliberately and accidentally. In 1792, the fifth mate on board the fur-trading vessel *Columbia*, plying its trade on the west coast of Vancouver Island, Canada, recorded in his diary on 27 March:

I am sorry to be under the necessity of remarking that this day I was sent with three boats, all well man'd and arm'd, to destroy the Village of Opitsatah (Clayoquot) it was a command I was no ways tenacious off, and am greived to think Capt. Gray shou'd let his passions go so far. This village was about half a mile in Diameter and Contained upwards of 200 Houses, generally well built for Indians ev'ry door that you enter'd was in resemblance to a human and Beasts head, the passage being through the mouth, besides which there was much more rude carved work about the dwellings some of which was by no means inelegant. This fine village, the Work of Ages, was in a short time totally destroy'd.

Fig. 1. "The town of Pomeiock". Drawing by John White (1585). Representations such as this provide a unique source of information about ancient settlements, and a guide to archaeologists in their efforts to retrieve and interpret evidence about past, extinct, human activities. See Fig. 47 for an interpretation based on historic records, and Fig. 48 for modern experimental reconstructions. (Reproduced in Cumming *et al.*, 1971, p. 197; courtesy of Trustees of the British Museum.)

Throughout the decades of observation and recording of data about ancient practices and habits, there run the white man's unthinking comments and inference about his own greater technical ability, his more stable way of life, and his general superiority. Time has revealed how inadequate was this patronizing viewpoint. As ethnographic recording went on, so too did both exploring and colonizing, and accompanying these latter went unimaginable destruction of unique monuments, records and traditions of indigenous groups in Africa, America and Australasia. The rifling of tombs and the looting of temples and strongholds were sufficiently destructive, but far worse were the deliberate extinctions of societies. When we speak of lack of information about particular pre-historic customs and habits, it is worth remembering that these losses were only a part, and a small part, of the loss to human society as a whole.

> We were entertained with all love, and kindness, and with as much bountie, after their manner, as they could possibly devise. We found the people most gentle, loving, and faithfull, void of all guile, and treason, and such as lived after the manner of the golden age.
> *The voyage of Philip Amadas and Arthur Barlowe to Virginia*, 1589

> They told us they only wanted a little land, as much as a wagon would take between the wheels. You can see now what it was they wanted.
> Black Elk, *c.* 1850

The culmination of this episode in North America, and the last opportunity to record aboriginal Indian traditions, occurred in California in 1865. A small group of Indians, the Yahi, living in the foothills of the Sierra Nevada, continued to practise their hunter–gatherer way of life, without agriculture or domesticated animals, although most of their territory was already utilized by white settlers. The inevitable conflict had a predictable result: the eventual slaughter of almost every Yahi in an encounter in 1865. A few survived in the desolate country of the chaparral, until in 1908, only 70 years ago, their camp was discovered by accident; all of their equipment, not a single item of which was modern, was removed by the discoverers, leaving the Yahi destitute. The last surviving member was found in 1911 (Fig. 2), and was eventually "adopted" by two anthropologists. He was apparently forbidden by his customs to speak his own name, and so he was called Ishi, the name for "man" in his own language. Ishi taught the anthropologists and others to flake flints, to make tools and weapons, to trap and to hunt and to gather; he identified hundreds of plants used in the past by his tribe, and he told of the traditions, the taboos and the organization of his people. Without Ishi, archaeologists would have lost perhaps 90 per cent of the information of this particular society. He died of tuberculosis in 1916, the last of his kind; his story is full of compassion, humour and frightfulness (Kroeber, 1961).

America was not the only continent where policies of extermination were operated, and the pursuit of the Bushmen in southern Africa, the Aborigines in Australia, and the total elimination of the Tasmanians in

1877, were no less reprehensible. Writing in the early twentieth century, W. J. Sollas pointed out that even where attempts had been made to protect the surviving remnants of indigenous tribes, "the white man's civilization proved scarcely less fatal than the white man's bullet". Sollas himself relied upon ethnographic information in interpreting prehistoric societies of the Stone Age; his book *Ancient Hunters and their modern representatives* made one-for-one comparisons between particular pre-

Fig. 2. Ishi, "the last surviving wild Indian in North America", at the time of his capture at Oroville, California, on August 29, 1911 (Lowie Museum of Anthropology, University of California, Berkeley).

historic communities and modern societies such as the Aborigines of Australia which he called "the Mousterians of the Antipodes". Such analogies were unfounded, in fact, in geography, in cultural development and in objective scientific terms.

The work of Ishi, the Californian Indian, in fashioning an arrowhead of flint or obsidian, was carefully recorded in 1916, and similar observations were made by many ethnographers and archaeologists in the late nineteenth century (Fig. 3); some of these are noted below, but part of Ishi's technique is described here in order to make the point that even a simple implement of stone requires not only an understanding of the

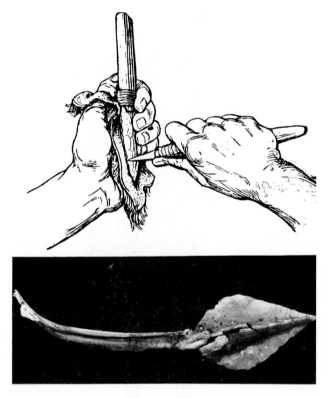

Fig. 3. *Upper*. Pressure flaking a flint point with a bone tool—one of many pressure techniques used by American Indians to produce symmetrical sharp arrowheads and other projectiles (after Holmes, 1919).

Lower. Flint arrowhead in part of its original wooden shaft, from Fyvie, Aberdeenshire, Scotland. Of the thousands of arrowheads discovered in both Old and New Worlds, only in a few cases have the wooden shafts survived. Length of arrowhead 4 cm, date *c*. 2000 B.C. (Courtesy of Anthropological Museum, University of Aberdeen.)

material and its theoretical properties, but an experience born only of tradition or long experimentation. The recording was done by Nels Nelson who produced a unique document outlining the general flint-knapping procedures and the particular tricks employed by Ishi. The advantage of this record over many others made in the late nineteenth century was that Ishi could be asked to explain the reasons for his actions and the consequences of changing his technique, and he could repeat the work again and again. Ishi first broke up the obsidian block to obtain long thin flakes, using a bone punch. Then he placed a flake on a piece of hide which he held in one hand; he pressed the wood or bone flaker against first one edge then another, turning the flake over often. Nelson comments:

Not having experimented very much, I am unable to say why Ishi proceeds as he does but he gets results which I cannot imitate try as I will. Ishi removes thin and fairly slender chips that extend two-thirds or more across the face of the flake, while my chips are thick and short. Consequently his arrowpoints when finished are thin and shapely, while mine, much to his disgust, are thick and clumsy affairs.

Nelson, 1916

Many other explorers and ethnographers were at work in the late nineteenth century, and records were made of flint, obsidian and glass flaking techniques used by indigenous African and Australian craftsmen. At first it seems remarkable that the techniques of pressure-flaking were so uniform throughout the world; obviously the properties of stone were well understood by those who relied upon it for their tools and weapons. Many of the ethnographers themselves became proficient in stone-knapping and their descriptions of the processes of flaking arrowheads in particular were the unique result of comparing experimental data with observed technologies practised by many aboriginal groups.

Consolulu, a Cloud River Indian, was watched by B. Reading, an anthropologist, in 1879 as he made obsidian arrowheads in the same way as Ishi did some thirty years later. H. Balfour recorded the same procedures in 1903 by Australian aborigines who used bottle glass and telegraph insulators to make their pressure-flaked arrowheads. The story, perhaps exaggerated, told that the only way the men installing the telegraph lines could ensure that the glass insulators were not removed by the natives was to leave a handy deposit of glass bottles at the base of each telegraph pole.

In addition to the many valuable reports about aboriginal flaking techniques in Australia, America and Asia, there was some rivalry among experimental archaeologists in their own proficiencies. F. H. Cushing, whom we shall meet later, worked among the south-western Indians in the United States and carried out a vast number of experiments. He claimed to be able to make an arrowhead by percussion flaking and pressure in under two minutes, which compared very favourably with Consolulu who took 40 minutes. Sir John Evans, writing in 1897 about arrowheads and pressure flaking, commented rather sourly: "Mr Cushing has described the process and claims to be the first civilized man who flaked an arrow-head with horn tools. This was in 1875. I had already done so and had described the method at the Norwich Congress in 1868." Apart from the disputable comment about "the first civilized man", Evans also seemed to overlook Cushing's inference in his own report of 1895 that he had discovered the technique, by accident, in about 1850.

There was much interest in the European flint mines which were churning out gun-flints in the later nineteenth century; the percussion techniques used by the gun-flint makers were carefully observed by Evans and others in 1860–70, and they noted with some amazement that the average weekly output for the 20 men at Brandon in Norfolk was 200,000 gun-flints and strike-a-lights. This suggests a rate of 3 per minute which is a remarkable performance over a long period of time. Metal hammers were employed, and a thriving sideline of the business was the production of small flint figures, in the form of capital letters, hearts and other tokens of esteem; entwined hearts made an impressive gift, so long as the recipient forgot they were of stone (Fig. 4).

Many thousands of other flint objects were also made by Victorian craftsmen in England, and by their contemporaries in America, and the products were not so easily recognized as being of modern manufacture. With the collection of ancient stone relics so popular in the nineteenth century, a thriving trade was set up by flint-knappers who could turn out replicas of prehistoric tools for sale, not as replicas but as the real thing. The most notorious of these craftsmen was Edward Simpson, alias "Flint Jack" (Blacking, 1953).

Born in 1815, he worked and travelled throughout England, and his ability as a flint-knapper was recognized by many. He supplied artifacts to those who were prepared to pay for them, and did not disguise from the few scientists who befriended him that he readily forged whatever was required. He did not do well in Scotland, as he found the Scots "too cannie", but in Ireland he forged and sold many axes, arrowheads, hammers and spearheads. He also did well in Cambridge, and in London he "found the demand for celts and other flint implements fully up to the measure of his power to manufacture them". Eventually exposed, he became an outcast, turned by necessity to crime and died unlamented. His extraordinary powers of working flint and stone were never fully recorded, and his skills in direct percussion techniques have probably never been surpassed. He does not seem to have used pressure-flaking in his work;

he used only hard hammers, mostly iron, and believed that the technique which produced the long flat scars on ancient arrowheads had been lost forever: "No man alive can do it: it is a barbarous art that is lost. I know the nature of flint as well as any man but I can't do that." He may well have known flint better than anyone, but the art of pressure-flaking had not been lost as we have seen. Many in America could produce the characteristic arrowheads, and in Britain there were several who had devised the technique. W. J. Knowles (1903) observed one forger in Ireland who made arrowheads by pressure, using his cloth coat instead of buckskin, and a stone flaker instead of antler, wood or bone. And one English forger produced pressure-flaked glass and flint arrowheads using the ivory handle of a lady's button-hook. The trade in such antiquities in both America and Europe must have been enormous, and many museums probably contain considerable quantities of these late nineteenth century masterpieces.

FIG. 4. A love token produced in flint by a Brandon knapper. Width *c.* 3 cm. (Photo: G. Owen, University Museum of Archaeology and Anthropology, Cambridge.)

Well before this time experimental archaeology had had its tentative beginnings. A definition of the subject will be suggested later in this chapter, but if we accept that any honest effort to understand ancient

artifacts by actually working with them represents experimental archaeology, then the earliest work was long underway by 1850. These early
archaeological experiments were carried out, not on the ubiquitous flints
and obsidians, but on a different material, bronze. The first of the experiments was disastrous in terms of the material tested, and soon after,
another test was equally destructive of the experimenter.

In 1768, a bronze musical instrument called a *carnyx* was dredged from
the river Witham in Lincolnshire, England (Piggott, 1959). This was
apparently almost intact and if it had survived it would today be unique;
no complete *carnyx* has ever been recovered. The report of the find from
the Witham appeared in 1796, when a careful examination of the *carnyx*
had been made. The character of the horn as a musical instrument is best
shown by representations on the Gundestrup cauldron from Denmark

FIG. 5. *Carnyx*-blowers depicted on the Gundestrup silver cauldron, Denmark,
c. 100 B.C. The artist has shown the instruments either with curved mouthtubes, or
with obliquely angled mouthpieces, probably the latter. As musical instruments they
would leave much to be desired, but in appearance and noise were undoubtedly
effective. (National Museum, Copenhagen.)

(Fig. 5), and by historical comments on its performance made by Polybius
in describing the Celts at war:

And the parade and the tumult of the army of the Celts terrified the Romans;
for there was amongst them an infinite number of horns and trumpets, which,
with the shouts of the whole army in concert, made a clamour so terrible and
loud, that every surrounding echo was awakened, and all the adjacent country
seemed to join in the horrible din.

The Witham *carnyx* was made of a sheet of beaten bronze, 1·5 mm thick, with a tin solder holding the edges and joints together. Not content with providing posterity with a description like this, the specialist Dr George Pearson, acting for the owner Sir Joseph Banks, continued his work by experimenting with the *carnyx*. In order to compare the metal of the instrument with other samples of known bronze compositions, Pearson decided that "to judge accurately from these appearances the metals to be compared with one another should be in the same state of aggregation ... I therefore melted the old implements, and cast them in the same ingot mould ... each of these ingots was fractured by a pretty smart stroke with a hammer."

We can only say that experimental archaeology is rarely so destructive of its materials, while commending Pearson on his enthusiasm, and Banks on his co-operation. Worse was yet to come, but not at once.

One year after Pearson's experiments were published, the first Bronze Age musical instruments from Denmark were recovered from their resting place in moorland at Brudevaelte, Zealand. Six magnificent horns, later called *lurer*, were found here in 1797 and they formed part of the collection of the National Museum after its formation in 1807. C. J. Thomsen, one of the founders of the Three Age system of prehistoric archaeology, was perhaps the first to experiment with these *lurer*, and he recorded that it was still possible to blow them. His successor, J. J. Worsaae, also recorded his experiments, and in 1843 he wrote: "Several *lurer* are so well preserved that they may still be blown; however the sound is not so dull as one might think; in this respect they may be placed only between a French horn and a trumpet." It is believed that Worsaae's specialist consultant was a trumpeter in the Royal Horse Guards. Subsequently, the *lurer* were tested again in 1893, 1902 and 1947; these results are discussed in Chapter 5.

Contemporary bronze horns have also been found in Ireland, and the first of these was recovered in 1698; when blown, it gave "but a dull, uncouth, heavy sound, that cannot be heard at any distance". In 1809, a larger horn, dated now to the Iron Age, was found at Ardbrin, County Down; the report states that the finder applied his mouth to the tube and produced a gong-like noise which attracted the attention of many people in adjacent townlands. Another horn found in 1827 was blown by a trumpeter of the 23rd Regiment of Dragoons, and the noise could be heard for miles, according to a contemporary account. However, a small controversy soon developed over these accounts, which some claimed had been written into the press cuttings by the editor in order to make good copy. One of the larger horns was apparently tested again, and a great variety of tones were produced, all of a rather low and dull nature.

One particular problem which much taxed the antiquarians of the time was that some of the Irish horns were not normal end-blown instruments, with mouthpiece at the smaller end, but were blown from the side (Fig. 6). In addition, the hole was quite large, much larger than normal, so it was doubly difficult to produce a musical note. In experiments carried out some years before 1860, the investigations proved fatal to one antiquarian, as the contemporary account sadly reports:

It is impossible for any one at the present day to produce a clear musical sound from (the horn), by any amount of exertion . . . , after the greatest effort, the only sound produced is a dull roar which is not heard to any great distance . . . the late Dr. Robert Ball, of Dublin, entertained a different opinion, and believed that trumpets of this construction were really musical instruments. By a strong effort of the lungs and lips, he was able to produce . . . a deep bass note, resembling the bellowing of a bull. And it is a melancholy fact, that the loss of this gentleman's life was occasioned by a subsequent experiment of this kind. In the act of attempting to produce a distinct sound on a large trumpet . . . he burst a blood vessel, and died a few days after.

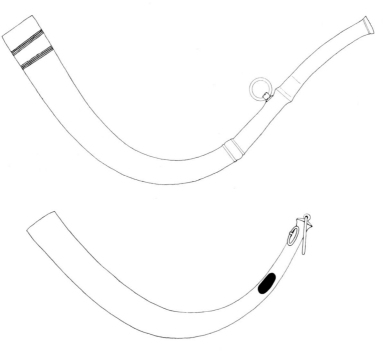

Fig. 6. Bronze horns from Drumbest, Co. Antrim, Ireland, *c.* 700 B.C. The upper horn, 86 cm long, is a normal end-blow type, and can yield 6–8 notes. The lower horn, 64 cm long, is a side-blow type, and the first experiments in blowing a horn of this type proved to be fatally unsuccessful. (Ulster Museum, Belfast; drawings from Coles, 1963.)

Many other objects and materials were subjected to experiments in the late nineteenth century, and these were often combined with ethnographic observations; together they form an important body of evidence for modern experiments on wood, bone, stone, metal and flints.

There was also great interest in human remains, of course, although the experiments upon these were still hampered by religious ideals. Among the many human remains recovered from the excavations of burial grounds in Europe, and elsewhere, there were noted a number of skulls, of varying antiquity, which had had discs of bone removed (Fig. 7). A physician

FIG. 7. Human skulls of the Later Stone Age of northern Europe. Both have been trephined, with a disc or discs removed. The skull on the left has been "shaved" by a sharp flint tool, the blade moving in at a very shallow angle, slicing through the tabula externa, the diploe (spongy bone tissue) and barely into the tabula interna. The skull on the right has had a disc removed by cutting perpendicularly down through the bone, hopefully not slipping through the tabula interna and entering the dura mater (brain membrane). Some Stone Age persons survived the operation, others did not. (National Museum, Copenhagen.)

undertook to experiment with human skulls recently deceased, and he scraped and cut holes in both an adult's and a child's skull; the former required 50 minutes of work with a glass flake, the latter only 4 minutes. Because it was believed that no one could withstand such an operation for almost an hour, the conclusion was that all prehistoric adults had been dead, or died, at the time of their operation for disc removal (Munro, 1897). Since this experimental work was done, further excavation has revealed the skulls of adults who clearly survived trepannation, whose heads had healed before death interrupted. Some ancient skulls had more than one disc removed, each hole healing in turn before the next was opened. The record seems to be 7 discs from one person, by the end of which he must have been very light-headed. Modern ethnographic records also show that the operation is carried out on adults as well as children, and they remain conscious during the work, which takes less than 30 minutes. The operation is carried out to cure the individual of an illness or an obsession, and it must certainly take the mind off the original problem.

The almost universal curiosity about stone tools was a reflection of the white man's own variety of materials—brass, iron, glass, rubber and the like—and his amazement that prehistoric man was able to base almost all of his equipment on the properties of one substance. This in a way was an inaccurate view, but relatively few antiquarians realized it; those who had participated in the recovery of prehistoric organic remains from the lake-muds of Switzerland or the desiccated wooden materials from desert environments, were aware of the widespread use of wood by almost all primitive people, but the sheer disparity in preservation between stone and wood persuaded most archaeologists to concentrate their energies upon the stonework. Thomas Wilson, writing in 1899, summed up the problem then, and it is still with us today:

> Among the hundreds of collectors throughout the United States, where tens of thousands of ancient arrowpoints and spearheads have been collected, we have no record of any of them having been found with handle or shaft attached. This is not strange nor is it peculiar to these implements. The published stone hatchets doubtless had wooden handles, yet of all of the thousands found there have been less than a dozen reported in the United States with their wooden handles.

Yet there were some oustanding finds of ancient wooden artifacts, and some experiments directed towards understanding them. G. V. Smith worked with a stone axe, hafting it in an elm or a beech sleeve, mounted in a maple handle, and he recorded his success in chopping through pine-wood, a thick log requiring over 1500 strokes before it was severed (1893). Others, working in Europe, experimented on oaks and other trees, and a primitive wooden hut was built using only stone axes and bare hands. Some work was also done with flint blades mounted sideways in wooden handles to serve as saws, and John Evans himself experimented on syca-more branches, sawing through these with some difficulty. More sophisticated mortise and tenon joints were made by Smith, using his stone axe as a chisel. The point of it all was to demonstrate that wood, the universal raw material for houses, fences, tools and weapons, was quite easily worked by stone and flint into a multitude of shapes, and that an abandoned and decayed campsite might once have contained a wide range of carved wooden pieces of equipment, but the only surviving element was the ubiquitous stone.

A few wooden arrowshafts survived, however, including a fine specimen found in 1885 in a peatmoss at Fyvie, Aberdeenshire (Fig. 3). This was examined by Joseph Anderson, Keeper of the National Museum of Antiquities of Scotland, and he attempted to replicate the shaft which in the original extended in a smoothly tapering manner up to the point of the flint. Using a set of flint blades, flakes and a hollow scraper (a flake with one edge concave), he cut, thinned, rounded and notched a pine shaft with little difficulty (Anderson, 1886). F. H. Cushing in America also carried out the peeling and shaping of arrowshafts including their straightening in grooved stone slabs after heat or water had been applied to the wood; he was also a proficient knapper of flints, as we have seen, and experimented with the *Atlatl* or throwing stick, and with primitive metallurgy (p. 23).

Of the manufacture of bows, little seems to have been done until Pope, one of Ishi's friends, began work in the early twentieth century. Ethnographic records, however, were taken in the last decades of the nineteenth century, when archery was fast becoming a lost art and the secrets of bow-making were already beyond most young Indians in America. P. H. Ray recorded in 1886 that only the oldest men in the Hupa and Klamath Indian tribes retained the knowledge of how to hew a yew. The heartwood was shaped by knife, then the sinew of a deer's rear legs was shredded and glued upon the wood with boiled sturgeon gland; the bow was then wrapped and hung in the sweat house to season before it was strung. It was reported that such a weapon could cast an arrow over 100 metres.

It is interesting to reflect on the procedures for working wood and to realize that fire was rarely applied directly to the material, but that heat in some form or another often figured in the process of shaping, fixing or hardening. In early experimental work there was little done on the use of fire in shaping or hardening wood, although A. Lane Fox, later General Pitt-Rivers, recorded in 1875 a number of observations concerning the manufacture of dugout canoes in America: fire-setting, or water boiled by hot stones, accompanied by the use of wedges, props and scoops, transformed a solid log into a dugout vessel.

In the last decades of the nineteenth century, Fox carried out a masterly series of excavations in southern England, a series which some have claimed to form the basis of modern excavation techniques. He was well aware of the limitations of archaeological evidence, of its fragmentary nature, and of the wide range of ethnographic observations already completed throughout many parts of the world. In his work, Fox attempted to combine these aspects, and he experimented with archaeological materials in order to solve particular problems. This approach was relatively new. Instead of deciding to test, say, flint or stone or wood in a general way, Fox devised his experiments to answer certain questions about function, reliability and competence of artifacts.

In excavations at Cissbury, Sussex, Fox recovered examples of deer antler tools and ox shoulder blades, implements which already had been found in other camps and flint mines in southern England (Fox, 1876). These sites are now known to be of the third millennium B.C. In his experiments, Fox produced a set of tools from one pair of antlers; this yielded two picks, 1 mandril, 2 wedges and 5 tine punches. The tools were cut from the antler with flints, and the wedges were ground smooth on wet sandstone. They were then employed to cut into a smooth chalk face, which represented a situation encountered by prehistoric man in either digging a ditch around the camp, or quarrying into the chalk in search of flint nodules. With the antler tools, one man could excavate almost one cubic metre in 1.5 hours, and Fox suggested therefore that the longest side gallery in the prehistoric mine, 9 metres long and of a diameter suitable for only one man, could have been cut in twelve hours.

Experiments were also carried out using antler picks to prise out lumps of chalk from the sides of the mine shaft leading down to the galleries. The wedges and punches were hammered into cracks in the chalk, and the picks and mandril used to detach the lumps. Fox observed that the marks left by his tools in the chalk matched those observed in the sides of the prehistoric shaft and galleries. The removal of the chalk blocks and rubble from the galleries and shafts would have been a major task. Fox considered that the ox-shoulder blades might have served as shovels in this work, and he attempted to test this idea. He cut off the sharp spines of three modern ox bones, and experimented with the resulting shovel-like blades. He found it easier to move chalk rubble by filling his wheelbarrow by hand rather than by using the blade which was sharp and difficult to manipulate. By attaching a wooden handle he produced a very efficient tool, which was twice as effective as bare hands for lifting the rubble as well as being easier on the skin. Fox concluded that the excavation of the flint mines at Cissbury was well within the capabilities of a small group of men, and required relatively simple tools easily made from local materials.

This work was continued in subsequent years by Fox, who adopted the name Pitt-Rivers in 1880. His complete excavations of earthen burial mounds in Cranborne Chase, Dorset, again created interest in determining how the barrows were built, and also how rapidly their quarry ditches had silted up. Chalk weathers and erodes, and chalk mounds spread and settle through the actions of water and wind. Pitt-Rivers emptied the ditches around the Wor Barrow, a Neolithic burial mound, and left them exposed to wind and rain. His aim was to discover the rate at which the ditches began to silt up with material eroded from their sides and edges. From this he hoped to calculate the time that had elapsed since the ditches were originally cut. He left the ditches open for four years, then excavated their silts and recorded that almost 70 cm of chalk silt had already accumulated. Rapid silting from the upper sides of the ditches had covered the base, so that the shape of the ditches had already altered; while the base retained its original character, the upper parts had weathered back extensively. In this experiment, Pitt-Rivers did not succeed in his objective, which was one of chronology, but his observations have been substantiated by more recent experiments which have led to far greater attention being paid to ditch sections, silting rates and stratified materials. Some of the more important conclusions are noted elsewhere in the book.

When this work was being undertaken, others were engaged upon the experimental investigation of hard stone quarrying, shaping stone blocks, and working stone into axes and hammers. Some of these experiments have not been repeated since, probably because they were so conclusive in their results. There had already been much conjecture about the engineering of the pyramids of Egypt, the stone monuments of central America, and the megaliths of western Europe. Few had attempted to try to recreate the ancient methods of quarrying, shaping, transporting and erecting large stones, and indeed few have done so even today. But some limited experiments were carried out in the late nineteenth century, and these were the first to approach the subject in a rational and objective manner. W. M. Flinders Petrie, one of the pioneers of ancient Egyptian studies, introduced his paper in 1884 with the remarks: "Though so much labour has been bestowed on the literary remains of the Egyptians, and there are now so many scholars who can now read an inscription with ease, yet not a single student appears to have given his attention to the mechanical evidences of ancient knowledge and skill." Petrie believed that the cuttings, sawing and drilling of stone in Egypt must have been performed with tools which were harder than the substances, granite and diorite, operated upon, and he suggested that diamonds, set in bronze tools, had been used by the ancient Egyptians. The spiral scratches seen in some of the holes in the stones suggested to Petrie the rate of drilling, and he drew the quite amazing conclusion that the rate of cutting through diorite and granite, both exceedingly hard rocks, was 2.5 cm in only 7 strokes of the saw, and not

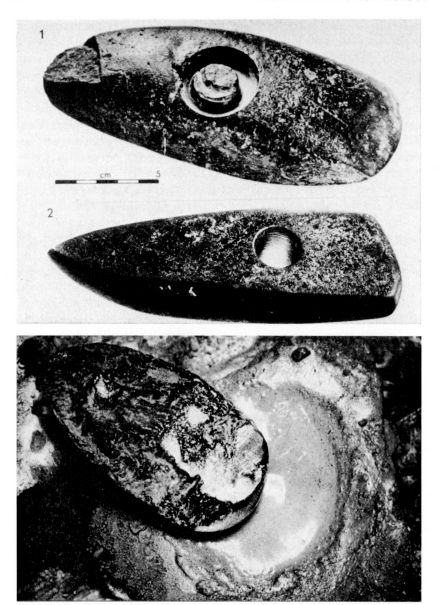

FIG. 8. *Upper.* Prehistoric stone tools perforated with tubular drills. 1, Adze partly drilled through, with an irregular hole caused by a wavering drillhead; the work could have been completed successfully. 2, Axe-hammer with complete perforation, probably drilled through from one side only. (From Rieth, 1958, taf. 22:1, 25.4.)

Lower. Polishing a greenstone axe by grinding it against a sandstone block (photo: Horreus de Haas).

much less in turns of the drill. This would be difficult even on sandstone or limestone, other substances extensively used in the construction of some of the major stone monuments.

Following Petrie's paper, which was read at a meeting of the Anthropological Institute of Great Britain and Ireland in 1883, there was a flood of comments from the audience, some of whom had actually experimented with the cutting and drilling of hard rock. John Evans in particular set out in some detail his objections to the need for, and therefore the use of, diamonds held in bronze. Instead, his experiments had shown that the drilling of hard stone, including diorite and jade, was accomplished by a soft tubular drill such as copper, bone, antler or wood, which was fed with a hard gritty substance, corundum being the hardest. This is pure aluminium oxide, occurring as a mineral in igneous rocks as well as in shales and limestones, and the only mineral harder than corundum is diamond. Evans suggested, and his experiments proved, that feeding the drill as it turned often resulted in spiral grooves down the side of the drilled hole, the particles following one another so that a series of parallel striations resulted. Evans' experiments were supported by observations among certain indigenous tribes of South America who were able to drill holes in rock crystal by rotating a pointed stem of plantain between the hands while feeding it with sand and water.

The technique of drilling stone was also considered by other nineteenth-century archaeologists (Fig. 8, upper). Dr. A. Keller, who patiently recorded the extraction of relics from the lake-muds of Switzerland, experimented on stone with tubular bones of sheep and goat, antler and yew wood cylinders, using a bow-drill and feeding the points with sand and water (Keller, 1878). His results exactly matched the relics from the prehistoric Swiss settlements. Dr. C. Rau carried out a series of experiments in drilling soft stones with flint points as drill head, and succeeded in perforating hard slate and other stones by hand-turning alone. When he attacked diorite, however, he used a wooden drill fed by quartz sand, and a pump-drill motion. Progress was slow, less than 0.2 mm depth was added to the hole after 2 hours' constant work (Rau, 1869, 1881).

Others experimented in the same way and there was general agreement that flint drill heads mounted on a rod of wood and turned by hand could perforate soft rock, wood, bone and antler. Hard rocks needed a tubular (either solid or hollow) drill fed with quartz sand or harder minerals of a fine consistency, and their efficiency was measured more by the quality of perforation than working speed. A particularly useful set of experiments by J. D. McGuire in 1892 employed the bow-drill, pump-drill and hand-drill in work upon limestone, sandstone, slate, serpentine, marble, catlinite and jasper. Sand was fed dry and wet into the wooden drills, and some work was carried out under water (the drill not the operator) in order to float off the dust which otherwise clogged the drill. The need to hold the drill point perpendicular to the work was stressed by McGuire, and he explained that the inevitable clogging of the drill in deep holes was the reason for the almost universal prehistoric method of drilling from both sides of the implement, thereby reducing the depth of each hole to be drilled.

Instead McGuire turned to the manufacture of stone tools and weapons, particularly hammers and ground axes. These implements had been found in many parts of the world, and were often made of high-quality close-grained rocks, beautifully smoothed and polished (Fig. 8, lower). Observations of indigenous people working on these objects had suggested that they were highly prized both as tools and as prestige implements. At the time, it was believed that they represented an enormous output of energy in their production, as an early eighteenth-century account by Lafitau, *Moeurs des Sauvages Ameriquains*, suggested:

> Hatchets have been used over the whole of America from time to time immemorial. They are made of a pebble hard and difficult to break. They require a great deal of time to make them serviceable. The method of preparing them is to sharpen them by rubbing them on a sandstone, and to give them, by means of time and work, very much the appearance of our hatchets, or of a wedge. Often the life of a savage was not sufficient for this purpose from which it comes that such an article, though rough and imperfect, is a precious heritage to their children.

McGuire set out to examine this claim by making stone hammers and axes of various substances; his work in 1878 was fully published in 1892. A hammer of black porphyry was pecked out and grooved in about 5 hours, using diorite and quartzite stones. Other rocks were also pecked and ground, and quartzite was considered to be a suitable hammerstone for most of these. A long experiment on nephrite, however, was more arduous. Nephrite is a variety of jade and is hard and tough. McGuire began work on a nephrite chunk knocked from a boulder and pecked away at this with quartzite hammers; most of these lasted for under 10 minutes before shattering and about 40 were ruined before a close-grained specimen was found that survived for about 8 hours. Other hammers, of gneiss and granite, were useless on the nephrite. Eventually a yellow jasper hammer was employed and this completed the pecking operation after another 40 hours of work. Both nephrite and jasper had lost the same weight of stone dust through this pounding. The roughed-out axe was then ground with granite for 5 hours, polished with a quartzite pebble for 6 hours and then rubbed with a piece of wood and animal skin. The result was an incomplete but recognizable grooved axehead, representing 55 hours of pecking and pounding with stone hammers, during which time over 460,000 blows were delivered upon it. Certainly not a lifetime, but nonetheless hard work.

Compared with this, other experiments on the working of stone were less ambitious and more easily completed as they were representative only, involving samples rather than the whole product. W. Gowland, working at Stonehenge around 1900, organized an experiment in the dressing of the sarsens which form the major uprights and lintels of the monument; he found that quartzite hammers used to peck and pound the surface of his experimental piece created a tooled face similar to those of the prehistoric structure (Gowland, 1902). McGuire also dressed several blocks of stone in this way before further decoration was formed by grooving, grinding and chiselling; his work was particularly impressive because of the apparent energy with which he attacked the problems, although more details might have been published. He set out his position clearly in 1891:

The views here set forth are supported by the experience of many years in the collection and study of implements, as well as by experiment. Whether or not they are accepted as sound, it is believed that an intelligent discussion of the subject by archaeologists will advance our knowledge of men in the age of stone.

But both McGuire and Cushing were men of wide interests and talents and they did not restrict themselves to investigations of wood and stone alone. Both seem to have had the ability and energy to turn to whatever finds were made, and they were many, and to make impressive contributions in experimental work. McGuire wrote more cautiously than Cushing who revelled in discarding the theories of others and was in the habit of throwing in lines such as: "In subsequent experiments I discovered many additional processes, and developed improvements on the earlier ways of working." The fact of the matter was, of course, that he often made discoveries because he had the widely travelled background knowledge acquired by few, as well as the curiosity and energy to pursue investigations of all kinds. Both Cushing and McGuire carried out experimental work on copper in the late nineteenth century, following the discoveries of flat copper-plate discs and other ornaments in the burial mounds of the Hopewell culture of Ohio. The objects were mainly of sheet copper and a high degree of technical skill was exhibited in their production and ornamentation, with intricate cut-out figures and embossed decoration. McGuire demonstrated in 1892 that copper nuggets from Lake Superior could be hammered, with annealling, until they formed plates only 6 mm thick. C. C. Willoughby carried out further work in 1894 on a pebble-strewn beach, where he had an unlimited choice of rounded and flattened

experiment was devised to test its deep-water capabilities. A World's Fair was being held in Chicago in 1893, in part to celebrate the 400th anniversary of the discovery of America by Christopher Columbus. What better experiment—one with a bite in it—than to try to sail in the Viking ship across to the New World, thereby demonstrating the seaworthiness of such craft and allowing those interested to draw their own conclusions. And so it happened (Fig. 10); the Gokstad replica, only 24 metres long, set sail and made the crossing in 27 days, reaching maximum speeds of 11 knots and withstanding Atlantic storms *en route*. Its reception at Chicago was tumultuous. The experiment has prompted over the years a quite remarkable series of lengthy voyages in unusual boats and rafts, and these will be described in Chapter 2.

Fig. 10. A replica of the Gokstad Viking boat, made in 1893, and moored here at the Great Exhibition in Chicago. Its voyage from Norway to New York took 27 days, proved the ocean-going capabilities of Viking craft, and was one of the pioneering events of experimental archaeology. (University Museum of National Antiquities, Oslo, Norway.)

By the close of the nineteenth century, experiments with ancient sites, materials, objects and techniques were well established as a legitimate exercise which could reveal much information about the life of early man. The great and unique advantage which nineteenth-century archaeologists had over their successors was the existence of a multitude of indigenous groups of inhabitants in North and South America, Africa, Asia and Australasia. Many of these communities, whose raw materials were entirely non-metallic, were already in decline in the nineteenth century; but in a number of cases it was possible for some records of their customs and practices to be retrieved. In other situations, the opportunities had already been lost with either the complete extinction of the society or the total transformation of their way of life. The precious records of full functioning societies were made the more valuable by what had already gone elsewhere.

Because of these opportunities experimental work was actively pursued, and in the preceding pages some of the pioneers have been mentioned. The stimulation created by ethnography was, however, shortly to be lost as more and more territory was seized by the white man, as more aboriginal societies were forced into unfamiliar situations, and as more of their traditional patterns of behaviour were lost. Recording of data continued of course, but its relevance to experimental archaeology was diluted or ignored, and there are few instances in the decades from about 1910 until quite recently that suggest much inspiration was obtained from the records of anthropologists or ethnographers. Their interests altered too as less attention was paid to technical aspects of material culture and more to social and political organization. For these reasons, as well as European political ones, experimental archaeological work languished in the early decades of the twentieth century The notable exceptions were those few individuals who seized the opportunities to observe, experiment and record archaeological evidence as it became available. Among these was Saxton T. Pope who based his experiments on archery upon the experience of Ishi in the closing years of the Indian's life; Pope's massive work is discussed in Chapter 5. S. H. Warren's contribution in 1914 was equally important.

The interest in early man which had been initiated by the mid-nineteenth-century revelations had a chronological direction in that explorers and archaeologists continued to seek the "missing links" in man's ancestry, as well as earlier and earlier human remains. Of course it was uniquely valuable to recover actual traces of man himself in his physical skeletal form, but it was readily acknowledged that the conditions for preservation of his remains were not likely to be suitable in many parts of the world. Instead, his industrial remains, being of stone and therefore imperishable, were sought in dated geological formations.

For the latter episodes of man's prehistory there could be no problem in identifying stone tools and weapons as these were of standard traditional forms, made to established patterns, and therefore of indisputably human origin. Earlier forms of stone tools, however, were less likely to be so firmly traditional in shape, and the very earliest tools would have no pattern yet fixed. The problem was to define a set of rules by which such early implements could be recognized in the field and accepted as showing human influence in their flaking. There were two distinct and opposing viewpoints. One saw that any and all flints which showed regular chipping and a symmetrical or uniform shape could be, and probably were, of human manufacture; the geological positions of such fractured specimens therefore provided a likely date for the presence of man. The opposing view was that natural geological agencies such as storm beaches, rushing streams, earthfalls and the movement of ice sheets could create conditions for fracturing flint in standard ways including pressure, and thus that entirely non-humanly worked flints could appear symmetrical and as if flaked with design and intent.

The dispute existed for almost half a century. Those seeking to prove the presence of humans in Europe in pre-Pleistocene times could point to flaked flints, called eoliths or dawn-stones, from suitable pre-Pleistocene deposits, and could collect from the multitude of fractured flints eroded from such deposits an array of plausible artifacts. They neglected to observe the fallacy perpetuated in such a practice, as Warren was quick to point out in 1914:

> It is so easy to argue in a circle to show that our series of flints indicates intelligence, and not to see that the intelligence has been put into them by ourselves, in our selection out of the infinite variety of Nature.

Warren carried out exhaustive experiments on flint fracture by direct percussion, pressure, grinding and crushing. He designed various devices to apply and measure the degrees of force needed to scratch flint, to squeeze and crush it, and to fracture it at different angles. These experiments were designed to show that natural forces could and would fracture, flake and scratch flints with sufficient force to produce the types of flaking and damage seen on specimens selectively recovered from ancient geological deposits. Warren concluded that the striations on the eoliths indicated that geological movements had taken place, and that such movements contained sufficient direction and energy to chip and shape the flints into eolithic forms. Certain fractures could not be produced experimentally because Warren was unable to create the conditions for enormous slow-moving pressures; nonetheless movement of ice was clearly indicated. Although claims for the recognition of eoliths as of human workmanship continued to be made following Warren's work, no adequate rebuttal of his results was ever produced; so the word "eolith" gradually came to signify a stone shaped to resemble something which man might have used but which he did not himself make. Warren did not compose this definition, but set his results out objectively and then stated:

> In conclusion, let me say that I have no prejudice against the existence of man in the Pliocene period: it is simply a question of obtaining the facts to prove his existence at that time. But in view of the evidence detailed above it appears to me imprudent—indeed, to my mind practically impossible—to accept these chipped flints as throwing light upon that early chapter of human, or immediately pre-human, history, which I, no less than the most enthusiastic of my opponents, should like to see opened up before us as clearly as the Palaeolithic Age now stands revealed.

The problem has now passed from Europe to Africa, where indisputable proof of man's existence in a remote period is now established through two decades of discovery in East Africa.

Following Warren's work, experimental archaeology lapsed into a phase of small-scale restricted work, interrupted only by Pope's great contribution to archery in 1918. A few useful investigations were carried out by English archaeologists in the years 1920–35, before the subject blossomed again through the stimulation of Scandanavian studies.

During this quiescent period, one man in particular was active. E. Cecil Curwen, working in Sussex, explored a number of archaeological theories by experiment. He and his father Eliot Curwen continued the work of Lane Fox in using ox shoulder-blades as shovels for chalk rubble, and they concluded that the shovels were really only effective if wooden handles were attached (1926). Curwen (1930a) also investigated flint sickles and the gloss which often appeared on their edges. In earlier experiments, F. C. J. Spurrell had deduced that harvesting of corn would deposit silica gloss on the flint sickles; Curwen obtained some serrated flint blades from a flint-knapper, Fred Snare of Brandon, and he then proceeded to saw wood and bone and to cut straw. A narrow lustre was produced on the edge of the flint after much work sawing the wood, but no gloss was visible after bone-cutting; a broad and diffuse gloss was deposited on the flint after only half an hour's work cutting straw.

These results seemed to confirm earlier experiments on corn, but other views were still expressed; so Curwen in 1935 mounted a more elaborate study. The silica gloss produced by his earlier work was easily removed from the flints by washing and brushing; this had not originally been realized. His later experiments involved spinning cylinders of oak, bone and compressed straw on a lathe and cutting into the cylinders with flint blades to determine how much lustre was deposited upon the flints and how permanent it could be.

The flakes cut into the wood and bone cylinders for 30 minutes at 2500 r.p.m. (which represented 17 km of cutting) and their edges were given a narrow dull lustre by the wood, but were splintered by the bone. When applied to the strawboard drum, spun at 3500 r.p.m. on the lathe, the best-quality black flint received a bright lustre on its serrated edge—a lustre which could not be removed by scrubbing. Curwen suggested that standing corn might be taken to represent the compressed straw in terms of polish at a ratio of 100:1; the 25 km of contact between the flints and the straw on the lathe therefore might represent 2500 km of cutting in the field. This would itself indicate a field of 40 ha which was clearly too large to think of in terms of the work of a single sickle. Thus the permanent lustre on prehistoric flint sickles might represent many seasons of work in the small fields. These experimental results seem to have settled the problem, although they are dependent on the quality of material for making sickles; also, more granular blades would react differently to the action of cutting corn.

Although there were other archaeologists, technologists and engineers who conducted experiments between the World Wars, no major projects were established, and the unending series of single isolated experiments, flint-knapping, copper-smelting, wood-chopping and the like continued only sporadically. Little work was done on the movement of large stones in the erection of megalithic structures, and little on boats and ships and the problems of transport. Few reconstructions of primitive houses were made, and no attempts to measure their decay. Experiments in farming, clearances, cultivation, harvesting and storage of food were hardly considered, although one or two projects were initiated in America. For all of these subjects, some of them of very considerable importance in archaeological efforts to seek and experience the events of the past, archaeology had to wait until the turmoil of 1939–45 had subsided.

Following the war, archaeology began to adopt many new approaches and techniques: analytical methods, geophysical dating procedures, new techniques for the recovery of material, numerical processes for arranging data, and imaginative ways of interpreting the evidence, all began to be employed by archaeologists. More objective recording of data was stressed; furthermore the limitations of the surviving evidence began to be acknowledged openly. The public's interest in ancient remains was stimulated by reports of discoveries made during the war, and during the clearing and rebuilding operations in many cities and towns. Radio and then television broadcasts played an important part in bringing new discoveries to the attention of a wide public; and in these the unique value of experimental reconstruction could be realized. In this the inspiring work of the late Paul Johnstone for the BBC was pre-eminent. The creation of three-dimensional models and full-size replicas of ancient pieces of equipment, weapons and armour, ploughs, houses and boats, should have been solely an archaeological responsibility, but the outcome was a spate of rather subjective re-creations and simulations—some entirely imaginary—for public admiration and stimulation.

At the same time, however, other archaeologists undertook programmes of experimental research that are still continued today by themselves or others. These programmes represent the beginnings of modern experimental archaeology. Although to select some and not others may seem unfair, there can be no dispute about the lead taken by Scandinavian archaeologists in the establishment of modern experimental archaeology. Five of these pioneers, who began work between 1943 and 1958, represent the major interests of current investigations.

The first of these was Axel Steensberg who carried out an exhaustive series of experiments on ancient sickles. He concentrated not on the silica gloss left upon them by the corn, but on the function, the methods of use, and the relative merits of flint, bronze and iron harvesting implements. Steensberg's interest in ancient agricultural implements has continued to the present time, and he was one of the founders of the journal *Tools and Tillage* which continues to provide a guide to research on every aspect of the subject of early agriculture. One of these subjects is forest clearance and the establishment of cultivated fields. The leader in this experimental work was J. Iversen who initiated a series of investigations into the procedures of clearance and cultivation and their implications for land fertility and land use in prehistoric times; many other experiments have since continued this work.

Completely separate from these aspects are investigations on the construction and function of musical instruments, a subject in which experiments have had a long and not altogether smooth history. A standard for all subsequent work was set in 1949 by H. C. Broholm and his collaborators in their publication of the Scandinavian Bronze Age *lurer*, where experimental testing of the instruments established once and for all their musical capabilities and implications. As a model for the experimental investigation of any complex piece of equipment this work has much to recommend it.

At the same time as the sonorous notes of the *lurer* were sounding in Copenhagen, another Scandinavian, Thor Heyerdahl, was beginning his long and adventurous career as an experimental sailor. His first major investigation, published in 1948, concerned the Kon-Tiki, a balsa raft which he sailed across the Pacific from Peru to Raroia in Polynesia in order to demonstrate that those islands could have been colonized from South America. This was only the first of Heyerdahl's voyages, and his work has stimulated others to attempt equally daring and hazardous journeys upon the oceans in order to better understand how ancient colonization and travel were accomplished. Even so, few of these have equalled the first crossing of the Atlantic by the Gokstad replic, or the first part-crossing of the Pacific by Kon-Tiki, and none at all the very first adventures upon the great unknown oceans untold centuries ago.

In the same tradition of these Scandinavian experiments, one other investigation demands a place here in the historical development of the subject, not only for its imaginative approach but also because it has laid the foundation for much subsequent work. In 1956, Hans-Ole Hansen arranged and carried out the work of building replicas of prehistoric Danish houses, using only those materials which had been found in earlier excavations, and only those techniques of building judged appropriate to the period. As a result of this work, and of Hansen's first experiments in actually residing in one of these houses, a very long and impressive series of house-building and house-destroying experiments was initiated in Denmark, and elsewhere. This particular subject has played a vital role in interesting both archaeologists and the public in the value of full-sized replicas as well as in the auxiliary work that can be conducted within and around these structures.

With all these crucial and inspirational developments the theme was total commitment to materials, technology and on occasion to human participants. There can be no doubt that they provided the encouragement, through their success, for further work and for the establishment of experimental archaeology as a uniquely valuable tool in the search for the evidence of man's origins, all of his first inventions, his achievements and failures, and his reliance upon the environment for his future. In this pioneering work of experimental archaeology there is the foundation of objective and observable truth which we will see in the succeeding chapters as the basis for a tangible understanding of man's past. But first we must attempt to define some of the objectives of experimental archaeology, its requirements, and its place in the whole field of investigation into human behaviour.

  The aim of imitative experiments is testing beliefs about past cultural behaviour.

                                                              Ascher, 1961, p. 793

The discipline of archaeology, as a science and an art, is bounded by the amount and variety of the evidence available, and it is shaped by the measures adopted to handle and interpret this evidence. Archaeologists devote much of their time to a study of the actual material remains left unwittingly by ancient man, and for some this study is sufficient in itself. To be able to describe, arrange and present this data in an orderly fashion is considered to be an end-result. For more archaeologists, however, this organization of the evidence is not enough. All are agreed that it is essential for the information to be arranged in such a way as to be easily assimilated, but this is merely a first step in understanding the evidence. It is not enough to ask "What is this evidence?": it is essential to ask "What does this evidence mean?" There is a whole series of questions to ask, about the "how" and the "why" as well as the "what". All are essential if we are trying to explain human behaviour.

In recent years archaeological investigations into man's past cultural behaviour have increasingly looked for patterns of activities rather than simple isolated events, and have employed the concepts of model-building in attempts to predict and understand ancient activities. These activities, consisting of the standardized production of implements, for example, or regular farming practices, or traditional ways of building houses, are obviously more likely to be represented in the archaeological record than a single perhaps unsuccessful action. And because they are more abundantly represented, they form the basic source of material evidence for the archaeologist to use in his interpretations and in his predictions. Models, real or imaginary, are constructed on the basis of this surviving evidence, and the more ways in which these models can be made and tested, the greater reliability can be placed upon their predictions. Direct copies of implements and structures, such as replicas of stone axes, boats or houses have been classed as "artificial hardware models" (Clarke, 1972, p. 13), and they are on a level with "real-world models" normally taken from historic or ethnographic records: experimental three-dimensional replicas can be handled and interpreted in the same way as these real specimens, and in some cases more objectively than historically observed but now-decayed artifacts. Here is not the place for a full discussion of the relative merits and demerits of "model-building" in its widest sense, but it is as well to note that the "hardware models" in this book form an important part of the whole concept.

The pioneering work in experimental archaeology has already been described and the main concepts of this early work will be clear. Subsequent and recent considerations have refined the approaches, the recording, the assessments, but they have not altered belief in the fundamental importance of the experimental approach (Ascher, 1961; Coles 1973, 1977; Hansen, 1974, 1977; Reynolds, 1977a, 1978; Callahan, 1976; Knudson, 1978; Ingersoll et al., 1977).

The basic principle behind experimental archaeology is that of testing, examining the quality of a site, structure, implement or weapon. All of these human artifacts can be viewed by experiment in their three dimensions. They may be handled freely, may be broken if required and may otherwise be subjected to all sorts of indignities. An axe-like tool can be used as an adze, a spade, and a knife to test its possible functions. A house can be built, lived in, pushed over, or burned down to see how its components react. A boat can be made, propelled in different ways, loaded to overcapacity, run aground or even sunk, simply to observe its capabilities. These examples are not frivolous; most of them have actually occurred, and the others should, but they serve to illustrate the potential for experiment. Almost every piece of work done with sufficient thought has yielded useful and valuable information. The information may be entirely negative, in that a presumptive implement or process or function does not work, but even this is of value. A flint flake may not work as an engraving tool, even though it has been called a burin by archaeologists, and the demonstration of this non-function is of considerable use to those attempting to reconstruct Stone Age tool kits. A sheet bronze shield may not resist a slashing sword, and, because it fails to do so, other suggestions for the use of such impressive armour may be strengthened (p. 180). The suitability of most archaeological materials for experimental testing is hardly in doubt.

The relationship between experiment and excavation is more difficult to define. In a sense, all excavations are experiments, dealing with the recovery of data, but few excavations in themselves are designed as experiments to test recovery as well as interpretative methods. Archaeological sites are generally considered too precious (and each is wholly unique) to squander on deliberate experimental principles, yet it could be argued that by adhering to traditional methods of excavation, archaeologists are perpetuating the mistakes of their predecessors and gaining little but repetitive information (Reynolds, 1977a). This is not entirely correct, of course, because the evolution of excavation and analytical techniques has been rapid and expansive; yet there still is a case for adopting bolder experiments in recovery techniques, particularly in different approaches to the same site in order to provide suggestions about the reliability of the evidence. If, for instance, even the topsoil of a settlement was to be excavated in part by machine, in part by spades, and in part by trowels after vegetation had been killed, the resulting time and yields of material would be varied. There would be a short period and no finds, a longer period and some finds but few *in situ*, and a very long period and many finds *in situ*. Whether or not the last was worth the effort and expense would depend upon the problems of the site and the sets of evidence needed. At a more advanced level, an occupation horizon could be excavated by entrenching tool and bucket, by trowel and hand shovel, by spatula and paintbrush and the material could be discarded at once, or put through a shaker sieve, or subjected to flotation and sieving. The results would be spectacularly different, as some few experiments have already shown (Payne, 1972). Again it is up to the excavator to decide his particular approach to the site.

A useful example of experimental excavating, but on an artificial site, has recently been provided by Fischer *et al.* (1979). Investigations on late glacial and early post-glacial occupation sites in northern Europe have naturally been concerned almost exclusively with flint tools, because flint is the sole surviving material; these sites have traditionally been excavated in units of 1.0×1.0 m or even 2.0×2.0 m, the finds from each square determining the unit density, and thus allowing "activity plans" to be drawn for the occupation. Some of the sites have yielded enormous quantities of flints, thus suggesting a long period of occupation, or a considerable population on site. In the experiment, a flint knapper sat on a low platform and produced long flakes of late glacial character from 15 flint nodules weighing 36 kg. After 2 hours and 40 minutes, the nodules were worked out, and a staggering total of 18 046 flakes had been produced, averaging 113 per minute. Most of the large flakes and also a majority of the very small ones fell immediately in front of the knapper, the medium flakes landing farther away. One presumes that the larger flakes would be removed for use elsewhere, and also some of the medium flakes, hence concentrations of very small flakes, too small for most purposes and too hard to retrieve from the ground if vegetation was present, may well mark the locations of flint workshops.

The majority of flakes lay within an area 1.0×1.0 m, but the site was then excavated in units of 0.5×0.5 m, and a density pattern was produced which naturally demonstrated the precise area of major concentration; density patterns using excavation grids of 1.0×1.0 m, and 2.0×2.0 m, were also produced, and showed very diffuse and unacceptable patterns, capable of several different interpretations.

Recent excavations on late glacial and early post-glacial sites have attempted to record artifacts *in situ*, but nonetheless the sieving on site has generally yielded a high proportion of artifacts which were not observed *in situ*. The experiment suggests that time-consuming procedures of hand excavation to locate and record individual objects, while relying on sieves for further material, should be altered to direct sieving of small units which will allow greater precision in locating workshops and presumably other activity areas, as well as speeding up the excavation. Even if the attempts to locate and record individual artifacts continues on sites, the reduced excavation unit is recommended.

We have already seen that experiments with archaeological materials have been underway for well over a century, and that these pioneering attempts met with varying fortunes. Within these early experiments, and more modern work as well, clear patterns of design may be seen, and these reflect the one basic and underlying determinant for all experiments, that of "setting the question"; the most suitable method of determining this is through a discussion of the various levels of experiment already established. This account is modelled on a recent assessment of the concepts, assumptions and problems of experimental archaeology (Coles, 1977).

Experiments can be broadly grouped into three levels. The lowest level is that of simulation, wherein a copy is made of an original artifact with attention paid only to its visual appearance for display purposes. The materials used may vary from the original, the technology employed in making the copy can be modern, and the copy itself is not tested for its function or purpose. Museum displays are a fair description of this level of experiment, and some scientists would totally exclude the category from experimental archaeology. Yet visual effects can be useful, essentially to give a third dimension to material culture, to provide a scale, and notably to lead on to further consideration and work. Above this, such experiments cannot rise, and their greatest value at the moment must be their public appeal which brings appreciation and support for further work. Examples of this level of experiment are numerous and include rebuilt prehistoric tombs, Celtic chariots, Roman forts and plenty of houses (Fig. 11).

The educational value of such simulations is important. A number of rather impressive experimental structures have been built to act as focal points for educational programmes generally involving young people who can be given the chance to appreciate the scale and character of former houses or forts, or who can actually assist in the work and thereby appreciate the tasks of their ancestors (p. 244). Some experiments of this kind have approached and attained the second level of research. The participation of Television authorities in work at this first level is welcome, although their apparent need to provide yes or no solutions may be irritating to some experimental archaeologists.

In these programmes, and in full-scale models of ancient sites, the quality of "simulation" and "reconstruction" must be faced. Many archaeological sites contain the decayed remnants of structures, with ground-plans visible, but few traces of surviving walls and none of roofing. To erect an impression of an ancient building, on the basis of the ground-plan alone, and to call it a reconstruction, is theoretically wrong. In similar fashion, to copy an ancient tool or weapon and call it a re-creation is also wrong. The words reconstruct, re-create, reproduce, replicate, give a false impression of authenticity and the word simulation is perhaps more accurate (Hobley, 1974). In this book the word reconstruction is used, by

Fig. 11. *Upper*. Roman gateway and part of turf rampart at The Lunt, near Coventry, England. (Photo: B. Hobley.)

Lower. Reconstructed Neolithic longhouse at Hjerl Hede, Denmark, based upon excavation plans from the site at Barkaer (photo: J. M. Coles.)

tradition, but we should not forget that the results are approximations of what might have been, not what was.

A second level of experiment, to which all work should in theory aim to reach, is concerned with testing for the processes and production methods used in the past. Here the experimenter is involved not only in making a copy or replica which looks like the original, but also in manufacturing it correctly. Appropriate materials must be used, and here the value of analyses of ancient objects, to determine their composition, cannot be exaggerated. Experimental casting of bronze axes, or the flaking of stone axes, can only be judged if the raw materials have exactly the same characteristics as the originals. The point is obvious, and needs no further comment here.

A second element in experiments concerned with the production methods is that of an appropriate technology. The greatest care may be taken in collecting the raw materials, but the working or assembly of such materials should be entirely in keeping with a level of technological ability appropriate to the society which made the original objects. We do not know how much effect a bulldozer will have upon a copy of an earthwork, or an electric drill upon a wooden framework for a Roman gate; the first has a more visually substantial effect upon the reconstruction, but friction, cracking and fraying all have a part to play in the build-up of pressures upon wooden timbers during drilling and hammering of pegs and nails. This has been seen most clearly in the experimental building of an Iron Age house at Moesgård, Denmark (see Fig. 50, upper) and it would be interesting to compare the laboriously drilled holes and the tree-nails from this site with the electrically driven holes and modern fasteners at the Roman gateway at The Lunt, Coventry, England (Fig. 11). This should not be taken as criticism of the latter work, because the objectives of the two experiments were different. The problem of technology is perhaps the most difficult for experimenters to solve because there is a limit to the degree of our knowledge about prehistoric or early technology and beyond this experimenters are in dangerous territory where subjective unsubstantiated opinions are rife. The experiment must obviously be conducted with as close an approximation to ancient techniques as may reasonably be assumed and expected; and as long as the reported results clearly signify the procedures used, appropriate assessment may be made by others as to their suitability and significance.

If it is possible to employ only those procedures and equipment likely to have been available in the contemporary society, then further experimental advances may be made. On the one hand, the implements used can themselves be observed for their own capabilities and the wear and breakages that occur. On the other, the more difficult question of time can be posed. In experimental production of stone tools, for example, the hammer-stones or wooden mallets can be recorded for bruising or chipping, and the time taken to produce a stone axe can be reasonably estimated. In casting a bronze implement, or forging an iron tool, the equipment used, furnaces, crucibles, moulds, hammer, all can and should be carefully recorded before, during and after use. This point again is self-evident, but its reliability is only acceptable when the experimenters are entirely familiar with their materials and technologies; whether this is ever completely possible is a matter for debate. Here, however, the use of ethnography can be of great importance.

Ethnography is one of the most neglected fields of experimental archaeology. Societies today which are totally isolated from the main technological advances of the world are rare, and becoming rarer, but much has already been recorded. Detailed records of stone tool manufacture, iron smelting, forest clearance, house building, pottery firing and many more such activities, provide unique guides to the technologies of the past. They are unique because the people who practised them knew no other ways and were entirely familiar with their materials and their procedures and the precise reasons for selecting them all. Craftsmen in modern industrial societies are unlikely to be familiar with ancient tools and processes, and it is to be regretted that ancient crafts and technologies are being lost at an alarming rate throughout much of the world today (Hansen, 1974). The criticism often levelled at ethnographic records is that they represent situations far removed in both time and space from the milieu of the ancient society under examination. The criticism is legitimate yet it cannot totally serve to dismiss the use of such an information source. In certain instances it may be possible to overlook environmental differences—iron working may be a case in point. In others, differences in environment will have had a major effect; simple forms of agriculture in tropical or sub-tropical regions should not be used as guides to prehistoric practices in northern latitudes. With care, the experimenter will find a vast source of "experimental" data already available, and one might hope for a compilation of such material from an ethnographer or archaeologist rather than a social anthropologist.

A third level of experiment is concerned with the function of the artifact, that is the use or uses to which the object is presumed to have been put. This level is a logical step up from that dealing with the production methods, and there are few experiments that can proceed directly to function-testing without the necessity for accuracy and relevance in manufacture. It would be worthless to test an earthen bank for erosion and weathering if it has been heaped up by an earthmoving machine; but it is little better to test an accurate copy of a wooden ard dragged by chain and tractor. Both aspects must be related in concept and approach. The visual appearance of a wooden boat might not be affected by the use of modern technologies in its making, but its handling and possibly its seaworthiness might be altered in ways that could combine to affect the conclusions drawn from the experiments. The question of the extent of alteration can probably never be resolved unless comparative tests are done, and this would be an expensive process. The general point, however, must be clear, that for function testing the object must be made in an appropriate manner. That there is scope for some choice in this will be emphasized later when the approach to experiment is discussed.

There are two aspects in this functional work which are vital, yet sometimes ignored or neglected. The first is that of manipulation and operation; the second is environment. The actual methods by which objects are used to carry out certain functions require more thought than untutored volunteer labour is likely to give. The reason why stone axes sometimes compare badly with steel axes in chopping trees, for instance, is in their mode of use because the angle of blow and back lift of a stone axe is totally unlike that of a steel axe to which modern man is accustomed. The lack of success in breaking up and transporting chalk and earth, using antler picks, bone shovels and wooden baskets is in part due to our unfamiliarity with these unusual implements. The same difficulties are present in efforts to cultivate soils with ancient forms of ard, which involved entirely theoretical and subjective methods of training the draught animals, devising the harness, and manipulating the ard. The results are conspicuously successful as experiments because of the care taken in recording and publishing the observations and problems.

The ard experiments are also concerned with the environmental conditions that always affect work of this sort. Here the questions of cleared ground, old turf, soils and climate are vital if the experiments are to have any relevance in terms of past situations. Other tests with other equipment are not so dependent upon physical environmental conditions which match those of the past, but even so this is an aspect well worth careful consideration. We must also not ignore or exclude the general concept of the social background of the experimenters, their outlooks on economies, time, their motivation, ingenuity and general philosophy of life, all of which may affect the experimental work in subtle and unconscious ways; these are mostly undefinable and certainly unquantifiable.

Among the experiments concerned with the functional testing of ancient remains, several may be distinguished because they achieve far greater reliability through repetition. Repetition is often boring, whether more so in writing than talking is uncertain, but in experimental archaeology the ability to sustain repeated tests has almost always led to augmented results.

Repetition in experiments concerned with the underground storage of grain has shown the relative ease by which seed-grain could be preserved by Iron Age man, but it is only by a long sequence of tests that this facility has become apparent. It was a question of gaining expertise in the work and in the small refinements of detail; this only became possible through a trial and error approach (p. 121).

Series tests are basically the same as repetition except that here a conscious effort is made to lead from one result, repeated if required, to a second, or to a redirection of effort. From an initial interest in basic archery, Pope extended his experiments to include a great variety of bows, arrows, bowstrings, arrowheads and targets, each test building upon previous tests and suggesting further work (p. 170). Another programme relevant here is that concerned with earthwork erosion and decay, where a series of examinations over a long period of time should augment our knowledge of the processes by which prehistoric earthworks achieved their appearance today (p. 240). Repetition and series of experiments have one other element probably worth mention here. This concerns the personalities involved in the work. Although it is true to say that a new approach and fresh insight in an experiment may ensue from a change in the personnel of a team, the maintenance of both continuity and understanding in experimental work is extremely important and can be best achieved by the constant presence of at least the instigator and/or chief technician. Personal involvement in experimental archaeology is generally maintained throughout the work through sheer interest and dedication, and it is notable that those few cases where the series tests have lagged behind the planned programme have concerned rather larger teams of specialists with no one single leader or director. Personal involvement is important, and excellent demonstrators of dedication and total immersion in the projects are not hard to find at places such as Little Butser (p. 114), West Stow (p. 146), Pamunkey (p. 213) and Lejre (p. 244), nor are they less abundant in experiments not involving full-time salaried staff, in situations of extreme hardship and some danger.

Not all who wish to experiment with archaeological material can afford the time or money to conduct major programmes of work which may involve heavy and abundant raw materials, massive expenditure of effort in the technology, and lengthy periods of function tests. An experiment concerned with a megalithic tomb, for example, would involve quarrying and dressing of stone, transportation, a very large work force, and the organization of a site to house the experiment. An ingenious way out of this impasse is to reduce the experiment in one or two ways. The first, as employed by Erasmus in Mexico, was to conduct short but full-scale exercises as samples of the entire procedures (p. 138): observations were made of short-term quarrying and digging, transportation, building and facing of stone and earth walls, and these time and energy records were then used to calculate the drain on a prehistoric society engaged in erecting a massive, partly surviving monument.

The alternative way to lower this cost factor is to reduce the entire experiment to a small scale, 1/10 or even less. Such reductions have been attempted for earthworks and for megaliths with varying results. At first sight, to attempt to understand such structures by miniature models seems absurd, and there can be little doubt about the uncertainty of observations concerned with erosion and weathering of small domes of earth. Yet one scaled experiment on the megalithic monument called Stonehenge has generally been accepted as demonstrating precisely how the large uprights were erected on the site (p. 240). The engineering work involved in the experiment consisted of exact scaled humans, ropes, timbers and stones, with much practical and theoretical reasoning attached. It would seem, however, that many experiments are of such a character as to remove much hope of a successful scale model approach.

A final stage in scaled experiments, if costs and opportunities are unrealized, is to do no actual work of reconstruction or simulation, but to devise and conduct the experiment on purely theoretical grounds. It should be possible to predict exactly how a structure could be put together, or how it would react to certain conditions, given all of the properties of the materials and the strength of the agencies acting upon them. The erection of parts of Stonehenge can be visualized in this way, just as the current, wind and navigation requirements for Polynesian colonization can be calculated (p. 65). The proof of the theory, however, must still lie in the actual event, where all the small and seemingly unimportant factors, such as temperament and variations in equipment, as well as exceptional conditions, may be inadvertently applied.

It is tempting to consider if a fourth level of experiment can be tried. This would logically involve an extension beyond the relatively simple functional testing of materials and artifacts, into the less clearly defined areas of the society as a whole. That tools and weapons "maketh man", or at least allow him to exert greater control over his physical world and his competitors, cannot be disputed. The success of material things, their acquisition, shaping and above all their efficient use, is in a way a measure of the ease with which a society could adapt to its environment, and hence an archaeological assessment of such materials must inevitably lead on to considerations about the society which invented or exploited such artifacts. Some of these social factors are easy to comprehend; for example, the communities necessary, and their overall leadership and persuasion, to plan and construct huge monuments of stone and earth. The underlying needs to seek out and colonize new territories, by deep-water craft or over-land travel, are also suggested by assessments of the quality and character of the vehicles used, and of the ways by which man could establish food production in new lands. In similar manner, the demonstrable care and expertise needed to produce objects of value, weapons, armour, containers or other prestige equipment, must lead to considerations about the societies likely to have required such items and to have possessed the organization to produce and to consume them. In all of these aspects, experiments with archaeological materials such as are outlined in this book must inevitably direct and focus attention upon the underlying reasons for the behaviour that yielded the bare artifacts we find today. This fourth level, dwelling as it should with the broader implications of technology and function to the society itself, takes us beyond the limits of clearly observable actions; some experiments have attempted just this, the observation and explanation of society in action, and several of these are described later in this book, but it is surely significant at this point to note that their results are heavily qualified by the participants themselves.

The basic approach to a successful experiment, at whatever level, must be through the setting and answering of a question or questions. Just as to dig, hoping to find something, is a totally valueless exercise today in terms of information and relevance, the experiment designed only for vague curiosity will probably yield nothing of permanent worth. The only way to approach either excavation or experiment is by questioning the evidence and current theories in an attempt to extend the present state of knowledge.

House building demonstrates the potential of the questioning approach and the relevance it has to the procedures adopted (Fig. 12). If an experiment is to test the materials, and consider time and motion aspects in the erection of the building, then care in recording details will have to be taken in order to determine the appropriate methods to be used. If the building is to be destroyed by fire, its refinements perhaps need not be so extensive, but its exact assembly and the position of each of its structures must be noted; also its physical condition must be recorded before the conflagration. If the building is to serve only as a display area, or to house museum exhibits, then its precision in erection need not be so carefully controlled. The same general conditions will apply to other experimental subjects, including boats, stone tools, and earthworks, although the details will naturally differ.

Finally, there remains the problem of how to assess the results of experiments and how much reliance to place upon the answers that emerge. First, the results should be repeatable in order to demonstrate that chance alone has not determined the result. A single successful firing of a particular type of pottery vessel must be repeated so that the process can be shown

Fig. 12(a)

(b)

FIG. 12. Construction of a replica of a Neolithic longhouse at Cuiry-les-Chaudardes, Aisne, France.

(a). The heavy posts have been erected in original post-holes; hurdle-work is ready for clay daub, and roofing members are being tied in place.

(b). The longhouse under construction.

(Photos: courtesy of Unité de Recherche Archéologique No. 12 du Centre National de la Recherche Scientifique.)

to provide a consistent result. A sophisticated stone implement, such as a Palaeoindian projectile head of flint, must be produced time and time again in order to eliminate a freak percussion blow or unusual raw material that might have yielded a first successful copy. A single sea trial of a boat should not be considered enough to prove, even disprove, its capabilities.

Second, in assessing results it is important to be aware of the options thus produced. One solitary answer may not emerge from the test: there may well be several possible solutions to an experimental problem. A stone axe-like tool may not function as an axe but may work well as an adze; it could also serve as a hoe, or spade, or mattock, or meat cleaver and if all the possible functions are not explored, then the range of optional answers remains wide. Only by series-testing can the list be reduced by elimination. And it will be more often a question of elimination rather than substantiation; it is easier to prove that an object does not work at a particular task than it is to show that the object did serve one and only one function in the past. Here microscopic examination for traces of wear on implements can help. Fortunately, for many ancient objects and structures only one or two possible functions need be entertained. A boat is presumably made for water and should therefore float! Likewise, a house is likely to have been built to shelter something beneath its roof, if it had a roof.

The procedures to be adopted for each experiment will clearly differ from others, either in substance or in detail. Yet, underlying all, are a few quite fundamental "rules of the game" some of which must be observed for all experiments; and all of them must be observed for some experiments. The acceptance of these, or versions of them, are essential for uniformity of procedures, reliability of observations, and acceptability of results.

1. The materials employed in the experiment should be those considered to be originally available to the society under examination; for example, in making replicas of ancient pottery local clays should be used, and in building copies of ancient houses, do not use plastic thatch.
2. The methods used in the work should be appropriate to the society and should not exceed its presumed competence. For instance, in building an earthwork, hand tools and manual labour should be used, and not machinery. But remember that it is unlikely that man can manipulate ancient implements such as stone axes as effectively as his ancestors —and even practice may not make perfect.
3. Modern techniques and analytical studies should be carried out before, during and after the experiments. So that the results can be fairly assessed it is important to include in the observations the analysis of materials and measurements of stresses and wear. For example, in watching the decay and collapse of a house, or break-up of a boat, it is important to know why it happened, how it happened and when it happened.
4. The scale of the work must be assessed and fairly stated. If scale models are used, uncertainties will arise and must be acknowledged; for example, scaled-down earthworks or modern earthworks cannot represent all of the factors of building and erosion of ancient banks.

A full-scale exercise on only a fraction of a structure may not represent the full impact on materials or manpower; for example, to use one timber cut with a stone axe and one hundred others cut with a buzz-saw in building a house cannot but deflect the objectives of measuring workrates, technology, stability or weathering.
5. Repetition of the experiment is important in order to avoid a freak result. For example, the production of a sophisticated flint blade may be achieved by a chance blow so the technique can only be demonstrated by repeated attempts.

Series of experiments, building on the results of previous work, can lead to greater understanding as well as exposing new problems. For example, the way grain was stored in underground pits is now easier to explain because of continued tests which show how pits can be maintained in a fresh condition. The useful life of houses is better understood now that multiple tests have been carried out over 10–15 years.

6. During each experiment certain problems will be examined in the hope of gaining answers. But improvisation should also be considered; and adaptability is of paramount importance. For instance, long-distance voyages in untested craft have always required considerable improvisation in handling the boats; firing of pottery in earth kilns has almost always meant last-minute on-the-spot repairs to achieve the appropriate seal.

7. Experimental results must not be taken as proof of ancient structural or technological detail. For instance, it is possible to sail a raft across the Pacific or the Atlantic, but these brave feats do not prove that ancient man made these voyages. In making and hardening leather shields, various methods were found successful. Any of them could have been used in the Bronze Age. But so could a number of other methods. Where a test has eliminated a possible answer, where a presumed function does not work, then the "negative" answer is likely to be a positive one, and that ancient function can be said not to have been performed by that tool. On the other hand, if a certain implement does function successfully in performing a certain act, it need not necessarily mean that the tool was actually used in this way in the past. It may have been used for another purpose not considered by the archaeologist. It is not often that absolute proof is claimed, yet in some cases it has. Work on Bushman rock art and their paints and media quite clearly indicated only one positive answer to the media problem (p. 203). Few other experiments suggest such a clear answer. The work of Heyerdahl is a case in point; although he has been able to show that voyages in reed boats across the Atlantic are possible (p. 87), he has not claimed that such voyages did take place in the past. His modesty is something that other experimenters might emulate.

8. A final test, at least as important as the others, can best be described as "honesty". The experimenter must assess the results of the experiment in the following terms: Were the materials right? Were the methods of using them appropriate? Were mistakes made? Were procedures recorded accurately? Was the experiment affected by personal opinions, idiosyncrasies, preconceived ideas, short-cuts, laziness, tiredness, boredom, over-enthusiasm? All of these must be honestly assessed, and those affecting the experiment should be stated in the publication of the results because experiments with archaeological sites and objects

are still sufficiently rare to be eagerly seized upon and used indiscriminately. They are nothing of the sort. For instance, the range of musical notes produced from Tutankamun's trumpet continues to be accepted as an entirely appropriate ancient Egyptian fanfare although serious musicians and archaeologists alike know that the experiment was a complete farce (p. 205). An honest appraisal of experimental archaeology can go as far as, but no further than: "... Where history is silent and the monuments do not speak for themselves, demonstration cannot be expected; ... the utmost is conjecture supported by probability ..." (Wise, 1742, p. 5). Experimental archaeology can provide or deny that vital "probability" to the "conjecture" about past human activities.

2 Discovery and Exploration

Wherefore Your Highnesses . . . determined to send me, Cristóbal
Colón, to the said ports of India . . . and ordered that I should
not go by lands to the East, as the custom was, but by way of the
West, by a course which no man, to our certain knowledge, has
taken until this day.

Cristóbal Colón, 1492

Man hoisted sail before he saddled a horse. He poled and
paddled along rivers and navigated the open seas before he
travelled on wheels along a road. Water-craft were the first of all
vehicles . . . were man's first major tool for his conquest of the
world.

Heyerdahl, 1978, p. 19

THE BRAVE WORDS of Christopher Columbus, calmly recorded in his
journal for 1492, mark the first historically documented attempt to sail
long distances into uncharted seas. It was not, however, the first voyage
into the unknown, brave though it was. Before Columbus many men had
undertaken voyages of equal length, longer duration and in smaller vessels.
The flagship *Santa Maria* was perhaps 25 m long and carried a crew of
about 40; small as these numbers are, they bulk large beside other voyages
which took place before Columbus, but which have not had the benefit of
historical recording. This should not reduce the impact or achievement of
the 1492 discovery of America. Columbus was the first to reach America,
to establish contact with the indigenous peoples, to return to Europe and
to set in motion the eventual recolonization of the New World. It matters
not that he was only the third or even fourth "captain" to make landfall
in the west.

Ships were the largest single movable objects known to early man
(Johnstone, 1974, p. 7). They released him from his dependence upon the
land, allowed him to travel widely, and eventually to circumnavigate the
world. All or almost all of the landmasses, continents and islands alike,
were visited, explored, colonized and exploited. The fact that remains of
early man have been recognized from many parts of the world shows that

ships and boats not only existed many centuries ago but were sea-going and capable of long voyages well outside the sight of land. The basic archaeological problem is not *if* man could travel long distances in pre-historic times, but *how* he actually did travel. The settlement of Australia, and of Polynesia in particular, are probably the best examples of long distance voyages of discovery and colonization; the short haul across the Timor Sea to northern Australia may only have required voyages of 300–500 km, but Pacific Ocean travel among the incredibly scattered islands of Polynesia would have necessitated voyages of well over 3000 km. The implication of these figures may only be apparent when we realize that voyages such as these first began 100–200 centuries ago; some assessments of these achievements are made in this book. The names of the sailors, their types of boats, their purposes and their successes are all lost in the dimness of prehistory, and it is only through the appearance of historic records of voyages, and fragments of ancient craft, that we can comprehend the seafaring abilities of early man; experiments to test both documents and fragments have helped illuminate this vital phase of human activity.

Some of the earliest recorded voyages that we know about are Egyptian, perpetuated by monumental inscriptions. An expedition *c*. 1500 B.C. to the land of Punt (Somalia) brought back cargo including "every beautiful wood of this god's country and heaps of resin of myrrh, with green myrrh trees, with ebony and ivory, . . . with baboons, lemurs and greyhounds, with natives and their children . . ." (De Buck, 1948, p. 100). The boats were not of papyrus but were of wood, and must have been large. Earlier Egyptian ships, in fact the oldest surviving ships in the world, were also built of wood (Fig. 13). In 1954, archaeologists working near the Great

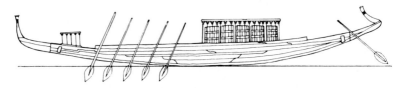

Fig. 13. The oldest "ship" in the world, made *c*. 2600 B.C. The ship, reassembled and restored, is 43 m long and displaces 40 tonnes; its survival was due to unique atmospheric conditions in its chamber, near the tomb of Cheops, Egypt. (From Johnstone, 1974.)

Pyramid at Giza (2600 B.C.) discovered a series of 15–20 tonne limestone blocks set beneath the enclosure wall of the pyramid; beneath the blocks lay the dismantled remains of a great ship, the ship of Cheops (Landström, 1970). Plank-built of cedar of Lebanon, with smaller pieces of acacia, hornbeam, juniper and soapberry, this ship was no mere funeral vessel, made only for the pharaoh's death, but had voyaged many times, and had been fitted out by different crews using a variety of rope knots and ties of halfa grass. The modern reconstruction of the ship took 14 years and it can now be seen as a flat-bottomed craft, displacing 40 tonnes, and fully 43 m long—twice as long as Columbus's *Santa Maria* yet ten times as old. Sea-going it is unlikely to have been, and yet other Egyptian boats were capable of Mediterranean and Red Sea voyages, as the land of Punt expedition shows. An early papyrus record describes such a voyage:

> I had ventured out onto the big green in a ship 120 cubits long and 40 cubits broad. One hundred and twenty of Egypt's best sailors were on board. They looked to the sky, they looked to the land, and their heart was braver than the lion's. They foresaw a storm before it had come, and a tempest before it had struck. . . .
> The sailor is worn out, the oar in his hand, the lash on his back, and his belly empty of food, while the scribe sits in the cabin, the children of the great row him, and there is no reckoning of taxes due from him.

The Cheops ship, large as it is, was not the greatest of the Egyptian craft. A stone relief of 1500 B.C. in the temple at Deir-el-Bahari depicts 30 rowing tugs hauling a great barge which brought Queen Hatshepsut's two red granite obelisks from the Aswan quarries 200 km downstream to Thebes. The surviving pieces of these obelisks, and texts, indicate that they may have been 57 km high and weighed 2400 tonnes; if so, then the barge with its cargo would have displaced 7500 tonnes and it would have been the largest vessel ever seen in the world until Brunel built *Great Britain* in 1843, and truly an amazing structure, the largest movable object known to early man.

Tantalizing records such as these confront the experimental archaeologist in his task of recreating ancient ships and journeys. How seaworthy were prehistoric and early historic craft? They must have been eminently suitable for river traffic, for coastal movements, and probably also for deep-water voyages. Herodotus (*Histories* iv) records that the pharaoh Nekós *c.* 600 B.C. ordered a Phoenician circumnavigation of Africa, starting in the Red Sea and arriving back through the Mediterranean; the voyage took two years and covered 25 000 km. Earlier craft doubtless were also suitable for long voyages, not perhaps as lengthy as this one but nonetheless in their own way as hazardous. The trouble is we do not really know what kinds of craft were built for these exploits, and the numerous representations of ancient boats and ships in the eastern Mediterranean region are fascinating for conjecture but leave much scope for argument. These craft cannot be considered here. Only those directly relevant to experimental testing will be discussed.

Two main groups of experiments relate to ancient ships and boats. Both are important, but experiments dealing with long voyages of discovery, exploration and survival are far more dramatic than those concerned with cross-channel, riverine or inland water traffic. Nonetheless each group has its own value in the field of early contact and communication.

Long-range voyages without doubt often took place in early times. Prevailing currents and winds would have been well known and understood by fishermen working along the coasts of the Atlantic, Pacific and Indian Oceans, but those men working from islands or peninsulas where currents and winds were less reliable, and the return point smaller, might have been more subject to accidental voyages. Storms have always created problems for small craft on the oceans, and it is likely that early sailors were occasionally driven off course, and contact with the home port lost, with the inevitable result of an impromptu and ill-prepared voyage into the unknown. In these circumstances new lands could be found, involuntary settlers landed, and new settlements established; their longevity was probably not guaranteed, either through the lack of their own preparations or the resistance of any inhabitants. Planned colonization is of course a different matter. It involves reconnaissance for knowledge of direction across the sea, navigational aids, the ability to sail in both directions, craft able to carry not only adult males but the trappings of the entire society, females, children, animals, plants, traditions and ideas. We know that many such colonizing voyages took place in the past, and they represent the most challenging aspect of experimental ship archaeology, and one hardly taken up. What has so far been substituted is the demonstration that such voyages, planned and deliberate, could have taken place with the equipment and technology available at selected times in the prehistory of the Atlantic shores and Pacific islands over the past four or five thousand years.

Experiments such as these create their own excitement and fascination, as they involve risk, danger and survival for both craft and crew. Food supplies including fresh water, navigation by ancient methods, and the strength of the boat, as well as the courage of the captain and crew, all combine to create an atmosphere of adventure and a bonus for the experiment which can be as serious and scholarly as any land-locked and comfortable piece of experimental work. The essential point of the long voyage experiment and one to which we shall refer again, is that to demonstrate the discovery and subsequent settlement of new lands by ancient mariners involves not only the initial voyage but also the return, when reverse conditions of winds and currents are likely to be met. There must have been many involuntary discoveries by unwilling sailors blown off course and unable to get back, but their contribution to human knowledge and settlement is less than that of the hardy souls who managed to discover and report for subsequent exploitation. Too many experimental archaeologists have been content with one-way voyages and an easy conclusion that the return journey was possible. For an explorer, the return journey must have been the more difficult. He lacked the home harbour and its craftsmen to fit out and repair his boat, and he lacked accessible and reliable supplies of food for his journey. He knew less well where he had landed and his navigation homewards was likely to be less reliable, particularly during the earlier part of the voyage. The condition of his crew may not have been as good as it was when he set out; and it was likely to deteriorate if either boat or food was unreliable. For these reasons experiments involving long-range voyages really should attempt the round trip; how much more successful would Heyerdahl's *Kon-Tiki* and *Ra* experiments have been had it been possible to turn and sail back to the homeland. *Kon-Tiki* could have, *Ra* could not, in theory, but the demonstrations would have been impressive. Both expeditions were successes in various ways, of course, and their contributions are discussed below.

The second group of experiments with boats is less impressive at first sight, and has not gripped the imagination as have the longer voyages. Nonetheless, for ancient settlement and movement of people, for the development of exchanges and trade, for culture communication, the short-haul voyages are equally if not more important than the voyages of discovery. The archaeological record of both Old and New Worlds speaks of coastal and riverine movement in the first penetration of new territories, in the preference for new settlements near major waterways, in the exploitation of marine and estuarine resources, in the establishment of ports for active trading networks, and in the gradual occupation of island chains and clusters. All of these activities required rafts, boats or ships, and a huge variety of craft must have been devised to cope with the opportunities. Experiments dealing with these aspects have not been numerous, and this remains an open field for work. Such crafts and crews would have to be capable of loading and unloading an adequate cargo, beaching on and launching from a variety of shores, propelling by sail, paddles or oars, manoeuvring in cross currents and unpredictable breezes; and these requirements could be met by vessels made of wood, wicker, skin or reed as the occasion permitted. Experiments on wooden or skin boats have greatly aided our appreciation of the potential worth of a few of the small boats of the last 4000 years, but much more remains to be done.

The experiments dealing with both large and small boats for long-range and short-haul voyages have been many and varied, and not all can be mentioned here. The major evidence for the experiments comes from

c

actual surviving pieces of boat, historical references to crafts and voyages, and representations of events and art objects (seals, reliefs, rock engravings).

Wooden parts of boats are all too rare, but some notable discoveries have been made. These allow the archaeologist to see and to handle the actual boat components, to gain a detailed knowledge of materials, sizes and workmanship which he cannot obtain in any other way. Each new discovery of an ancient wreck can yield important information, often of far greater value than the yield of its cargo which is often the sole reason for modern exploration. Most ancient boats have, of course, been discovered beneath the sea where conditions for preservation of wood may be extremely poor, but silts and muds of estuaries and coasts in particular can also preserve major parts of boats and ships. The humid conditions which allowed the Cheops ship to survive were almost unique. In all cases, however, conservation of the wooden remains must be immediate, as otherwise the character of the components will be lost by shrinkage, warping and cracking of the drying timbers. Reconstructions based on actual wooden remains are likely to be more accurate and hence more reliable than those based upon records of parts now lost, or interpretations of what was probably there before. The development of techniques for recording and recovery of ship remains from beneath the sea has allowed far more accuracy in reconstruction than was previously possible. One of the earliest such rescue attempts concerned the Cape Antikythera wreck, off the Greek coast, discovered in 1900 and explored by spongedivers wearing copper helmets, lead weights and metal shoes, with air supplied by a hand-compressor. At 55 m depth, working time was 5 minutes per man; most divers suffered from nitrogen narcosis. The task can be seen in the perspective of another famous excavation on dry land; the effect must have been as if Tutankamun's tomb had been explored in 5-minute shifts by drunken stevedores wearing coal-buckets on their heads, never having seen a tomb before (Throckmorton, 1970). The contrast between the first underwater investigations and the most modern recoveries is beyond measure. One of the finest examples of the latter is the project for the Skuldelev Viking ships which were scuttled in a channel of the Roskilde fjord *c*. A.D. 1000, discovered in 1957, lifted in 1962, conserved in pieces ever since, and steadily reconstructed in a new museum at Roskilde. Experiments based upon these ships have the immeasurable benefits of actual materials, sizes and technologies preserved in the originals; there is room for conjecture still, but serious flaws can be largely avoided (Crumlin-Pedersen, 1970).

Another source of evidence about ancient boats survives in documented records of types of craft, methods of manufacture, and voyages. Allowance must be made for exaggeration on occasion, and rarely are technical details included, but references to actual voyages provide the stimuli for experiment. The Viking voyages to North America, now established beyond doubt, are outlined in Icelandic sagas but it is often difficult to distinguish contemporary records from those additions made later when the sagas were written (Jones, 1964). Nonetheless, the role of Viking ships in the ravaging of England *c*. 1000 A.D. was and is undisputed, just as the reliability of the ships was unquestioned during the explorations and settlements on coastal America at about the same time. Less certain are the facts about a possible earlier landing by St Brendan, *c*. 500 A.D. Historical records of the tenth century describe his voyages in the north Atlantic, and a recent experiment to test this history is described in this book. Ethnographic records of boats and technologies from many parts of the world are another and more reliable source for reconstructions and experiments, as they show certain aspects of woodworking which may be reflected in archaeological materials, such as the use of fire for hollowing logs, wedges for plank splitting, and types of rafts and skin boats which may have been in use in earlier times. The balsa rafts of Ecuador were first described by Europeans in 1735, and serve to support the form of experimental raft, the *Kon-Tiki*, which Heyerdahl built; the *guaras* or planks used to guide the raft allowing it to sail near the wind were also recorded at this early date (Fox, 1875, p. 426). A caribou skin boat made for an ethnographer by Newfoundland Indians in 1874 foreshadowed in the same way the more recent exploits with a version of St Brendan's boat. Such ethnographic records are a valuable, but increasingly rare, tool for the experimental archaeologist.

A final source of material for reconstructions of boats and ships are representations of various craft on tomb walls, living rock, paintings, seals and models. These give rise to the difficulties of scale, artistic mis-representation, political exaggeration, and lack of specific detail, yet even so they can provide a guide to further studies as well as serving as models for experimental reconstructions. Clay models, paintings and engraving of boats from Egypt and Iraq date back to *c*. 6000–4000 years ago, and some of the paintings show rigging and sails which are generally lacking in other sources (Krzak, 1971, 1972). They also sometimes depict the methods and arrangements for propulsion; a later depiction, of the fifth century B.C., on the Siren Vase, shows Odysseus bound to the mast while his crew row past the sirens with the men's ears filled with beeswax. The boat is shown from the side and we can see four oarsmen, six oars and seven oarports (Fig. 14). This suggests that each bench held three men, two of whom pulled oars on one side of the boat, the third working alone on the other side; alternating in this way, the four benches held twelve men, six oars per side, with the seventh oarport used on occasion to counteract sidewinds. A small experiment tested the feasibility of twelve oarsmen working from only four benches; it showed that no difficulties were likely (Tilley, 1971). Other pictorial representations from the eastern Mediterranean have been the subject of discussion and argument concerning the types of boats as well as the occasions when they were used; but most theories have not been tested by experiment. Engravings on rock surfaces in northern Europe, however, often depict Bronze Age boats *c*. 1500–500 B.C., and these have been subjected to both interpretation and experimental reconstruction (p. 92). In the total absence of any surviving Bronze Age boats from northern Europe, the problems are great and the results controversial but nonetheless fascinating.

FIG. 14. Sketch of the design on the Siren Vase, showing Odysseus bound to the mast of his ship as his men, their ears stopped with beeswax, row past the sirens (not shown on this sketch, but depicted as winged creatures on the original). Note the six oars, seven oarports, yet only four men, on the port side; this has led to the suggestion that each bench held three men, with alternate pairs rowing on starboard and port sides.

These three sources, surviving boats, documentary evidence, and artistic representations, form the basis for an understanding of ancient exploration, colonization, transportation of goods and exploitation of the sea. Such an understanding is imperative in any attempts to reconstruct how ancient societies lived, how contacts were made and maintained, how goods and ideas travelled. Too often it is assumed that boats and ships were available, that navigation was easy, and that contacts were therefore easy to establish and maintain. This may be so, but it is necessary to demonstrate *how* such events took place rather than assume them. Experimental testing may not be able to prove conclusively that particular events did take place in the past, but they go some way towards the demonstration that ancient man was a capable boat-builder and an intrepid sailor (McKee, 1977).

Without doubt, pride of place in any list of boat experiments must go to the *Kon-Tiki* expedition (Heyerdahl, 1950, 1955). This was not the first experiment dealing with boats, it was not the first long-distance voyage, and its results have not led to a major revision of views; but as a dramatic yet academically sound event, it has not really been surpassed by anything before or since. The theory behind Heyerdahl's expedition was that parts of Polynesia could have been colonized from America: the current view, well-documented by physical anthropology and archaeology, is that the multitude of islands of Polynesia, from the Marianas and Hawaiian Islands in the north to the Solomon, Samoa and Society Islands in the south were progressively colonized from south-east Asia. Heyerdahl's thesis that parts of Polynesia could have been reached and therefore settled from America was based on similarities in material culture between coastal South America and Polynesia. Most authorities dismissed the idea by accepting a dogma of 1875 that the coastal South American boats and rafts were incapable of deepwater voyages; the balsa raft of Peru was described as a "floating bundle of cork-wood" (Hutchinson, 1875). Other authorities did not even accept this view, and stated categorically that the balsa raft "absorbs water rapidly and loses its buoyancy completely after a few weeks" (Lothrop, 1932). Further scorn was poured on the craft in an interesting demonstration of how a single ill-founded remark can be magnified and come to represent the main argument for or against a theory: " . . . it was obviously a type of boat that would awake nothing but scorn in the breasts of shipbuilders of almost any other maritime people in the world." (Means, 1942.) Finally, in 1945, the possibility of an American contribution to Polynesian culture was totally dismissed: "Since the South American Indians had neither the vessels nor the navigating ability to cross the ocean space between their shores and the nearest Polynesian islands, they may be disregarded as the agents of supply." (Buck, 1945.)

It is amazing, now, to turn to the historical records of west coastal South America, carefully researched by Heyerdahl (1955, 1957), and read the numerous and unambiguous reports of the ocean-going capabilities of ancient indigenous Peruvian balsa rafts (Fig. 15). In 1526, Francisco Pizarro's expedition encountered a large balsa raft well out to sea. The Spaniards captured a crew of twenty Indian men and women aboard of whom eleven were at once thrown overboard, four left to sail on, and five taken into captivity to train as interpreters for the next peaceful contact.

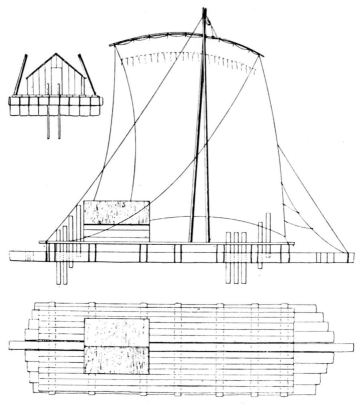

FIG. 15. The balsa raft of South America, drawn by F. E. Paris (1841–43). Heyerdahl's *Kon-Tiki* was constructed in the same way. The guaras or steering boards extend between the logs. This raft could be up to 25 m long, 8 m wide and could carry loads of 20 tonnes. Only 9 large balsa logs were needed, with 7 smaller crossbeams. (From Heyerdahl, 1978.)

The raft itself was a cargo ship of 36 tonnes displacement, nearly as heavy as the Spanish caravel; it was carefully described by Pizarro's officials as a flat raft made of logs with a deck of slender canes, the whole tied together by rope. It carried masts and yards of fine wood, cotton sails with rigging of henequen rope. Many other reports of sightings and contacts were made over the subsequent decades of Spanish exploration. In 1560 a Spanish missionary described Indians as "great mariners; they have large rafts of light timber with which they navigate the ocean, and while fishing they remain many leagues out to sea". The most important of these early records suggested that a South American army had sailed from Peru in the decades before Pizarro, had been gone for one year, and on return had reported landings on two inhabited islands far out in the ocean.

An early historian of Peru, Bernabé Cobo, described the ocean-going rafts in the sixteenth century:

> The largest rafts used by the Peruvian Indians living near the forests...are composed of seven, nine or more logs of balsa timber, in the following manner: the logs are lashed one to another lengthwise by means of lianas or ropes tied over other logs which lie as cross-beams; the log in the middle is longer than the others at the bow, and one by one they are shorter the closer they are placed to the sides, in such a way that, at the bow, they get the same form and proportions as seen on the fingers of an extended hand, although the stern is even. On the top of this they place a platform so that the people and the clothing on board shall not get wet from the water which comes up in the cracks between the large timbers. These rafts navigate on the ocean by means of sail and paddles, and some are so large that they are easily able to carry fifty men.

The dispute about possible American contributions to Polynesian culture became centred upon the balsa raft, presumably because few if any authorities were aware of, or acknowledged, these early reports. Hence Heyerdahl's decision to demonstrate the seaworthiness of a balsa raft was perfectly justified in the situation. Neither the majority of authorities nor Heyerdahl was aware of the existence of balsa sailing rafts in a small area of Peru at the present time (Edwards, 1960). Heyerdahl's raft, the *Kon-Tiki*, was made of nine balsa logs, each 0.7 m in diameter and varying in length from 14 to 10 m; these logs were felled in the deep forests of the interior and floated down to the port of embarkation at Callao, Peru. The logs were slightly grooved to hold the hemp rope bindings, and they were tied together to make a raft 14 m long and 5 m wide with the longest logs at the centre forming a pointed raft with a squared end. Upon the logs a platform of thinner logs and a deck of bamboo slats were fastened by rope; and a bamboo, reed and banana leaf cabin was positioned at the centre. A bipod mast of mangrove wood was set forward of the cabin, and held a square canvas sail, 6 × 5 m; a steering oar was attached to a balsa block at the stern, and five guaras or centre-boards were placed between the balsa logs projecting about 1.5 m into the water beneath the raft. In the water, the heavy balsa logs were about half-submerged, and further slender logs were tied along the sides to prevent too much water shipping across the deck. The contraption as completed looked totally unseaworthy. Heyerdahl records the disappointment felt by him and his crew of five men at the comments of his friends and advisors. The only dispute among them was which of the fatal mistakes would first cause disaster on the voyage—the balsa logs becoming waterlogged or breaking in two; the ropes wearing through and collapsing the structure; the men being washed overboard; or the whole thing being totally unmanageable. With these cheerful comments ringing in their ears, the crew set sail on 28 April 1947. Food for four months was taken, as well as 1250 litres of water. But in retrospect they realized it would have been possible to manage on far less; a constant stream of flying fish, bonitos and dolphin was available, and rain provided extra water.

The various problems encountered on the voyage were minor, once it was realized that the balsa logs would indeed float for a long time and were strong enough to avoid breakage in heavy seas. The raft was judged to be a perfect carrier for heavy cargo: it had minimal freeboard, but it rose with every swell and wave, overriding the threatening weight of water which would have crushed more slender craft. Even so, the topsy-turvy ride would have alarmed most sailors at first, and certainly did the *Kon-Tiki's* crew until they realized its strength and safety:

> When, swallowed up by the darkness, we heard the general noise from the sea around us suddenly deafened by the hiss of a roller close by, and saw a white crest come groping towards us on a level with the cabin roof, we held on tight and waited uneasily to feel the masses of water smash down over us and the raft. But every time there was the same surprise and relief. The *Kon-Tiki* calmly swung up her stern and rose skyward unperturbed, while the masses of water rolled along her sides. Then we sank down again into the trough of the waves ...'
>
> Heyerdahl, 1950, p. 79

The raft's other secret was its openwork construction which allowed all water to wash through it and fall back into the sea: no weight of water could ever accumulate long enough to create damage, and the raft could never be broken up by waves or swells. The other threatened problems also did not materialize. The ropes soon forced their way into the soft outer part of the balsa logs, but then were stopped by the green sap-filled wood: as the ropes were then buried, no friction could develop between ropes and logs. The sap in the logs prevented waterlogging, and *Kon-Tiki* could have continued in use as a cargo-carrier long after her maiden voyage. Even so the strain on the crew was great. Steering the raft was the greatest problem. The stout mangrove steering pole with pine oarblade attached was pinned to a heavy balsa block at the stern and tied with ropes to the sides of the raft in order to check extreme movement.

Sailing steadily westwards, the raft averaged 79 km per day, with a minimum of 16 km and a maximum of 130 km. After 45 days, 3700 km had been covered, and on 17 July (80 days) island seabirds were sighted. Currents carried the raft past Angatau at the end of July although the inhabitants made an attempt to tow *Kon-Tiki* into the lagoon. On 7 August, after a voyage of 6900 km and 101 days, the raft was washed on to the Raroia reef in the Tuamotu Islands; although the cabin and masts were wrecked by waves, the crew and most of the cargo were safely landed (Fig. 16). The theory that the coastal rafts of South American Indians were totally unseaworthy, and therefore that the question of American involvement in the Polynesian settlement was invalid, was shown to be wrong.

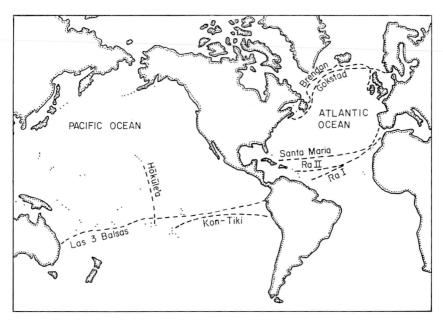

FIG. 16. Some routes taken by ancient and experimental boats in the Atlantic and Pacific Oceans: the *Gokstad* replica across the north Atlantic; St *Brendan*'s boat across the north Atlantic; *Ra I* and *Ra II* across the central Atlantic; *Kon-Tiki* into the Pacific; *Hōkūle'a* between Hawaii and Tahiti; *Las 3 Balsas* across the Pacific.

Nevertheless, Heyerdahl had not succeeded in manipulating the centre-boards of the raft in such a way that he could tack into the wind. The five guaras or centreboards enabled the raft to sail almost at right angles to the wind; and by raising or lowering a guara fore or aft the raft could be steered without the steering oar. Yet the inability of *Kon-Tiki* to sail into the wind was a serious blow to any theory of close and continuing contact between coastal South America and the Pacific Islands. Heyerdahl returned to this problem in a series of later experiments not generally well publicized. A smaller raft of nine balsa logs was made with square sail held on a bipod mast, and six guaras inserted between the logs (two in the bow, two in the stern). No paddles, rudder or steering oar were carried on the raft on its test off the coast of Ecuador (Heyerdahl, 1955, 1957). By experiment it was learned that the interplay between sail and guaras allowed the raft to tack into the wind, and to sail back to the exact launching place. The effect was simplicity itself: the centreboards provide sideways resistance to the water as well as preventing leeward drift just as the keel of a modern sailboat does. By raising the sternboard, for instance, less resistance is felt at the stern and it drifts away from the wind, thereby altering course. This discovery was not new because in about 1615 a Dutch explorer had drawn a picture of a balsa raft arriving in a Peruvian harbour after a two-month fishing trip; two of the crew were shown attending to the sail, and the other three members were raising or lowering the guaras. In 1736 Spanish naval officers observed and recorded balsa rafts sailing into the wind (Juan and de Ulloa, 1748); subsequent histories are emphatic on the same point. The guara as a tool by itself is useless: it only works as a steering board on a vessel with a sail. The abundance of guaras in ancient Peruvian graves therefore suggests that it was a well-established tradition for coastal South Americans to sail vessels in the Pacific waters. Heyerdahl's experiments had again only confirmed what we should have known all along from European explorers, sailors and historians. Ocean-going craft could and did move out from the coastal waters of South America well into the Pacific; the indigenous balsa raft, almost universally despised by marine historians, could set its course with the wind to any port and could, as well as any sailing vessel, find its way back against prevailing winds.

> I shall never forget the sensation produced in a ship I commanded one evening on the coast of Peru, as we steered towards the roadstead of Payta, so celebrated in Anson's voyage, and beheld an immense Balsa dashing out before the land wind, and sending a snowy wreath of foam before her like that which curls up before the bow of a frigate in chase. As long as she was kept before the wind we could understand this in some degree; but when she hauled up in order to round the point, and having made a stretch along shore, proceeded to tack, we could scarcely believe our eyes. Had the celebrated Flying Dutchman sailed past us, our wonder could hardly have been excited more.
>
> Hall, 1833

The contributions made by the *Kon-Tiki* expedition are not restricted to the simple argument about American Indian participation in Polynesian settlement. Whether or not contact was made and maintained is in a sense immaterial to the problem. What Heyerdahl demonstrated was the urge and necessity to experiment, to test a theory, not to accept blind dogma and popular ideas. He has conclusively shown that coastal American Indians possessed vessels capable of carrying heavy cargo, of voyaging on the ocean, and of navigating back to home port from any location. Against the weight of scientific archaeological evidence for a south-east Asian origin of Polynesian settlement any American contribution overall must have been slight if it was ever present in the westernmost islands of Polynesia. Nonetheless, *Kon-Tiki* and its successors keep alive the possibilities for further research in this subject, although their major contribution to the world of archaeology must be seen within the field of concepts of experiment and the testing of theories.

Since the *Kon-Tiki* sailed from Peru to Raroia in 1947, there have been a dozen other experimental voyages in balsa rafts from Peru and Ecuador in South America westwards into the Pacific. *Seven Sisters* sailed to Samoa in 1954, *Tahiti Nui II* (made from bamboo) sailed to Rakahanga in 1958, *La Cantuta* sailed to Matahira in 1959, *Age Unlimited* sailed all the way from Peru to Samoa and on to Australia in 1963–64, *Tangaroa* sailed to Fakareva in 1965, *La Balsa* reached Australia in 161 days in 1970, and three more rafts in convoy sailed through Polynesia and Melanesia to Australia in 1973, taking 179 days. *La Cantuta I* sailed in 1955 from Peru to the Galapagos Islands where it entered a current which allowed it to sail neither west nor east; the same happened to *Pacifica* which struggled for 143 days to return to America before abandonment. The captain of *Pacifica* was Vitale Alsar, who, with *La Balsa* and the three-raft expedition, has now travelled by balsa raft a total distance of 42 500 km—more than the circumference of the earth at its equator.

Eric de Bisschop, the captain of the log raft *Tahiti Nui II*, had previously attempted to sail a Chinese junk from west to east—from Indonesia to Polynesia—to test a presumed route of colonists. He spent three years in his ship but did not succeed as the currents were opposed to him. De Bisschop sailed in a Polynesian canoe from Hawaii back to Indonesia easily, then tried to sail a bamboo raft from Tahiti eastwards to Peru, to reverse the *Kon-Tiki* voyage. After seven months, still 1600 km west of Chile, he abandoned his craft as it was on the point of drifting back to Polynesia. His final effort, in *Tahiti Nui II*, ended in a successful voyage, but he lost his life on the reef at Rakahanga. Truly he was a brave adventurer.

Another experiment to sail from west to east, and one which told anthropologists much, was the "Projekt Pazifik"; this was an attempt to sail an Asiatic junk, based upon a first-century A.D. clay model, from the China Sea to Ecuador. In 1974 the junk *Tai Ki* set sail and was soon dragged northwards into the north Pacific currents used by European explorers. After 114 days, the junk had reached 40°N and was still 3200 km from north-west America. The collapsing vessel was abandoned, the crew picked up by aircraft, and the wreck was later seen drifting near Alaska. This experiment in fact demonstrated the route to America: across the north Pacific, winds and currents flowed west to east, and upon reaching

America turned southwards towards northern Polynesia. Hawaiian canoes were formerly built of North American pine which had drifted down. Fifty years ago a canoe was sailed direct from Vancouver Island to central Polynesia and on to New Zealand.

Polynesia is a term which embraces a multitude of islands in the Pacific, forming a rough triangle with the Hawaiian Islands in the north, Easter Island in the south-east, and New Zealand in the south-west. Decades of archaeological and anthropological work in the islands of the Pacific have conclusively demonstrated the sequence of colonization of Polynesia from an original base in south-east Asia (Bellwood, 1978); the mechanisms of this have yet to be experimentally established. The earliest settlements in the Pacific are known from Melanesia, including New Guinea, where occupation dates back as far as 25 000 years ago. Archaeological finds in the Solomon, New Hebrides and Fiji Islands demonstrate that Melanesia was gradually colonized over the succeeding millennia, and between 3000 and 2000 b.c. the small islands of Micronesia in the north were settled. The evolution of distinctive Polynesian culture, however, began to take place with the major settlement of Tonga and Samoa in the centuries between 1500 and 1000 b.c. About the time of Christ, Polynesians founded colonies in the Marquesas and the Tokelau Islands. The Marquesas Islands probably served as the base for settlements established from *c.* 500 a.d. in the Society Islands and then Easter Island, followed by further expansion north to Hawaii and south-west to New Zealand. Subsequent episodes of colonization by specific groups of Polynesians throughout the whole area are not our concern here. The point is that there is overwhelming evidence for a south-east Asian origin for the first settlement of Polynesia, and for an indigenous development of Polynesian culture in the Pacific. The success of the *Kon-Tiki* expedition has not altered this basic model.

One of the most fascinating subjects in Polynesian settlement was the character of the boats which must have been used to explore and to transport groups of people from island to island. The development of vessels capable of sailing long distances was a vital necessity for this settlement, and should rank high in any list of human inventions. Watercraft capable of sailing thousands of kilometres across the ocean, carrying not only crew but passengers, as well as food, livestock and plants, must have existed before 1000 b.c. The character of historically recorded boats in Polynesia suggests that these earlier craft were large double canoes. Twin-hulled canoes were favoured by recent Polynesians for any long-distance travel because they had far greater carrying capacity and greater stability than the single-hull canoe with outrigger. Nonetheless, the problem concerning these canoes was simply stated: Could migrations have taken place intentionally by voyages of exploration, report and planned colonization? Or were all the migrations of people the result of accidental drift of canoes? The first view involved a Polynesian ability to send out exploring parties, and for them to return and guide settlers to the new-found land. The second view insisted that colonization took place from canoes lost at sea and drifting by wind and current; or that groups of Polynesians had been exiled, by choice or force, from their homes and had to set sail in the hope of finding new land. The quality and character of the double canoe is an important part of this discussion because its ability to sail to windward was crucial if the Polynesians were to attempt return voyages to report discoveries and to organize colonizing parties. As the general direction of Polynesian settlement was from west to east, against the prevailing easterly trade winds and currents, it seems likely that their canoes could sail to windward, but in the absence of surviving early forms of canoe or historic records of such long voyages the problem of demonstrating this theory still remained.

An interesting computer simulation of winds and currents, as they would have affected canoes, suggested that accidental drift voyages were unlikely to have been the cause of west-to-east movements of Polynesians, and further that drifting canoes had virtually no chance of reaching Hawaii, Easter Island and New Zealand from other regions of Polynesia (Levison et al., 1973). Even so, the absence of surviving original Polynesian canoes, the loss of traditions of building such canoes, and the lack of historic records of canoe performances, all combined to create a gap in vital information about the vessel's abilities to sail to windward.

The last surviving double canoes of Polynesia were Hawaiian, and adequate records existed of these so that a recreation was possible. The Hawaiian double canoe was up to 20 m long and could carry as many as 80 men. The freeboard was low, perhaps 60 cm, and the twin hulls were linked by cross pieces, carrying a narrow platform between the hulls which left room for inboard paddlers. One or two masts carried woven pandanus sails of triangular shape with the apex held down to a curved boom. Steering paddles were held against the hulls near the stern.

The first experiments, designed to test the theory that such canoes could sail into the wind, used scale-models (Bechtol, 1963) and then fibreglass copies of the modern canoes were constructed (Finney, 1967). Two identical models of a Hawaiian outrigger canoe were made; then the two fibreglass hulls were joined to form a double canoe called *Nalehia*. By sailing and paddling in sheltered waters it was found that the canoe could sail downwind at 16 km per hour in a moderate wind and at 55° to windward. The canoe when carrying an overall load of 3 tonnes could be paddled by a crew of 12 men at an overall rate of 3 knots in calm conditions, and 6 knots at full stretch; with a 20-knot headwind and virtually no current, only one knot could be achieved.

These results were stimulating but inconclusive for a variety of reasons which are self-apparent. The decision was then made to undertake a further more authentic experiment to demonstrate the ability of canoes to sail from island chain to island chain across Polynesia (Finney, 1977). It was not merely the canoes that were to be tested; the calculation of position, the navigation beyond the sight of land, and the ability to find small and remote islands many hundreds of kilometres away were tests of the sailors themselves.

The islands of Polynesia are widely scattered (Fig. 16), but many of the groups are also very large, the Society Islands measuring 250 × 460 km, the Hawaiian Islands three times this size; so the precision necessary to guide a vessel towards such groups is reduced. Nevertheless, navigational skills exhibited and recorded by Polynesian sailors are of the highest order and would allow them to sail to particular islands with little difficulty. A Pacific navigator used the paths of stars, ocean current, zenith stars, flight paths of birds, the colours of the ocean, driftwood and seaweed, cloud formations and ocean swell distortions, each of these telling him of his course, his need to alter direction, his proximity to landfall (Lewis, 1972; Gladwin, 1977). As examples, navigators steered towards sequences of stars as they rose from a point on the horizon, leading to the destination islands. Ocean swells of known direction and strength could be compensated for by angling the canoe's pitch and roll. Stars known to pass directly over an island provided latitude readings for navigators, as an island could be approached upwind until the star was overhead, then the canoe could turn due west and sail with the wind straight to landfall. Nesting birds on flights to or from their feeding grounds gave indication of their island homes. Warm updrafts from islands held cumulus clouds high above the land while allowing smaller clouds to drift away to sea; clouds reflected the green waters of lagoons; deepwater blues changing to greens heralded the proximity to reefs. Driftwood signalled land to windward. Seaweed suggested an upcurrent and a reef. Ocean swells, deflected off islands, bent and betrayed the position of the land by its angle. All of these phenomena were known to Polynesian navigators, who, by aiming towards the centre of an island block, could achieve sighting of land before altering course to the precise island port once the landmarks were clear. Nevertheless, this bare statement does less than justice to the incredible skills once held by Polynesian navigators, now increasingly rare. The careful recording of these skills by marine anthropologist David Lewis, himself no mean navigator, may help to preserve the traditions. Much of Lewis's documentation was provided, through example, by Tevake of the

Santa Cruz Islands, perhaps the finest recent navigator of all Polynesia.

The double canoe for the sailing experiments was built in Hawaii. *Nalehia*, mentioned above, was 13 m long, and *Hōkūle'a*, a reconstruction of a two-masted early Polynesian canoe, was 19 m long (Fig. 17). *Nalehia* had been based on nineteenth-century drawings and fragments of old canoes. But *Hōkūle'a*, representing the oldest type of sailing canoe, had to be devised from sources drawn from all over Polynesia; the sprit sail,

Fig. 17. The *Hōkūle'a* under sail, voyaging between Hawaii and Tahiti (from Finney, 1977).

found throughout Polynesia, was selected, as was a semi-V-shaped hull in preference to the rounded U-shaped hull of *Nalehia*. The *Hōkūle'a* hull gave greater resistance to leeway and considerable cargo capacity, both useful features for long voyages to windward. Because traditions of building double-hull canoes from suitable native materials were difficult to find in Hawaii, *Hōkūle'a* was also made of modern materials, and cannot therefore provide data on the strength and lasting nature of Polynesian canoes. This seems a very serious drawback to the experiments; however, the canoe was basically of native design in hulls, in rigging and sail plan, and was probably comparable in displacement (11 400 kg fully loaded) to original canoes. The sailing trials took place in 1975 and 1976, with the major experiment a voyage from Hawaii to Tahiti and back to test the ability of Polynesian canoes and navigators to move freely in any direction across the ocean. The voyages were sponsored by the Polynesian Voyaging Society. In the trials, *Hōkūle'a* achieved a maximum of 18.5 km per hour, much less than modern catamarans whose use of modern crosspieces allows much wider spacing of the hulls and therefore larger sail areas. The wooden crosspieces and coconut fibre lashings of Polynesian canoes could not permit wide spacing of the hulls because of the dangers of breakage, and hence the sails had to be rather small to prevent capsizing. *Hōkūle'a* carried 50 m² of sail, whereas modern catamarans often carry over 125 m². The concern about the strength of the double-hull design also extended to swamping, because once this occurred it was very difficult to recover: as one hull was bailed out, its buoyancy depressed the other into the water. In rough open waters a crew might have difficulties. *Hōkūle'a* proved to be sensitive to heavy seas and light winds when heavily loaded, but it could sail quite close to the wind, and made about 10 km per hour at 70°–75° off the wind in moderate-to-strong conditions.

The voyages between Hawaii and Tahiti in 1976 tested the theory of sailing against the wind and therefore of controlled Polynesian colonization, navigation by traditional methods, and *Hōkūle'a* itself. Hawaii lies well to leeward of Tahiti, and a wind course of 75° to wind and current was projected. The strategy was to sail the canoe against the prevailing north-east and south-east trade winds and equatorial currents in order to reach Tahiti along a curved course, first sailing south-east against the north-east winds and currents, then allowing the current to push the canoe eastwards in the doldrums, and finally taking a course slightly west of south using the south-east winds and current (Fig. 17). The voyage, of 17 men and a dog, began on 1 May 1976; the crew consisted of Hawaiians and *haoles* (non-Hawaiians) with the navigator, Mau Piailug, from the Caroline Islands far to the west. In 1974 he had navigated his outrigger canoe from Satawal to Saipan and back, between the Caroline and Mariannas

Islands, a voyage of over 1700 km, using the traditional methods of star sightings and sailing distances for the hundreds of islands of Micronesia (Gladwin, 1977). For the Polynesian voyage he was advised by Lewis and a Tahitian navigator, but his own mastery of traditional methods was of paramount importance.

The voyage from Hawaii was not without incident, but the canoe behaved well and after 32 sailing days and 5370 km, landfall was made in Tahiti. After a short stay, the return journey was completed in 22 days with more favourable winds; and the voyagers were given a wild reception in Hawaii. The performance of *Hōkūl'a*, which could sail a course of 75° off the wind over long open ocean waters, suggests that Polynesians with more experience and knowledge than the experimenters could have explored and settled all the islands. It would have been useful to have had further trial sailings due east. Although the modern materials used in *Hōkūle'a* make it impossible to calculate the exact strength and durability of the original canoes, it seems logical to conclude that native materials would have been sufficiently well chosen to permit the building of vessels capable of extended voyages.

These experiments, computer simulation, and observation suggest that many of the island groups of Polynesia could have been linked by regular voyages in past centuries. But this is unlikely to have been the case for all Polynesian islands; voyages from Tonga to the Marquesas, for example, were not possible in normal trade-wind conditions. The journey from Tahiti to New Zealand involves unfavourable winds and two-way voyages would have been rare—certainly they would have involved extraordinary navigational skill. Easter Island, too, would have been a difficult landfall, as it lies far to windward and does not have a cluster of islands around it to provide a broad target. Doubtless many canoes were lost at sea through inexperience, uncertainty and misfortune. However, the combined weight of archaeological research, historical records and experiments indicate the strong possibility, some would say certainty, that two-way voyaging played an important part in the colonization of the many islands of Polynesia.

Basically the same thing can be said of the early settlement of North America, not of course the first settlement by hunters and gatherers crossing the dry Bering Straits many thousands of years ago, but the discovery and subsequent colonization by Europeans within the past thousand years. In the north Atlantic ocean, conditions were obviously different from those of the central Pacific. The problems for early explorers involved extreme cold, fog and ice; furthermore, there were no island groups as sightings or landfalls across the 3000–6000 km (depending on the route) between Europe and America, unless the northern route was taken to Iceland and Greenland (Fig. 17). Both the central Atlantic and the north Atlantic crossings have been attempted by archaeologists hoping to test particular boats or theories, but the earliest experiments were concerned with the exploits of the first European colonists of North America, the Vikings.

Viking sagas, particularly the "Greenlanders' Saga" and the "Saga of Eirik the Red", record the discovery of a land west of Greenland in 985 (Jones, 1964; Cumming *et al.*, 1971). In this year, Bjarni Herjolfsson was blown southwards in attempting a voyage from Iceland to Greenland. Bjarni sighted three lands in five days of sailing northwards to Greenland. In 1001, Leif Eiriksson sailed in Bjarni's ship to explore these lands, and he named them Helluland, Markland and Vinland. His records of the length of the shortest day suggests that Vinland was south of the St Lawrence river. Further settlements were made in succeeding years, and in the first encounter with native Americans, the Greenlanders killed 8 of the 9 men they found sleeping beneath skin boats. The subsequent settlements were unsuccessful, and the Greenlanders abandoned the country in the early eleventh century.

Throughout the accounts of exploration, the Viking ships are not recorded in any dramatic way, but only as vehicles for sailing along the coasts, up the rivers and fjords, and back to Greenland; they were clearly well adapted to this sort of coastal travel. We know little of the size of these ships except that Thorfinn Karlsefni, an Icelandic merchant who attempted a colony in Vinland *c.* 1010, had three ships for 160 people and all necessary supplies. The type of ship is unknown, but many remains of these ships have been recovered in the homelands of the Vikings (Christiansen, 1968).

Among the numerous burial mounds of the Viking period in northern Europe, protecting the inhumed or cremated remains of men, women and children, a few have contained traces of Viking ships and wagons. Many ordinary graves consist only of a male with his weapons or a female with her jewellery. But others are much more elaborate, and these provide the basis for reconstructions of both sea and land transport in Viking times, as well as interpretations of the burial rites devised for persons of high rank. Viking burial ceremonies were extremely varied, and the one eye-witness account may represent an extreme version of the burial ritual for a chief; nonetheless, it does provide a glimpse of Viking society in the tenth century, and it paints a detailed and horrific picture of the rites (Brønd-sted, 1960). The witness was an Arab merchant trading along the Volga, who observed the ceremonies executed on the death of a northern chief. The man was temporarily buried while preparations were made for his formal disposal. A young woman, one of his slaves, volunteered or was chosen to accompany him, and was put in the charge of an old woman, "a massive and grim figure" called the Angel of Death. The girl was provided with food and drink, was cared for, and spent her few last days in singing. The dead man's ship was drawn up on the bank and made ready for burning by piling timber around and beneath it. The corpse was taken from its temporary grave and dressed in fur-trimmed and gold-embroidered clothes made for the occasion; it was then laid in a tent on the deck of the ship, with weapons and a banquet of food and drink placed beside the body. Various animals were sacrificed: a dog was cut in two and thrown into the ship, two horses were run about until covered with sweat and then chopped up, two cows were slaughtered, and a cock and hen as well. The female slave walked along the bank and entered each tent where she had intercourse with each owner; then she was led to the ship, drinking from a cup and singing. She entered the tent where her master lay, and other men entered and had intercourse with her. Finally she was placed beside the corpse, held by the men and had a rope twisted around her neck. The Angel of Death who had conducted the ceremonies then stabbed her between the ribs with a knife, while the crowd outside beat on shields to drown her cries. When she was dead, the men and the old woman went from the ship and the pyre was ignited by the dead man's nearest kinsman; all the people threw burning brands onto the pyre, and the ship, the tent and the corpses were consumed by flames. On the spot a large mound was raised, with a wooden post inscribed with the chief's name. The archaeological remains of this series of activities would consist of the mound and a large pyre of ash and charcoal buried beneath it, and this single surviving record of Viking funerary ritual gives a clear indication of the problems facing the archaeologist in his efforts to interpret the surviving remains of other totally undocumented periods in man's prehistory and early history.

Not all Viking burials involved the burning of the body, the grave-goods and the ship, and from a number of particularly large mounds in northern Europe have been recovered the remains of the notorious Viking boats which provided the speed and strength for travel across open waters to the British Isles, to Iceland and Greenland, and to America. Some were used for peaceful transport of goods for trade, or for carrying people to new settlements; but others were the basis for raids and assaults along the coasts of northern and western Europe. One of the victims of the latter gave a somewhat extreme and doubtless biased impression of it all:

... though there were an hundred heads on one neck, and an hundred tongues in each head, and an hundred voices in each tongue, they would fail to tell what the Gael had suffered of injury and oppression from these heathen foreigners; and though numerous their kings and their champions, yet none was able to give deliverance from the cruelty and wrath of the brutal, ferocious, furious, untamed, implacable hordes ...

War of the Gaedhil with the Gael

FIG. 18. *Upper*. Excavation of the Viking ship at Oseberg, Norway, 1903.
   Lower. The reconstructed ship from Gokstad in the Viking Ship Museum, Oslo.
(University Museum of National Antiquities, Oslo, Norway.)

In 1867 an enormous mound was dug into on a farm at Tune in Norway, on the eastern side of the Oslo fjord (Brogger and Shetelig, 1970). When large timbers were found within the mound, archaeologists from Oslo were called. On arrival, they found that a large wooden ship had been partly uncovered and lay cracking and crumbling as the sun and air dried it out. Hardly anything of the ship could be saved, but thirteen years later, across the fjord at Gokstad, another large mound was excavated. This time the archaeologists were on hand and could rescue almost all of the well-preserved wooden ship which had been buried in a trench before the mound was heaped up. The ship was 23 m long, and had to be sawn in two in order to transport it to Oslo for study and conservation (Fig. 18, lower). The ship had a burial chamber built over it, and this contained the remains of an elderly male, probably a Viking king, laid upon a bed with richly decorated clothes, weapons and eating utensils beside him. Within a few years of his burial, in the ninth century A.D., robbers had broken into the tomb and had stolen most of the gold and other precious objects, but a few traces of silk worked with gold thread remained behind. The ship also contained three rowing boats, a huge bronze cauldron for the crew's meals, 12 horses and 6 dogs, as well as the body of a peacock. The ship itself was, and still remains, perhaps the best preserved Viking vessel ever discovered; its preservation was due to burial in a trench dug into a blue clay which created conditions of waterlogging. The ship was 23 m long, maximum width 5·2 m, and height from keel-base to gunwale amidships just over 2 m. The ship probably displaced over 20 tonnes when equipped for sail with sixteen pairs of oars in place. The planking was of oak, all grooves and joints caulked with animal hair and tar. Important for the studies and experiments noted below are the details of the strakes; the bottom nine, below the water line, were pliable and only 2·5 cm thick. The tenth strake, strengthening the vessel and transitional between the bottom and the sides of the ship, was 4·3 cm thick. Above this the strakes were again thin up to the fourteenth, where oarholes were cut through and furnished with shutters to keep the water out when the ship was under sail. A shield rack ran along the gunnel, with the remains of 64 round shields hanging outside the vessel. A steering oar of oak was placed on the starboard side and extended about 0·5 m below the keel. The solid oak keel was a remarkable piece of timber obtained from a tree standing straight and tall to at least 25 m. The stem and stern of the vessel had unfortunately disintegrated, but the internal fittings were in recognizable condition; the floorboards were movable for storage of equipment beneath. Lacking any carving or decoration, the Gokstad ship was a heavy vessel built for work both in the fjords and on the ocean. It has been conserved and is on display in the Viking ship museum near Oslo.

Also preserved in the museum are the remains of another magnificent Viking ship, from a mound at Oseberg excavated in 1903 (Fig 18, upper) (Sjøvold, 1959). The ship contained the bodies of two women, an elderly arthritic woman of 60 years, identified from the sagas as Queen Åsa, and a younger female, perhaps a servant. The very rich furnishings of the burial chamber included beds and quilts, looms and textiles, oak chests laden with small tools (the jewellery chest had been plundered), three carved wooden sleighs, a cart (p. 94) decorated with Viking events and themes; there were also slaughtered animals—15 horses, an ox and 4 dogs. The whole array of the Queen's household was here, it seems. The ship itself was 21·5 m long, 5·1 m wide amidships, and had a stout oak keel 19·8 m long to which were fastened the tall stem and stern destroyed at Gokstad. The stem and stern were also of oak, high and curved, ending in spirals, and on the prow was a serpent's head. Fifteen pairs of pine oars were found, in length from 3.7 to 4.0 m, and the mast, also of pine and 13 m long, rested on a keelson and mast partner of massive oak. It can be seen that these two vessels, the Gokstad and Oseberg ships, were broadly similar and together they provide a very accurate picture of Viking ships of the ninth century A.D. They do not, however, represent all the Viking sea-going vessels that existed, and for some of these we must turn to the remarkable recovery of five ships of the eleventh century from the Roskilde fjord in Denmark (Olsen and Crumlin-Pedersen, 1967; Crumlin-Pedersen, 1970). These ships were scuttled in order to provide a barrier to Viking raids upon the rich trading town of Roskilde; and a narrowing of the channel at Skuldelev, 20 km to the north of the town, was selected for the blockage. In 1962 a cofferdam allowed all the ships to be exposed, recorded and lifted as individual pieces of timber; conservation and re-construction has taken place over the past fifteen years and the ships are being reassembled in a special ship museum at Roskilde.

The five ships are of five different types, a stroke of great good fortune for those interested in Viking vessels. One of the merchantmen is a deep-sea trader of the type that regularly sailed between Scandinavia, England, Iceland and Greenland; built of oak, pine and lime, it was 16·5 m long, 4·5 m broad and 1·9 m high amidships. Another merchant ship was of a type used for the protected waters of the Baltic, with a crew of 4–6 men restricted to half-decks both fore and aft (Fig. 19). A third ship was a small ferry or fishing boat. The remaining pair were warships. One of these was a 28 m long ship, for a crew of 40–50 oarsmen. The other ship resembles those portrayed on the Bayeux Tapestry, only 2·6 m broad, 18 m long and height amidships only 1·1 m and is closely comparable to another Danish Viking ship excavated at Ladby in Funen in 1935. Both these ships have recently been duplicated and tested for their sailing and steering qualities.

In 1963, a group of Boy Scouts from Gram in Denmark undertook the reconstruction of the Ladby ship (Crumlin-Pedersen, 1970). Although the planks were sawn rather than wedged and cleaved, and were rather thicker than the originals, the modern version proved to be easily handled, and could be beached almost anywhere; it could carry heavy cargo, and in fact transported four horses in an experimental loading and unloading of potentially difficult cargo, just as is shown in the Bayeux Tapestry (Stenton, 1957). More valuable, however, was another experiment with this ship which involved fitting a Viking steering oar to the starboard side with a withy which went through a knot or wart on the ship's side; the oar pivoted on this wart, and a tiller-like projection from the oar ran inboard for the steersman (Crumlin-Pedersen, 1970). Viking steering oars or side rudders are assymmetrical both in plan and in thickness, and the experiments on the Scout's ship showed why. The oar had been devised so that whichever way it was turned the area of the blade actually in the water was equally divided forward and aft of the axis. The result, like a counter-balanced lift, is that very little effort is needed to turn the steering oar, and a boy of ten could steer safely even in a strong wind. The performance of the rudder in one experiment was remarkable. A competition was held between rowers and the helmsman, the crew rowing on one side only against the opposite helm. The 20·6 m ship answered the side rudder and turned against the oars "and it was possible to hold the helm in position with a single finger in spite of energetic efforts on the part of the rowers to

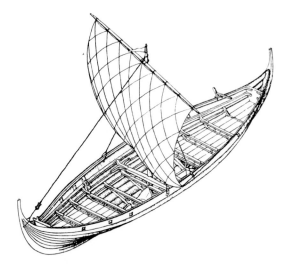

Fig. 19. Viking boat of the eleventh century from Skuldelev, Denmark, reconstructed (from Crumlin-Pedersen, 1970).

turn the ship the other way" (Crumlin-Pedersen, 1970). With the later
invention of the stern rudder, this Viking device was lost to Atlantic waters.

The copy of the Ladby ship is only one of a number of replicas of
Viking vessels, including a recent copy of the Skuldelev warship, also
made by a Scout group in Denmark. These replicas were made with hand
tools by traditional Viking methods so far as could be deduced; but the
projects were not designed to be rigorously recorded and tested scien-
tifically. In contrast, a very exhaustive series of experiments have been
directed recently upon the smallest of the three rowing boats found inside
the Gokstad ship in 1880 (McGrail, 1974; McKee, 1974).

The boat, or *faering*, selected for the experiment by the National Maritime Museum in Greenwich was 6·5 m long, 1·4 m wide amidships, and
had only three strakes on each side; the sheer strake was pine, and the
remainder of the boat was oak. The planks were very thin, only 10–12 mm
in thickness, fastened to the three ribs by tree-nails. The rudder and probably the tiller were similar to those of the mother ship, with a withy tie and
a boss or wart on the planking. When firstly recovered in 1880, the boat
was in fragments and it was only reconstructed 50 years later, when some
new wood had to be used. The inadequate records of this work may mean
that the boat's appearance today is not exactly ninth-century Viking
design (Crumlin-Pedersen, 1975). The problems of building a replica of
this boat were very considerable, and the experiment was perhaps more
rigorously carried out than any other known boat replication. Modern
boats considered to be close in origin to the Viking *faering* were carefully
studied. These included Shetland *fourerns*, the four-oared imports from
Norway, where the *oselver* boats are closely related to the modern version
of the Viking *faering*. The replica of the Gokstad *faering* was built at a
barge works on the Thames, and suitable oak and pine planks were sawn
to appropriate thicknesses. During the preparation of the main members,
some unacceptable distortions appeared due to the drying-out of the wood;
consequently alternative hardwood had to be used for one or two pieces,
and some oak used in place of the original pine bottom boards. The vessel
when completed was painted with a mix of tar, linseed oil and turpentine.
The *faering* as completed was not a precise copy of the Gokstad boat, but
was certainly close enough to justify a number of sea trials and some
general conclusions about the Viking *faering* as a rowing boat.

The trials took place in Devon and Cornwall, and were devised to test
rowing and steering. With two experienced oarsmen, and sheltered conditions, it was possible to achieve 4–5 knots stroking at about 40. Sprint
speeds of over 7 knots were also achieved (McKee, 1974). In rougher
water, the *faering* handled well, and the only problem seemed to be the
side rudder which was effective only for small angles of helm. If a sail had

been carried, it would have been difficult to turn to windward without an oar to help pull her about; but in the absence of sailing trials, we do not really know. The experiments with this vessel were carefully carried out, and the variations from the original clearly stated in the full report. The problems were probably due in part to the use of laminated hardwood instead of solid oak for the stem, sawn planks instead of split planks; but, most important of all, the use of glue in some of the scarves would certainly make the boat less flexible than the original (Christensen and Morrison, 1976). Nonetheless, the final comments of McKee, who was responsible for the sea trials, seem entirely appropriate:

This boat is a classic...Not only does she look, row and ride better than she should, but there was the added pleasure of finding a boat that would pass the ultimate test. This was the feeling that the boat could look after herself when the weather had so tired and perhaps frightened her crew that they were no longer able to do their best for her.

McKee, 1974

The most spectacular experiment with Viking ships remains the first one, which was based upon the remarkable Gokstad ship. Even before the Oseberg burial had been discovered, the opportunity was seized by Norwegians to test a copy of a Viking ship. The Gokstad vessel was uncovered in 1880; in 1893, the Great Exhibition was held in Chicago on the occasion of the 400th anniversary of the discovery of America by Christopher Columbus. A decision was taken in Norway to participate in this important event, and what better and more ironic way than to build a replica of the Gokstad ship and sail it across the Atlantic to the Great Exhibition, thereby commemorating the real discoverers of America? The impetus for this venture came from Captain Magnus Andersen, a sailor and editor, eminently qualified to organize both shipbuilding and publicity. The replica was built of Norwegian oak except for the keel, which needed a tree larger than any available in Norway. An oak tree providing a piece about 25 m long was obtained from Canada. The mast for the single sail was Norwegian. The launching took place from the shipyard at Sandefjord in February 1893, and as is usual on these occasions there were numerous comments made about the unseaworthiness of the vessel, its likelihood of breaking-up or sinking or capsizing. On April 30 the vessel set sail from Bergen, and it arrived in Newfoundland only 27 days later. According to the reports, the ship had behaved well even in the particularly bad weather encountered. For the crew the most striking thing was the way the ship flexed to meet the changing conditions of the sea. Andersen wrote:

The bottom of the ship was an object of primary interest. As will be remembered, it was fastened to the ribs with withy, below the crossbeams. The bottom, as well as the keel, could therefore yield to the movement of the ship, and in a heavy head sea it would rise and fall as much as three-quarters of an inch. But strangely enough the ship was watertight all the same. Its elasticity was apparent also in other ways. In a heavy sea the gunwhale would twist up to six inches out of line. All this elasticity, combined with the fine lines, naturally made for speed, and we often had the pleasure of darting through the water at speeds of ten, and sometimes even eleven knots.

The ship carried 16 pairs of oars but these were apparently never put to the test for speed. Upon arrival in New York the plan to row her into her berth using students as crew turned into a farce, and complete chaos ensued before the captain took charge again and calmly sailed her into her berth. The vessel eventually reached the Great Lakes, and was sailed and rowed upon Lake Michigan and into Chicago where she took her place in the Great exhibition (Fig. 10).

The objective was not to provide a scientific record of the properties of Viking ships, nor was any attempt made to use Viking methods of navigation. Nonetheless, as a propaganda exercise, and a dramatic expression of Viking achievement (Fig. 20), the experiment was a resounding success. At the time there was no tangible evidence of Viking settlement in America. Since 1893 a number of findings have demonstrated that the sagas of

Fig. 20. A modern version of a Viking ship, beside its competitors (courtesy Royal Viking Line).

Viking discovery and settlement in Vinland do indeed record the first European settlement of America; for instance, the site of L'Anse aux Meadows in northern Newfoundland, dated *c.* 1000 A.D., almost certainly represents one of the Viking landfalls, and may even be Leif Eirikson's settlement. We still know little of Viking methods of navigation, but some hints of the latter are provided by their reports of voyages to Iceland, and Greenland, and we can assume that the sun's position, cloud caps over islands, reflection of glaciers on clouds, sea birds, currents and winds were regularly used to guide the navigators. Yet even the Vikings did not feel entirely sure at times (Brandt, 1972): when King Olaf sent a rival into exile he ordered the Icelandic captain Thovarin to conduct him to Greenland. Thovarin objected, saying that he himself had never been there. The king suggested that it was high time he went, but in case he could not find Greenland he was to leave the man in Iceland, or even in Scotland, and if this was not possible he should throw him overboard. No modern experiments with Viking navigation methods have so far been carried out in the north Atlantic, but there can be no doubt that the Vikings travelled far and wide with confidence in their ships and in their ability to retrace their course. Whether or not they were the first Europeans to discover America still remains a mystery. That honour may belong to an earlier time, 500 years earlier than the voyage of Bjarni Herjolfsson in 985 A.D.

Following the collapse of Roman civilization in Europe, Celtic Christianity was spread through parts of the north and west by missionaries. Some of these missionaries were monks who established religious communities, or who wandered, more or less alone, seeking and spreading the word of God (Cumming *et al.*, 1971). In north western Europe, the native Celtic traditions of seafaring were strong and missionaries travelled from mainland to islands, and between islands, carrying the new religion with them. By 600 A.D. they had reached Scotland, the Orkneys and Shetlands and soon after the sea-crossing to the Faroes, 300 km of open water, was accomplished; a settlement in Iceland, only 500 km, was established before 800 A.D. according to the Irish monk and geographer Dicuil (825 A.D.). He had discussed these voyages with monks who had made the same journeys in curraghs, boats made of green wood and ox hides. Fifty years later the first Norseman arrived in Iceland and found the relics left behind by the departed Irish monks. Where the monks went is not known, but they had decided "they did not wish to live there with heathen men" (Jones, 1964, p. 102). From this geographical point in the historical narrative the records of Celtic exploration in the north Atlantic become obscure. Celtic legends mixed with histories tell of the exploits of Irish monks and saints who roamed the Atlantic, and they refer in particular to a sixth-century sailor, Saint Brendan of Ardfert (*c.* 484–577 A.D.). His travels are chronicled in a remarkable document, the *Navigatio Sancti Brendani Abbatis*, written down on the basis of oral traditions some 2–3 centuries after his death. Many manuscripts of this document exist but recent editions provide most of the essential details of St Brendan's voyages (Selmer, 1959; O'Meara, 1976).

The *Navigatio* describes how Brendan was visited in the west of Ireland by a monk who described a land far across the ocean, and who advised Brendan to go there himself. Brendan built a boat of wood and ox hides, loaded it with food and spare hides, and set out with 14 monks. The descriptions of the conditions, landfalls and phenomena encountered on the voyage suggest that he visited the Faroes (with sheep and sea-birds in abundance), Iceland (where a volcanic eruption occurred), possibly the Azores and the Sargasso Sea ("a thick curdled mass"), and a land forty days west of the Faroes where whales, "pygmies and dwarfs black as coal" (Eskimoes in fur suits?), and a "sea-cat" with huge eyes, whiskers and tusks (walrus) were encountered. This land may have been Greenland where the first Norse settlers in 982 found ancient settlements, stone implements and the remains of hide boats. Brendan's narrative also mentions a thick white cloud (the Grand Banks fog off Newfoundland?), a floating pillar of crystal (iceberg) and the land of Promise where he explored for forty days. He then returned to Ireland.

Parts of the *Navigatio* are obviously fantastic and imaginative. Brendan and his crew landed on what they first thought was an island but which they found to be a whale once they had started to cook a meal over an open fire; and on another occasion they were chased by a sea monster (Fig. 21). However, enough exists in the tale that could be authentic, embroidered no doubt by three centuries of the telling by Irish monks, but with landmarks still recognizable. In 1973 an experiment was devised to test the possibility that Brendan could have voyaged across the north Atlantic in the type of craft described in the *Navigatio*, a vessel built of ox hides stretched over a green wood frame (Severin, 1978). The modern reconstruction of the vessel, called the *Brendan*, was made in Ireland; the boat frame was of greased oak and ash, with two ash masts set in socketed mast-steps of oak. The frame was lashed together with leather thongs, each thong stretched, soaked and tied in place while wet. The skin of the boat consisted of 49 ox hides, each about 1·2 m square and 6 mm thick, tanned with oak-bark, double stitched together with waxed "fourteen cord" (14 threads rolled into one), with the hide edges overlapped by 5 cm. At the prow, where beachings and collisions would put extra stress on the cover, four hide thicknesses were overlapped; the stern was also strengthened. A keel-skid of oak was attached through the hides with copper rivets, but otherwise the leather cover was not perforated or fixed to the hull frame; instead it

FIG. 21. Marvellous adventures of St Brendan at sea, encountering a siren, meeting a holy man afloat, and attacked by a sea monster (from the *Navigatio*, Ulm, 1499; reproduced in Cumming *et al.*, 1971).

was stretched over it, that is pulled over the upper gunwale and tied down to the lower gunwale inside with hair-on belting. A steering oar was held by a yoke on the starboard side. The *Brendan* was 11·5 m long, 2·5 m across, and with her two sails of leather (later replaced by Irish flax), full cargo and crew, she displaced nearly five tonnes with a draught of only 30 cm (Fig. 22).

The *Brendan* set sail from south-west Ireland on 17 May 1976. She journeyed along the Irish and Scottish west coasts to the Faroes, then on to Iceland, landing on 16 July; here it was decided to postpone the next phase until the spring of 1977. The autumn gales off Greenland, and the pack ice, were considered to be potentially too strong for the boat. Saint Brendan himself had taken seven seasons to reach his most westerly point. On 7 May the *Brendan* set out once again, and made landfall in Newfoundland on 26 June 1977 (Fig. 17). The major problems encountered and overcome were strong headwinds, which effectively halted progress for a time, pack ice which could have crushed the boat, and a puncture in the hide cover which had to be repaired with a hide patch in appalling conditions. This bare recital of only a few episodes in the voyage disguises the very real dangers to which the crew of five exposed themselves. Venturing into the pack ice, the gales and heavy seas of the cold north Atlantic in a minute boat is something that most people would avoid.

The performance of this remarkable boat was not measured with great precision during its ocean voyages, partly because it was grossly undermanned. However, after arrival in America, rowing trials were held in Boston. These trials showed that a crew of ten could make headway in most conditions, and that even six men could edge upwind. But essentially the curragh was a sailing vessel. Under sail the vessel averaged *c.* 65 km a day during her voyages across the Atlantic, and a cruising speed of 2–3 knots was judged satisfactory in a force 3–4 wind; a following wind of force 5–6 allowed speeds of up to 7 knots, and occasionally 12 knots was recorded. Adverse winds actually drove the boat backwards as she sat up in the water and her stretched sides caught the wind. Against a headwind, *Brendan* could point 50°–60° off the wind, but she could not sail closer. Her most impressive quality was her safety even in rough weather; the stability of the craft was in part due to 0·8 tonne of fresh water ballast, which helped prevent any tendency to capsize.

The success of the voyage clarified some of the descriptions in the *Navigatio* of Saint Brendan which could not otherwise be understood. The inability to row upwind, the method of beaching the craft, or towing it up a shallow stream, the necessity of carrying spare ox hides and grease, as well as the many geographical features already noted, closely link the

FIG. 22. The *Brendan* at sea, en route to America (from Severin, 1978).

Navigatio with modern observations. Whether or not Saint Brendan actually did reach his promised land, and it was America, cannot be proved on the basis of the experiment; nonetheless the possibility still remains open and is, in fact, strengthened by the experiment. There are few other pieces of evidence which are archaeologically acceptable at the moment. The Icelandic saga describes a country called Ireland the Great, lying west in the sea near Vinland the Good, and tells of an unfortunate Norseman who was driven there by bad weather, was unable to escape and, worse still, was baptized by the inhabitants. Perhaps Saint Brendan was ultimately responsible for this indignity?

This, however, is still not the end of the story of explanation, or possible explorations in the Atlantic, nor of potential discoverers of America. For many years, anthropologists and others have investigated many sites and reports in the New World which purport to indicate that cultural connections existed between the Americas and the western coastlands of Europe and Africa (summarized in Heyerdahl, 1978, pp. 67–95). Such similarities range from the stepped pyramids of central America and Egypt, to Negroid and Mediterranean features of figurines and engravings in Mesoamerica, to African root vegetables in Amazonia, and to trepannation and mummification procedures for the dead in Egypt and parts of America. Many anthropologists cannot accept any or all of these as demonstrating human contact before Columbus, or the Vikings, or even Brendan, and they point to human solutions to common problems throughout the world, to inadequate and incomplete documentation of the similarities, and to the need for caution in accepting theories of transatlantic contacts without very rigorously tested evidence (e.g. Cowan, 1974).

One of the principal protagonists of the "possible contact" school is Heyerdahl, and in 1969 he set out to test one of the major problems, the seaworthiness of ancient Egypian craft in venturing out into Atlantic waters (Heyerdahl, 1971). As a basis for his boat he studied the representations of ancient Egyptian vessels which exist as rock engravings, wall paintings and models dated to prehistoric periods. Some of these representations depicted double-pointed sailing boats of papyrus reed, carrying up to fifty men. Smaller boats like these are still in use in various parts of the world, including the Middle East, central Africa and South America. Basically they consist of bundles of reeds tied together to form a slender cushioned shell, which floats well, can be repaired easily, and is light in weight. Heyerdahl required a large vessel to attempt the Atlantic crossing from North Africa to central America or wherever the currents and winds took him.

The first experimental reed boat was made in Egypt by shipwrights from Lake Tchad. The boat, called *Ra* (the Egyptian sun god) was 14 m long and was made entirely of bundles of papyrus reeds soaked in water and tied with rope. Twenty bundles were used to shape the vessel, each bundle extending from bow to stern; approximately 200 000 reeds were used. A woven reed cabin was placed amidships, behind an A-frame mast carrying the sail. Nearer the stern was a bridge with two long steering oars of iroko wood, joined together by a horizontal beam to move in unison. The craft weighed 12 tonnes without its supplies and its crew of seven men. After transport to Safi on the Atlantic coast of Morocco, *Ra* was made ready for the voyage. The doubters were not slow to gather, and the vessel's stability and manoeuvrability were questioned. The major cause for concern, however, was how long it would take for the papyrus to become totally waterlogged, shredded or broken.

On 25 May 1969 the boat was gently towed out to sea and set sail to the west. Almost at once the two steering masts broke, and the yard which held the upper part of the sail cracked. The result, not generally known to the thousands of well-wishers, left *Ra* almost totally without any command over wind or current. The experiment was in effect at an end. The boat was going to America and no one could do anything to prevent it. Objects or men swept overboard could not be collected by turning back because there was no turning back. Repairs were made to the craft, and many lessons learned by necessity. The major and irreparable problem was the stern of the reed boat: the ancient representations of Egyptian vessels had sometimes shown a thin line from the upturned stern extending down to the afterdeck, but as no one had been able to interpret this, it had been ignored in the replica. In contrast, the bow, similarly upturned, had a rope joining it to the mast which itself was tied to the sides of the boat. The stern was not supported in this way, and it soon began to sag under the weight of water, to act as a brake, and to drag down the afterdeck of the boat.

After 25 days at sea *Ra* had travelled nearly 200 km and was in difficulties. Another steering oar broke, the bridge collapsed, the liferaft was chopped up and used to prop up the sagging stern, the spare bundles of reeds were used in the same way, and a list to starboard developed as the reed bundles absorbed more and more water. After another 15 days, and another 1200 km towards the west, the ropes which held the outermost starboard bundle broke through and *Ra* began to crumble in the sea. Sharks prevented the continuation of underwater repairs, and after struggling on for 16 more days, and another 1100 km, the boat was abandoned only 970 km from landfall in the Barbados. The story of this voyage is a quite extraordinary one, calmly setting out the succession of minor and major disasters which culminated in forced abandonment of the once-proud *Ra*.

A lesson once learned the hard way is rarely forgotten, and Heyerdahl set up a second experiment using all the new evidence from the first. Another reed boat, *Ra II*, was made in Morocco by shipwrights from

D

Lake Titicaca in Peru. The vessel was made on different principles from the original *Ra*. Instead of many long thin bundles, the 280 000 reeds were used to make only three bundles, two of them extremely thick and rigid. Each thick roll was tied to the central thin roll by continuous spirals of rope. After tightening, the thin roll was quite submerged and formed a perfect central core or spine of the vessel (Fig. 23). The upswept bow and stern were formed by smaller bundles lashed to the hull, and a bundle along each side added breadth to the craft. The first *Ra* had suffered a

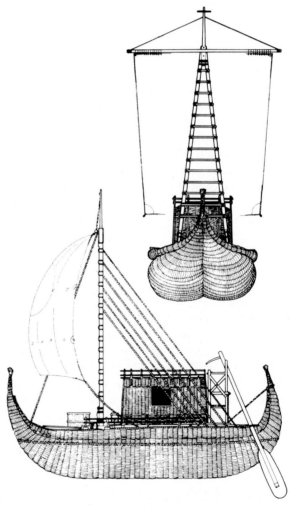

FIG. 23. *Ra II*, formed of two gigantic rolls of papyrus, squeezing a third smaller roll (invisible); length of vessel 12 m (from Heyerdahl, 1978).

fatal collapse. To prevent this from happening to *Ra II*, the stern as well as the bow was securely tied down to the sides. Cross-beams formed a base for the cabin, the steering bridge and the footplates for the mast. The boat was 12 m long, 5 m broad and almost 2 m deep. The cabin was 4 × 3 m, just sufficient for the 8 members of the crew. *Ra II* was far more rigid than the first *Ra*, which had undulated over the sea. *Ra II* bounced and cut through the waves, and produced a much rougher ride for the sailors.

Setting sail from Morocco, heavily laden with supplies, *Ra II* travelled rapidly while the papyrus was still dry. The first day's run was 177 km. On the fourth day, however, in calm water, every man could see that *Ra II* was sinking, and in an anonymous opinion poll the score was 6 to 2 in favour of the notion that the voyage would fail. Heyerdahl apparently does not know to this day who the other optimist was. After some frantic thinking, it was decided that the cargo was too heavy. The first objects to be jettisoned were two reed liferafts. These were followed by sacks of potatoes, rice, flour, grain, timber, rope, iron tools, books, a stove, lavatory paper. Then the boat stopped sinking.

Finally underway again, *Ra II* sailed westwards into the Atlantic, making over 100 km a day, even 150 km on occasion. It survived a moderate gale with fierce squalls, running before the sea, stern lifting high as the waves, some 10 m high, approached and overtook the boat. One of the strongest waves finally cracked the rudder-oar, but the boat survived although it began to settle lower with the weight of soaked reeds and inboard water. By tilting the mast, the sail was shifted forward and this improved the downward steering; but by now the deck was scarcely above water even on a calm day, and barnacles began to grow along the starboard deck. The bow and stern peaks were sawn off, the former to avoid fouling the sail, the latter to balance the boat and reduce weight. Even the lowering of the lines holding up the stern failed to distort the vessel. After a total of 57 days, and 6100 km, *Ra II* made landfall in Barbados (Fig. 16). The reed boat had survived, and so had the crew. Whether or not ancient explorers from North Africa had made the same voyage, and had survived, centuries before the Vikings, and Brendan too, we do not know. The crossings have not proved anything other than that the Atlantic winds and currents could have taken courageous sailors, voluntarily or involuntarily, westwards to a new and different world.

The reed boat as a vehicle for long distance voyaging is not well attested in ancient records, although the historian Eratosthenes recorded that Egyptian papyrus rafts travelled as far as India and even Ceylon, taking 20 days to reach the latter. This distance would be about equal to 20 days' sailing for *Ra* and *Ra II*. Certainly the seaworthiness of papyrus rafts and boats is not in much question, and the latest expedition using a reed boat has attempted to show that the Sumerians, who developed one of the world's first civilizations in Mesopotamia (Mallowan, 1965), could have sailed as far as India in setting up their trade and colonies. There is, in fact, a representation of a sailing vessel from Mesopotamia dated as far back as *c*. 5000 B.C., and the discovery of pottery of Mesopotamian character some 600–700 km south in the Arabian Gulf must surely indicate seafaring activity (Oates *et al*., 1977). Sumerian clay tablets and pictographs dating back to 3000 B.C. depict curved sailing vessels, and a modern replica, called *Tigris*, was built in 1977 by Heyerdahl (Heyerdahl, 1978). Sumerian records suggest vessels of up to 100 tonnes, and Babylonian tablets refer to cargoes of as much as 50 tonnes. The *Tigris* was made of 30 tonnes of reeds gathered in the swamps of southern Iraq, and the vessel was constructed on the same principle as the *Ra II*, two long tapered rolls being joined to form the hull. The *Tigris* was 18 m long and extremely heavy; it carried a large sail and 12 oars each 6 m long. With an international crew, it set sail from the Tigris and Euphrates rivers' exit into the Persian Gulf, and successfully negotiated the Gulf and the Strait of Hormuz, before venturing into the Arabian Sea. Due to a combination of physical and political circumstances, the expedition was abandoned off the north-east coast of Africa by the deliberate burning of the *Tigris*. In projects such as this, involving the possibility of landfall in any of several countries, the political problems are often extremely difficult to overcome and in this case it proved impossible to continue. But nevertheless the reed boat had again demonstrated its strength in open waters, and the experiment had by no means eliminated the reed boat as a possible mechanism for seafaring activities in the Sumerian period.

But not all the vessels of the Near and Middle East were made of reeds; the boat of Cheops was, and is, of wood, and the legendary boats of the ancient East were also of wood. The Sumerian epic poem of Gilgamesh records the warning of the god Ea to the hero Utnapishtim to "pull down his house and build a ship of determined size, equal in length and width . . . on the fifth day I erected the ship's wooden frame with a surface of one *iku* [3500 m²], its walls were 120 ells long [60 m] and every side of the square roof had also 120 ells . . . I equipped the ship with six decks, dividing it thus into seven parts and the inside into nine. I drove wedges into the middle against the submersion of the sea, chose a boathook and ranged all necessary things . . . On the seventh day the ship was ready . . . the builders added weight to its deck plunging two thirds under water." A similar vessel is mentioned in biblical references; one version is as follows:

Thou shalt build a ship out of resinous woid, divide it into compartments, covering them with pitch inside and outside. Such are to be the ship's dimensions:

300 ells long, 50 ells wide and 30 ells high. The cover, allowing the penetration of light, should be one ell high; thou shalt make an entrance in the side wall and establish three divisions: bottom, second and third.

From her measurements such a vessel would be 150 m long, 25 m wide and 15 m high, truly an enormous ship, and as big as the Sumerian vessel which would be well over 4000 years old if the epic refers to an actual event. Neither of these arks have been reconstructed; to build them would be a gigantic task.

Precisely where the voyage of Noah's ark took place is unknown. But other ancient journeys, and their experimental re-creations, are better understood (Fig. 16). It is perhaps of interest to list their durations and the distances sailed in order to appreciate some of relative sizes and speeds (see Table 1).

TABLE 1

Vessel	Length m	Crew	Approximate distance km	Sailing days
Santa Maria Spain to San Salvador	?25	c.40	6000	36
Gokstad replica Norway to Newfoundland	23	c.30	5000	27
Kon-Tiki Peru to Tuamotu	15	6	6900	101
Ra II Morocco to Barbados	12	8	6100	57
Tigris Iraq to Djibouti	19	11	6700	144 (afloat)
Hōkūle'a Hawaii to Tahiti	19 19	17 13	5400 5400	32 22
Brendan Ireland to Newfoundland	12	5	4200	50
Atlantic schooners Britain–America	—	—	5300	12

Most of the experiments with rafts, boats and ships have been devised for long-distance voyaging, but the other and perhaps more important aspect of sea travel in ancient times was concerned with shorter distances in more protected waters. The Viking merchantmen, the South American balsa rafts, the Egyptian reed rafts and boats were more often employed along the coasts and within the major estuaries and rivers than they were out upon the broad oceans and seas. In earlier times the establishment of settlements in new areas, and the development of trading patterns among various communities, demanded forms of transport able to carry heavy loads, or to move swiftly and to be beached and launched without difficulty. We know hardly anything of these smaller craft, other than that simple hollowed logs were used for the construction of many groups of such craft. These dugouts or logboats were practical for short paddled or poled journeys, as ferries to cross rivers or for line and net fishing; but their limited size, their weight and inflexibility did not provide solutions to all the needs of ancient communities. There are many historical records which outline the differing techniques used to manufacture logboats, and there have been very few experiments carried out which add to this evidence. A logboat was built in 1959 by 8 Scouts, who took 21 days to axe and adze an oak stem into shape. The finished boat was 4·5 m long and could carry a crew of 7 in very calm water, but 3 was a more suitable number for paddling (McGrail, 1978, p. 115). More recently, another logboat has been made by students in Denmark, who successfully paddled across open water to Sweden, although again the freeboard in calm water was very slight.

Representations of sailing and paddling vessels appear in many areas of the world as carvings on rock, impressions and paintings on clay and other substances. Near Thunder Bay in Canada, for example, a rock painting clearly shows a canoe, or perhaps a dugout, with eight passengers (Fig. 24, lower). Paintings at other Lake Superior sites are more definitely bark canoes—some associated with totemic symbols (Dewdney and Kidd, 1962). These representations can be interpreted as canoes because native canoes were historically recorded, drawn and photographed by European settlers and historians. Many other regions of the world have comparable representations, and some as historically identified.

More difficult are representations of vessels in areas of the world where no traces remain of the actual craft, and where we cannot be sure that such artistic work did not depict entirely imaginary vessels of some ceremonial significance to the ancient society. The best example of this problem is the rock art of the Bronze Age in Scandinavia. In northern Sweden and Norway, rock carvings of simple rather square vessels have plausibly been interpreted as depictions of skin boats rather like *umiaks* (Gjessing, 1936). Farther south, in southern Sweden and Norway, and in Denmark too, the rock carvings show different craft, more elaborate, and with many variations (Fredsjö et al., 1969). As comparable representations occur on

Bronze Age implements, particularly bronze razors, the rock carvings can be assigned to the period 1500–700 B.C. Archaeologists know that during this period Scandinavians were engaged in quite intensive and widespread trading with other regions in order to obtain copper, tin and gold. As most of the northern lands are near to the North Sea or the Baltic Sea, maritime activities must have been a regular feature of life. There was, of course, the ubiquitous dugout; but what other types of boats were available is not known. The recent Danish experiment succeeded in forming a 5·5 m dugout frcm a heavy lime tree, using stone axes and other prehistoric

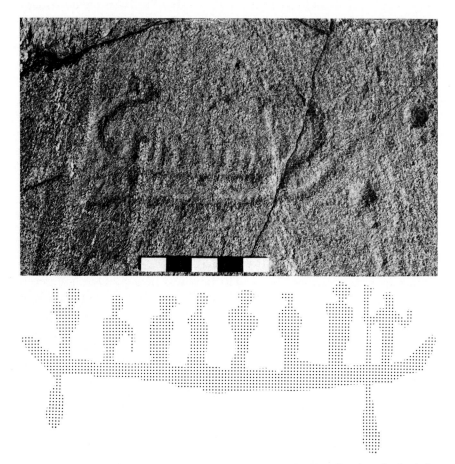

Fig. 24. *Upper*. Rock engraving of a Bronze Age boat, Hällby, Sweden, the basis for the experimental reconstruction. Note the upturned prow and stern, and the extended keel line. The scale totals 25 cm. (Photo: J. M. Coles.)

Lower. Dugout or bark canoe with passengers: rock painting near Thunder Bay, Ontario, Canada (after Dewdney and Kidd, 1962).

tools. The boat was subsequently paddled the 13 km between Zealand and Scania in about 5 hours. Nonetheless, any heavy seas would probably swamp such a shallow craft, and the rock carvings of Scandinavia provide a hint of other types of vessel. These too have been tested experimentally.

Among the great variety of representations on the rocks are a large number clearly recognizable as animals, carts, ards pulled by oxen, boats (Fig. 24, upper) and weapons; the realism shown by these pictures suggests that the boat-like designs may also be realistic. Even so, their details are not clear enough to exclude their interpretation in a variety of ways, as dug-outs, skin boats, plank-built boats, or even rafts. The boats have a straight or curved keel-line, with strongly upturned bows, and sometimes sterns curved upwards as well. Above the keel and parallel to it is the line of the gunwale, the two joined together by vertical or diagonal lines or the whole area lowered by pecking. Above the gunwale, and between the inner bow and stern lines, are vertical strokes which may represent the crew or up-right paddles or neither. Sometimes one or more of these strokes is substi-tuted by a distinctly human figure carrying an axe or other object.

Although there are many theories about the type of craft represented by these engravings, only one has been tested by a full-scale experiment (Johnstone, 1972; Marstrander, 1976). The view was taken that the en-gravings represent skin boats; the commonly curved hull and the double prows suggested something other than a dugout or a raft, and the lines between the gunwale and keel looked like the internal framing of a skin boat, seen from the outside as stretch marks on the skins. The experimental building of a vessel on these principles was undertaken by the British and Norwegian television authorities, the work being directed by specialists in both rock art and ancient boats. The boat was built by Odd Johnsen in his boatyard at Frederikstad in Norway. Only wood, hide and twine were put into the construction, although modern steel tools (axe, knife and needle, but no saw) were used to prepare the wood and sew the hides. Twenty-four young alders, and one lime tree, were felled. After debarking and shaping, the alder poles were used to make 9 U-frames which were attached to a 7-m keel; to the frames were lashed the gunwales, stringers or strakes, and floor timber (Fig. 25). Some of the wooden members were also pegged together with wooden nails, the holes having been made by electric drill. There is no evidence for treenails in the earliest northern boats, and this was probably the greatest deviance from a reasonably authentic Bronze Age technology. Preparing and assembling the frame took the builder about 150 hours.

The cover for the boat was made from eight cowhides, tanned but with the hair still upon them. The Eskimo method of preparing skins for a boat is to soak them in seawater for a considerable time before the women clean them, make them soft and supple, and rub fat into them; however, the archaeologists could not persuade their wives to do this. The skins were stitched together with pitched twine, and were then stretched over the frame, pulled down over the gunwale and sewn with a zig-zag stitch around one of the stringers. Using a single piece of hide thonging allowed it to be tightened all around the boat, and also permitted the skin to stretch in any place should a collision occur. The skin lay on the outside of the keel, and now the craft had another true keel placed outside it and attached to the boat at bow and stern, as well as pegged through to the inner keel; this, of course, involved perforating the skins. Subsequently the experimenters felt that it would have been better to put the skins beneath the main keel and only make two major holes for the bow and stern pieces. These pieces were attached by pegs and lashings, and cross-pieces added to join the gunwale prow and the keel prow. An animal-headed post was set up at the bow, and thwarts were put in place in the boat. Attaching the hides to the framework, and finishing the boat, took about 50 hours; so the entire job occupied one man for about 200 hours. This compares quite well with a recorded building time of three weeks for three Eskimos making out of wood and sealskin an *umiak* of slightly smaller dimensions than the Bronze Age replica.

The vessel was 6·8 m long, 1·3 m across at the centre, and it weighed only 180 kg. After launching in July 1971, it was paddled by six students from the Oslo University rowing club, and timed trials in good conditions indicated a cruising speed of 2·8 knots. More interesting was the way the boat rode through the water, the double bow cutting the waves and lifting the boat. The outer keel and upturned bow also allowed very safe and easy beaching. Unladen, the boat had a freeboard of 50 cm, and with an astonishing one tonne of cargo, including the crew, it still had 32 cm freeboard. However, its freeboard sank to 25 cm with a load of 1.4 tonnes, and beyond this level of loading it would not have been possible to sail in even a moderate sea.

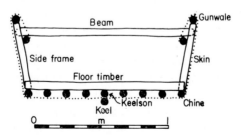

FIG. 25. Cross-section of the wood and skin boat devised on the basis of Bronze Age rock carvings.

The experiment set out to test only one of a number of possible interpretations of the rock carvings of Bronze Age Scandinavia, and in this it seems to have succeeded, demonstrating that skin boats could be made which in side-view resemble the carvings. The experiments, of course, could not prove therefore that Bronze Age craft were made of skin. What they did show was that Bronze Age technology could have made skin boats, and that these would have been both seaworthy and serviceable for transport in the protected waters around Scandinavia. The major alternative view, that the carvings represent plank-built boats, remains to be explored and tested; even then, there is unlikely to be a single answer or one that applies to all the carvings. This should not be a handicap in experimental boat archaeology because it is surely the range of possibilities that we seek to discover and understand, rather than rigid assumptions of imagined "facts". All of the experiments described here have avoided dogmatism in their results and conclusions, and such work will continue to advance our knowledge of ancient voyages of discovery and exploration as well as the methods of transport for colonization and trade.

Experimental work with boats has the advantage of a uniform environment, water, upon which to test the replicas, and there is little reason to doubt that conditions at sea now are broadly comparable to those of the past: wind patterns, ocean swells, areas and seasons of storm and calm are likely to have been in the past as they are today. The same cannot be said for experiments with land transport because soils and vegetation are probably unlike those of past times, and details of the precise terrain of trade and travel routes are unknown. Nonetheless, some work has been done on ancient methods of land transport, ignoring the actual or presumed routes.

Within the burial mound of Queen Åsa and her servant at Oseberg in Norway was a wide variety of equipment from a thriving manor, among them elaborately carved sleighs, a sled and a wagon. The body of the wagon, its box, was $c.$ 2 × 1 m, and it had curved sides and flat ends, like a cradle. Recent excavations in Denmark have yielded further examples of Viking wagons, none of them preserved as well as the Oseberg wagon, but all showing the same curving character of the box. Most of these Viking wagons have been associated with, and sometimes contain, female burials; moreover, they all date to the tenth century (Roesdahl, 1978). Reconstructions of the Oseberg wagon suggest a heavy vehicle (Fig. 26), suitable for considerable loads and probably drawn by oxen rather than horses. But these copies can only hint at the importance of land transport at this time; and, furthermore, finds of harness as well as actual wheel tracks across the land suggest that emphasis on Viking ships disguises the fact that transport by land was a vital element in Viking settlement, and perhaps in raids as well. Each wagon box seems to have been detachable from the chassis, in effect making the Viking wagons the first "container-vehicles". These boxes were perhaps hoisted on board ship loaded with supplies on outgoing journeys, and booty on the return trips. This may be fanciful, but there can be no doubt Viking expansion depended upon the efficiency both of sea and land vehicles. Experiments demonstrate the care taken in the manufacture of both types of vehicle, and in their high yields of capacity, speed and adaptability.

FIG. 26. Reconstruction of a Viking wagon, based on excavated finds in Scandinavia. (Forhistorisk Museum, Moesgård, Denmark.)

Many other vehicles for land transport and travel are known from earlier times, in the Near East and in Europe, but little work has been done on reconstructions. Versions of the Celtic chariot, a two-wheeled light cart drawn by paired horses, have been made by modern methods in order to give a visual impression, but these do not allow us to test the ancient records of such vehicles:

> I see a chariot of fine wood with wickerwork, moving on wheels of white bronze. Its frame very high, of creaking copper, rounded and firm. A strong curved yoke of gold; two firm-plaited yellow reins. The shafts hard and straight as sword blades.
>
> Emer's Maid, in *The Wooing of Emer*; Cross and Slover, 1936, p. 61

Ancient British chariots, of the later Iron Age, were observed by Caesar who clearly appreciated their manoeuvrability and the skill of their charioteers; and the discovery of the parts of such vehicles in many graves should allow closely detailed reconstructions to be made:

> ... they display in battle the speed of horse and the steadiness of infantry; and by daily practice and exercise attain to such expertness that they are accustomed, even on a declining and steep place, to check their horses at full speed, and manage and turn them in one instant and run along the pole, and stand on the yoke, and thence betake themselves with the greatest of celerity to their chariots again.
>
> Caesar IV, 33

What a well-disciplined Roman soldier thought about a naked and woad-painted Briton, leaping about his chariot and dancing along the pole between the plunging horses, cannot be imagined, or perhaps it can, but in the end it presented no more than a minor divertissement in the conquest. In a recent experiment with chariot, harness, ponies and charioteers (Fig. 27), the slightest jolt over rough ground tended to propel the tartan-clad Celts off the back in a most undignified way (Coles, 1973, and personal observation).

Roman horses were equally well trained; the fort at The Lunt, near

Fig. 27. Celtic chariot with Celtic ponies and driver, Hawick, Scotland—a version made for display purposes, light in weight and bumpy in ride (photo: J. M. Coles).

Coventry, with rampart and timber gateway (p. 135), also contained a circular structure or *gyrus* which has been interpreted and reconstructed as a military horse-breaking and training facility (Rylatt, 1978). The *gyrus* consists of a 30 m diameter circular enclosure with a funnelled entrance, the whole represented by a slot with sockets at intervals for uprights. The reconstruction was carried out by a small group of Royal Engineers in only ten days using prefabricated planks which were set into sleeper beams held in the slot. The uprights are considered to have supported an external elevated walkway for observation of the training session within. We do not know the precise methods for training horses but experiments within the *gyrus* demonstrate that the horses could walk, trot and canter, but not gallop, and that the circular walls contain and reflect noise, producing a considerable din, doubtless an essential part of any preparation for Roman or any military horses (p. 12).

Much more extensive experimentation has been carried out on a range of harnesses, carts and chariots of Near Eastern and north African types (Spruytte, 1977). Based on wall paintings, rock engravings, fragments and a detailed practical knowledge of carting, a variety of vehicles have been made and tested. These include a reconstruction of a chariot of the pharaoh Tutankamun (Fig. 28), with six-spoked wheels of wood and metal holding a wicker-floored box, with pole and double yoke, the entire vehicle weighing only 34 kg including harness. The driving tests proved entirely satisfactory, the vehicle pulling easily (by automobile!) at 38 km

FIG. 28. Inscribed design on the handle of a fan for Tutankamun. The text on the handle states that the fan was made of ostrich feathers obtained by His Majesty when hunting in the desert; the two-wheeled chariot is of wood, with a light frame, and the pair of horses are held by reins passing around the king while he shoots with bow and arrow at the ostriches. (From Carter, 1923–33, vol. II.)

per hour over a 1-km earth track. Further tests with paired ponies demonstrated speed and mobility. However there was one spectacular crash: the chariot had no brakes. Another reconstruction was based on fifth-century Greek representations of chariots on pottery, and the tests included full-tilt gallops with paired horses. Experiments were also carried out on wheels of many types, and a series of fixed-axle wheels and free-turning wheels were made without the use of a saw; but tripartite and more complex wheels required a saw and copies were made of Sumerian, Assyrian and Etruscan types. A Chinese cart of the second century B.C. with a pair of curved traces for a single animal, like modern racing carts, was reproduced, as well as two interpretations of chariots depicted on the Tassili rock paintings of northern Africa. The Tassili vehicles are extremely slight, consisting of hardly more than a pair of spoked wheels linked by an axle holding a small platform and central pole with crossbar for paired horses or other animals. One of the reconstructions was made entirely of wood, using only stone tools: axe, adze, knife, scraper, bow drill, and various points. The vehicle remained firm, strong and stable even when pulled at maximum speed by two horses; however, the quite remarkable aspect of this work must be the realization that metal, or metal tools, are not prerequisites for chariot or cart making. Only experimental archaeology could have made this observation.

3 Subsistence

...the countrey in fertilitie apte and comodious throughowt to make sugar and to beare and bring fourthe plentifully all that men would plante or sowe upon it. There be every where the highest, fayrerest and greatest fir trees that can be sene, verry will smelling and whereowt migght be gotton with cutting only the bark, as muche rosin, turpentyne and frankinsense as men would have; and to be shorte there lackethe nothing.

Ribauld, 1563

Food production—the deliberate cultivation of food-plants, especially cereals, and the taming, breeding, and selection of animals—was an economic revolution—the greatest in human history after the mastery of fire. It opened up a richer and more reliable supply of food, brought now within man's own control and capable of almost unlimited expansion by his unaided efforts.

Childe, 1954, p. 23

THROUGHOUT THE DECADES, and centuries, of exploration and colonization of new lands in America, Africa, Australia and the Pacific islands, the chroniclers tell of the immense fertility of the virgin lands, barely touched by indigenous peoples, whether they were agriculturalists, herdsmen, hunters or gatherers. In some regions, however, conditions were less suitable for settlement by farmers and stock-breeders, and these were the areas to which the native people often retreated, or into which they were forced as landtake by stronger groups proceeded inexorably. These conditions, untouched fertility, hunting grounds, conflicts of interest, must have been present in far earlier times in Europe and Asia, as well as Africa and America, when the first agriculturalists began to assert their need for land for clearance and cultivation. We are not concerned here with the origins of agriculture, indigenous in many parts of the world, introduced in many others, but rather with the nature of the earliest forms of food production. One of the constant and continuing interests of archaeology is the character of the "neolithic revolution", the establishment in many parts of the world of agriculture and domestication. Decades of research in the Near

East, in Mesoamerica and in Europe have revealed many aspects of early agriculture-based communities, their farmsteads and villages, their imperishable equipment of flint and stone, and the remains of the animals they herded and hunted. Radiocarbon dating has allowed a broad picture to be drawn of the chronological development of agricultural economies, showing the primary areas where cultivation of plants and domestication of animals first occurred.

In the Near East the indigenous wild wheats (einkorn and emmer), and barley, formed the basis of the transition from human mobile economies founded on hunting and gathering to more sedentary economies in part reliant on plant cultivation and the herding of animals. In middle America, the extinction by hunting of large animals led to increasing reliance upon the harvesting of wild plants, supplemented by the cultivation of beans, pumpkin, squash and maize in different regions. In both these areas of the world, the processes of agriculture were well underway by 8000 B.C.

The fact that Europe lacked almost all the native prototypes of early cereals, as well as sheep and goats, demonstrates that some agricultural practices must have been introduced in a developed state into the virgin lands of Europe; and radiocarbon dates again point to the earliest agricultural settlements in south-eastern Europe, with progressively later establishments to the west and north. The introduction of new animals and plants to the alien environments of Europe has been a source of continuing fascination on the part of the archaeologists, and experimental work has been able to assist in understanding the processes involved.

Most agricultural activities are seasonal in that land preparation precedes planting, a growing time ensues before the harvest, and both the yield and the land must then be made ready for immediate or future use. The relevance of studies of ancient land use is today not restricted to archaeologists. Recent crises in food production in many parts of the world, through climatic drought and humanly induced erosion and land exhaustion, have focused attention on the need for conservation of natural resources.

For almost 10 000 years, a balance existed between agricultural exploitation and natural recovery. Although ancient man was intensively exploiting his land, his methods were not destructive. Today, many areas of the world are seeing the dramatic effects of over-use of the land, with no chance of recovery. To trace the development of land use through time may well encourage some reflection on methods for the future. And to seek to understand the prehistory and early history of agriculture, experimentalists have provided clear guides to the processes involved and their consequences to both humans and the land. Two major aspects of early agriculture have recently been studied by experiment and by observation. The first of these relates to primary settlement in regions hitherto unoccupied except by hunters, and it involves clearance of forest and preparation for the first cultivation of plants. The second set is concerned with the pattern of farming life established by tradition and involving rounds of activities determined by seasonal conditions. Winter clearance of the land, spring cultivation and planting of crops, summer hay-making and silage production, autumn harvesting and storage of crops are but a few of the many activities. Both investigations are of course related. The primary farmers were anxious to develop a regime for their land, the established farmers were concerned to maintain their land and to take more into cultivation as needs arose. We will look first at the experimental work done on primary farming activities, sometimes called forest farming.

The choice of land for cultivation must have been absolutely basic and essential for early farmers. We have very little evidence of the criteria used by prehistoric farmers, but recent historic clearances in Russia and Canada indicate that the choice of site was so important that a "seeker of new land" was sometimes selected on the basis of his experience and previous success. He would choose the new land, often using the type of trees growing as a guide to the most fertile and appropriate soils. In this way, woodlands with stands of alder, oak and elm, birch or spruce were regularly chosen for the new farming community. Wild foods, both animal and plant, were also important to have at hand, because farming is never an instant food-producing exercise. Once chosen, the work of clearing could begin, and here many archaeologists have experimented with axes, and with fire, to see how easily ancient man might have coped with a mature, untouched and primeval forest.

The cutting equipment used by ancient man to fell trees could be of stone, bronze or iron. Stone axes were employed in almost all parts of the world, because stone was always available and because it was so effective in dealing with all but the hardest of woods. Iron too appears in many regions as a material suitable for cutting and chopping; but bronze was more restricted in its distribution. Although very few of the thousands upon thousands of ancient axes have been found with their wooden handles, there is no doubt that most axes were more efficient when hafted because greater speed and force of blow could be applied. Experiments have often been used to test stone axes, and sometimes iron and steel axes, but rarely bronze; however, all have recently come under investigation (e.g. Stelcl and Malina, 1970; Harding and Young, 1979). In actual use, it is found that the axes cannot often be swung boldly from behind the head; instead a shorter stroke is more effective in directing the blow. The reasons for this contrast between a modern steel axe and a primitive axe, whatever its material, lies in the balance and in the thickness (not width) of the blade. Many stone axes are fat, deliberately so, thereby giving weight to the tool but also ensuring that its physical shape will not easily fit into a deepening cut unless it is swung with great accuracy. It is likely that prehistoric man was an expert both in hafting and in using these axes, and experimenters probably suffer from inexperience. Recent tests have in fact shown that full-blooded swings are possible and that confidence increases with practice.

There are various ways of measuring the efficiency of axe work and many are the trees felled by experimenters using a bizarre variety of hafted or unhafted objects. Most trees have been felled at knee height, with the axe cutting in at an acute angle of about 50° to the trunk in order to splinter off long chips; the felled stems are therefore like pencils with sharpened ends, while the stump, receiving the downward blow, is thoroughly smashed and splintered (Fig. 29, left). It seems rather pointless to list the individual results of the tests as these depend on the condition of the wood (hard or soft), of the axe (blunt or sharpened), and of the experimenter (fit or unfit); however, a general guide, based on work done in Scandinavia, Czechoslovakia, Britain, America and Canada, suggests that any tree up to about 20 cm in diameter could be knocked down by a stone axe in under 15 minutes, while larger trees could take three or four times as long. Metal axes, of bronze or iron, prove to be much more efficient on the trees than are stone axes. This is because the metal axes are thin and can bite deeply into the stem without jamming. Stone axes are generally much thicker than metal axes, and they cannot bite deeply into the tree unless a very wide cut is made. One way to create sufficient width is to start two separate cuts, one 30–50 cm above the other, and direct work so that the two cuts eventually meet well within the trunk. This helps avoid the tiresome widening of a single cut. The comparative efficiency of stone, bronze and iron axes is of some interest, and there seems little doubt that a bronze axe was 2 or 3 times as efficient as an ordinary stone axe, and yet was itself rather less effective than an iron axe. The implications of these tools for the clearance of forests, which in north-western Europe at least was accelerated in the Bronze Age, and then again in the Iron Age, is a subject worthy of further investigation.

One way of measuring the worth of varying axes is by calculating energy expended in their use; one such test suggested that a steel axe was perhaps four or five times as effective as a stone axe. In New Guinea, ethnographic observation of sweet potato cultivators showed that steel axes were twice as effective as stone axes in clearing land, and lasted eight times as long. It should be remarked, however, that steel axes were not available to prehistoric man in Europe; hence the comparisons are a bit like contrasting

FIG. 29. Comparative tests with stone and bronze axes.
Left. Splintered stump and stem of spruce tree, 13 cm diameter, felled with a stone axe in three minutes (from Stelcl and Malina, 1970).
Right. Chopped stump and stem of birch tree, 20 cm diameter, felled with a flat bronze axe in three minutes. Note the wide, deep scars produced by the thin sharp blade. (Photo: J. M. Coles.)

smoke signals and the telephone, or slingstones and grenades. The alternatives were just not available to early man, and comparisons are valuable
only for the scale they indicate to modern man, who may not even know
much about steel axes today! The indisputable fact that enormous trees
of oak and other resistant woods were regularly felled and cleanly split into
planks suggests that more work is needed on very substantial timber, yet
here the modern and pressing necessities of conservation of our timber
must override the experimenters' problems. It seems likely that large trees,
over one metre in diameter, would have been felled by burning, or by
ringing (debarking) and then cutting down after death. In west Africa,
hardwood trees are totally resistant to axes, the axes merely bouncing off
the timber, yet by careful fire-setting the huge trees can be felled in 2 or
3 days (Shaw, 1969). In temperate zones, drying before burning would
have been necessary, as historical records attest. In western Canada,
within the past 40 years, attacks on virgin forest still involved only axes
and horses (Harding and Young, 1979). Lighter soils were taken first as
they were less heavily wooded, and only areas with hardwoods were
chosen; softwoods did not create topsoil essential for successful agriculture.
Ringing of large trees was standard practice, and these when dead were
pulled from the ground by a team of horses in order to remove the stump
and roots. After a year or two of drying, the smaller trees and underbrush
were burned *in situ*, and the heavier tree stems cut up for fuel.

All of these observations, and experimental work, indicates that forest
clearance was not an insuperable task for ancient man, but was one that
required planning and forethought. Although the time taken to clear
woodland was relatively short, we know that clearances were likely to have
been kept small (at first perhaps only 1–2 hectares) in order to allow forest
regeneration and prevent the development of heathland.

In contrast, modern farmland hewn from the forests of Brazil beggars
comparison with ancient practices. Recent landtake has involved enormous clearances of primeval forest, with the trees felled by steel axes. The
wood is burned over two or three years, grass is planted, cattle are driven
in, and ranches are thereby established. Some of the ranches achieve
$\frac{1}{2}$ million hectares in size. The herds reach over 20 000 head of cattle,
hardy beasts able to stumble over and graze between the burned stumps
and stems of the slaughtered trees, to withstand heat, floods and the
tabanid flies. The achievements of prehistoric man with his miniscule
holdings seem puny, but we must not forget his pioneering position, his
invention of techniques to cope with alien environments, and his success.

Experiments concerned with the whole range of early agriculture have
not stopped here. Instead they have often continued with the preparation
of the land for sowing seed. In Denmark as in America, the felled wood

was burned in order to get rid of it, to yield ash fertilizers, and to kill weeds and roots. Control areas were left cleared but unburned. Thereafter the experimental plots were planted with cereals (Steensberg, 1955; and see Reynolds, 1977b). However, all these experiments tend to neglect another essential reason for felling trees, that is to obtain timber. A rapid inspection of modern, recent and ancient traces of farmhouses, barns, sheds, fences, wagons and tools will show that most if not all were traditionally of wood, whether American, African or European. Land for cultivation would be chosen for its yield not only of soil but also of timber. Some few experiments dealing exclusively with woodworking are described in Chapter 5.

Burning of the felled wood in the clearances has been shown to create or help maintain a high fertility in virgin soils. In these experiments, wheat and barley sown directly into the warm earth and raked in with a stick soon sprouted and yielded a strong crop; in an unburnt plot nearby, the crop was very feeble in comparison. Moreover, the second and third years' crops from the burnt fields were also much reduced as the effects of burning were washed out, and the soil fertility was depleted by the plants. In northern latitudes of America the same results are attested in historical records of the "land butchers" who would roughly clear and burn an area, take a crop or two, then move on. Recent experiments in England, at Little Butser (p. 114), have carefully contrasted burned and unburned areas of cleared land, and have recorded the steady decline in yield from the emmer sown annually. After only two years the unburned ground was uneconomic, and after four years the burned plots were also found to yield only the equivalent amount of seed corn planted (Reynolds, 1977b).

In central America, closely related experiments have shown the obvious, that soil fertility is the major factor in plant growth; but they have also shown that weeding contributes in no small measure to the success of a series of crops where depletion of nutrients puts plants under stress (Hester, 1953; Steggerda, 1941). These experiments have not involved crop rotation, or the combination of cereals and beans which complement one another in their needs; beans will add nitrogen to the soil, whereas cereals exhaust this element. In Colorado, an interesting experiment involved annual crops of corn, beans and squash, in order to test soil exhaustion over many years (Frank and Watson, 1936). Navajo Indians used traditional methods of planting and regularly prepared and tended their plots. Each group of seed corn was planted at the bottom of a large hole which was left open until the shoots emerged and reached the ground surface. The hole was then filled in and the earth heaped up around the plants. In the early years of the work, older Indians put a "prayer" into each of the hummocks, but these were neglected by the younger Indians who continued the experiment. It is sad to report that no noticeable difference could be detected in the crops. The yields did not fall steadily over the years through soil exhaustion, and only extreme drought caused dramatic collapse of the crop. Due to consumption of the corn by rodents, and by other Indians (doubtless in the interests of scientific experiment), no crop-yield figures could be maintained. Such are the problems encountered by archaeologists who often feel their efforts are appreciated for the wrong reasons.

All of these experiments have yielded useful information about the practices of forest clearance and primitive cultivation; moreover they suggest that early farmers probably required quite large areas of land. Some of this land would be under crops, other parts would be undergoing clearance of trees by felling and burning, and further larger areas would be lying in fallow after one or several years of cultivation. For prehistoric agriculture, the experiments suggest that a small farmstead would require perhaps 5–10 times the amount of land actually yielding crops each year. In some modern farming communities, fields are abandoned for 20 years, and so a very large area is needed in which the actual houses near certain parts may also be abandoned periodically. All of these observations are clearly of significance to the archaeologist, but only if they are considered as part of the programme of investigation into early farming communities, and not accepted as demonstrating indisputable facts.

These experiments have been concerned with primary agriculture, that is the establishment of farming practices in areas of forest. Archaeological evidence from America, Asia and Europe in particular suggests that we cannot make any generalizations about the ultimate success or failure of these forest farmers. A feature of some of their activities was abandonment of the clearings to allow regeneration of woodland and soil fertility after a crop or two had been taken, and yet we know from historical records that often this slash-and-burn process was unsuccessful. Intense cold could kill the pioneer grain, warm wet weather could cause mildew on wheat, drought and heat might dry the crop to a crisp. Archaeological methods are not exact enough to obtain the evidence in order to determine if clearings were abandoned in despair or as a planned programme; but experiments certainly suggest that the pioneer farmer did not automatically have his way, and they therefore serve to caution those who consider that the establishment of farming was a smooth progression.

Even so it has been documented that farming was introduced and developed in many areas of the Old and New World between 6000 B.C. and 1000 B.C., and that areas of land were increasingly cleared of trees in order to allow the more permanent cultivation of crops. Rotation of plots and fields would continue of course, but woodland could be prevented from heavy development, and grassland for domestic animals established over wide areas; furthermore, the value of manure would soon be recognized, although it is difficult for archaeologists to identify clear traces of deliberate manuring of fields. In order to cultivate wider areas where the tree stumps had been removed by axe, fire, levers and ropes, tools were developed to cut and groove the soil. A number of different implements have survived, and most have been tested by experiment to determine their probable value to ancient man.

Digging sticks and wooden spades are obvious tools for breaking up the ground, and some spade marks of the Bronze Age are known from Cornwall. Of equal interest is a traction ard of ash, about 6000 years old, from northern Germany (Steensberg, 1973). This implement consists of a heart-shaped blade, with two holes near the upper part, and a long slender handle (Fig. 30, upper). As the actual tool was a valuable museum specimen it could not be tested itself, and so an exact replica was made from ashwood. The balance, blade shape and length of handle were inappropriate for digging or shovelling, and in any case the two holes and wear marks suggested a use as a rope traction ard. In the experiments, the blade was pulled slowly through light soil by one man hauling on a rope attached to the blade by the holes, with another man pressing the implement into the ground. The furrows produced were 5–6 cm deep, appropriate for depth of seed in this area today.

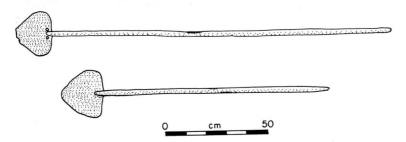

Fig. 30. Two wooden implements from Satrup Moor, Germany, *c.* 4000 B.C.
Upper. Ashwood tool with long handle and perforated blade, interpreted as a traction ard.
Lower. Shorter ashwood tool interpreted as a winnowing shovel.
(After Steensberg, 1973.)

More elaborate wooden implements for tilling the soil have also been recovered from ancient peatbogs where their preservation has been assured by waterlogging. These tools have been subjected to exhaustive tests as they represent the few survivors of the ards and ploughs which were the principal farming machines of the past. Many grooves and furrows created by the tools have been recorded by archaeologists, although their preservation depends upon random burial of the soil by landslip, or by the placing of burial mounds and the like over cultivated ground. One of the most elaborate experiments with these tools was based upon a series of replicas of an Iron Age wooden ard from Jutland of a form also depicted in Bronze Age and Iron Age rock engravings in northern Europe (Fig. 31).

Fig. 31. Rock engraving of the Bronze Age from Tossene at Haga, Sweden, showing paired oxen and simple ard with ploughman. Scale totals 25 cm. (Photo: J. M. Coles.)

The wooden ard consisted of a curved one-piece stilt and ard-head which passed through the beam; on top of the ard-head was a stout wooden bar-share which must have been held in place by wedges. Replicas of the prehistoric ard were made and tested in various ways (Hansen, 1969) (Fig. 32). The rock engravings show paired oxen pulling ards, so a pair of bull calves were trained to walk evenly and slowly in a straight line, harnessed to a yoke set behind the animals' heads and attached to the beam. In the event, the experimental ploughman needed three helpers to guide the oxen and to encourage them when they flagged or when the ard bit too deeply into the soil. Light and sandy soils could be cut easily, but old fallow ground proved too dense and hard. The oxen could produce draught power up to 200 kg but any load of 150 kg slowed them, and sudden dips of the share into the ground would stop the team even with the most vigorous "encouragement" of the helpers. Various parts of the

FIG. 32. *Upper.* Experimental ploughing with a reconstructed ard of Bronze Age type at Lejre, Denmark. The ard is made of ash, and consists of a one-piece stilt and ard-head passing through the beam, with the wooden bar-share held upon the ard-head by wedges.

Lower. The yoke with neck-ties and horn-loops; this is only one of a number of possible ways by which the paired oxen could be attached to the ard, which in this case is held by the central rope.

(Historical–Archaeological Research Centre, Lejre.)

ard broke, and wear marks developed on bar-shares and ard-head; these could be compared with traces on prehistoric fragments of ards in order to deduce the probable methods of original use. In particular, the bar-shares wore down rapidly, and it was estimated that 6 would have been needed to plough 0·5 hectares; the prehistoric share was almost new when it was lost, abandoned or stored in the wet peatmoss. The experiments created many furrows in the various soils, and these too could be recorded, and compared with prehistoric and early prehistoric marks in the earth. The result of this work, which is still continuing, is that new thoughts are being produced about the agencies which had formed the marks, about the shapes of bar-shares and ards, about the method of use, about the survival of ancient furrows and about the difficulties of working fallow ground. This experiment as much as any other dealing with the land demonstrates the value of such approaches in creating and answering some questions, and suggesting new ways of looking at old material.

This ploughing experiment, and others as well, have initiated research into the shape of ancient fields. In areas where developed and intensive farming was practised, fields rather than irregular plots were laid out, and tree stumps removed, so that organized ploughing could take place. Many such fields have survived destruction by modern deep ploughing, plantations and other land disturbance. In general these fields date from about 1500 B.C. to 500 B.C. in western Europe, the majority created in the Bronze and Iron Ages. The prehistoric fields in question are marked today by terraced edges called lynchets, and they are often rather small (0·1 ha, $\frac{1}{4}$ acre) although larger fields are also well known. Rectangular or square in shape, the fields often lie in groups with common lynchet borders; droveroads connect the groups with one another and with farmsteads and enclosures, the whole forming a unit of settlement (Fig. 33). Many of these Celtic fields, as they are called, lie on gently sloping ground and they were probably originally laid out by merely ploughing a convenient shape in two directions (hence the square or nearly square field), leaving an untouched strip between fields. Or some turf may have been cut off before ploughing and piled at the proposed field edges. With ploughing, with rain and wind, soil crept down and banked up at the lower border of the fields; on the upslopes of the fields, however, the plough gradually cut more deeply into the soil and thereby exaggerated the lynchet effect of the adjacent higher field. Through experimental work with ploughs and with fields, we can see the effects on borders as well as on the actual soils and furrows.

The plants of the experimental plots and fields in America and Europe had been naturally selected on the basis of ancient forms recovered from archaeological sites. In America, corns, beans and squash are grown, as well as water melon, cantaloupe and potato. In Europe, cereals such as emmer, spelt and barley are those generally planted in the experimental fields, but vetch and Celtic beans have also been grown. Unfortunately most experiments have been concerned mainly with soil fertilities and gross yields over a period of 1–5 years, and little attention has been paid to the quality of the plants, their nutritional values and their individual

FIG. 33. Celtic fields at Smacam Down, Dorset, clearly marked by lynchet formation. These fields were probably crisscross ploughed—hence the nearly square shapes, and the untouched edges form the base of the lynchets. Note the traces of a native settlement in the centre, perhaps contemporary with the fields. (Committee for Aerial Photography, Cambridge University Collection; copyright reserved.)

hardiness. In the set of experiments in Colorado, the quality of corn was clearly high as the crop was systematically raided by both animals and humans; but this is hardly a scientific observation. The crops grown at the Butser Ancient Farm (described below) are being carefully observed and measured, and have already presented some highly interesting data. Emmer and spelt have been grown as both winter and spring grown crops, without fertilizers and within Celtic-type fields prepared by ard, spade and digging stick. The yields have been very surprising, emmer averaging over

2 tonnes per hectare (16 cwt per acre); in addition, the protein levels of both wheats have been calculated as twice that of modern bread wheat. Information of this nature is likely to revolutionize our thoughts about ancient foodstuffs and requirements for land, crops and agricultural methods.

Mention has already been made of protection of crops, and there can be no doubt that ancient farmers had to somehow guard their plots and fields against animals both wild and domestic. Ethnographic records assert that fencing is always an important activity in the annual work. We may assume that stump fences and rock piles would have dissuaded only a few of the most faint-hearted animals and human raiders. Horizontal pole fences, upright palisades, woven hurdles and living hedges would have kept out a greater proportion of animals including cattle but probably not deer. Little experimental work has been done in fencing, except in the fabrication of hurdles to a known prehistoric design. Waterlogged peats in Somerset have preserved alder and hazel hurdles 3 m long and 1·5 m wide, laid flat in the marsh over 4000 years ago; the hazel rods and sails forming the hurdles were from coppiced woodland, almost the earliest evidence of woodland management in the world. In this practice, the stems or stools of hazel are cut back to ground level so that new straight shoots spring up from the base; after 3–7 years they are cut for fencing poles and for other uses, and the stool is left to produce new shoots. The prehistoric hurdles consisted of about 60 rods and 6–8 sails, with twisted willow ties holding the edges together. The experiments were designed to time the manufacture of hurdles of this type, and coppiced hazel rods were felled with stone axes or broken from the stools by hand or foot. The rods were trimmed of twigs and leaves, and woven into the hurdle, the time from start to finish representing 1·5–2 hours of work by two men (Fig. 34). The hurdle weighed only 30 kg and could be carried by one man. The experiments suggested that prehistoric hurdles were rapidly made, easily transported, and formed effective panels suitable for long lengths of fencing of heights up to perhaps 2 metres (Coles and Darrah, 1977).

The experiments described above have dealt with some of the basic needs of prehistoric farmers, whether they were pioneers or more established settlers. By attempting to reproduce some of the actions of ancient man, we can hope to gain a clearer insight into the reasons for specific operations which we know about, and also to obtain hints about the activities which have not survived in clearly recognizable forms.

There is one aspect, however, which is not entirely satisfactory in the work already done. We still cannot begin to understand the rates of success or failure of ancient farming from simple examination and testing of isolated activities, whether this be ploughing or fencing. We know from historical records in both America and Asia that primitive farming methods were not always successful, and that spectacular failures occurred not infrequently. In Canada, for example, some pioneer farmers tried to force the whole process of felling, burning and sowing into one season, generally with a chaotic result of half-burnt timber strewn across the plots where cereals struggled for light; other pioneers let their burning escape into the surrounding woods and thereby created a shambles unfit for man or beast until nature herself cleared away the debris by decay. Only half the settlers in Upper Canada managed to plant any crop at all in their first year, so it is little wonder that the failure rate was so high. Yet they persisted, and so doubtless did more ancient settlers of prehistoric times. By experimenting with only one or two aspects of land use, felling trees or growing a crop for example, we are artificially isolating the work from the competition that other activities created. Moreover, we are assuming that events on the land were not related. Of course they all were: farming

Fig. 34. Experimental manufacture of a hurdle or fencing panel of Neolithic type, 2200 B.C., in Suffolk. The rods (horizontals) and sails (uprights) are of hazel cut from coppiced stools with stone axes. The entire operation took only 1·5–2·0 hours. (Photo: J. M. Coles.)

above all else is a single related whole, each activity connected to the next in a sequence of seasonal work. By treating each action in isolation, we cannot come to grips with overall rates of success or failure on the part of ancient farmers, and these matters are of the greatest importance in attempts to learn more about early settlers, communities and societies.

A logical way to attempt to overcome this problem is to create an entire Ancient Farm, in which all experimental work is directed towards the success of the farm rather than the single exercise alone. At the moment, only one project has attempted this, and it is premature to assess its record or even its full potential. The Butser Ancient Farm Project in Hampshire exists as an operation designed to reconstruct and work a farmstead of the Iron Age, 300 B.C. (Reynolds, 1977a, 1979). It is based upon the evidence obtained from prehistoric farmsteads of this period, and upon documentary sources in which classical authors wrote about the Celts. The site itself consists of 23 hectares of chalk ridge, upon which are housed fields, plots, domestic animals, buildings and workshops, storage pits and kilns, all of which relate directly to a functioning and essentially self-sufficient Iron Age farmstead (Fig. 35). It is important to note, however, that human occupation in the sense of permanent dwellers is not attempted; after all we know far too little about the personal habits of Iron Age people to risk distortion of the working farm by introducing twentieth-century customs, and this matter is more fully examined in Chapter 6.

The Ancient Farm buildings consist of two roundhouses based upon actual plans from Iron Age sites at Maiden Castle (Dorset) and Balksbury (Hampshire); the latter has now been dismantled. The construction of the Maiden Castle house took the straw from 16 Celtic fields, over 30 trees, 7 tonnes of daub, one tonne of thatch and 3 cowhides. Such an undertaking would clearly have stretched the inhabitants of the farm in its early days, yet this house is small in comparison with those known from many prehistoric sites. The fields at Butser are worked by spade and ard, with boundaries already marked by lynchets. These fields and other plots hold experimental crops of emmer, einkorn, spelt, barley, oats, beans, flax and woad, all of which are monitored for yield and strength, the whole forming a planned programme for the next 20 years. Storage of the cereals following the harvest by sickle is another particular research project, already yielding important data. The manufacture of silage in pits for winter feeding of cattle is a recent subject of investigation. Silage is produced if the bacteria *Streptococcus lactis*, present on ordinary grass, can produce lactic acid on grass held in a pit in an anaerobic condition. The experiments may help to indicate the ways by which archaeologists could retrieve evidence for silage pits on ancient sites. Pottery firing in pits and the use of pits as debris receptacles also form part of the Iron Age programme.

An important element on any farm is livestock, and here the value of a long-term and permanently worked experiment is obvious. There have been few research experiments dealing with animals, although there is widespread interest in back-breeding of cattle, sheep and pigs. At Butser, long-legged Dexter cattle are being trained to pull carts, sledges and ards; these animals are close in size to the extinct *Bos longifrons* known from many Iron Age settlements. Similarly, Soay sheep, closest relative to pre-historic sheep, are kept behind high hurdle fences; lightweight, agile and rather goatish in appearance, the Soay will yield meat, milk and fine soft wool which can be plucked rather than sheared each summer. The wool is spun into yarn and woven into cloth on a replica of an Iron Age loom

Fig. 35. Artist's impression of the Ancient Farm at Little Butser, Hampshire, England. A hurdle-lined passage leads into the Iron Age enclosure with two round houses, Celtic fields, storage pits, and other areas for farming activities. (Drawn by R. Walker.)

of wood (p. 196). Other animals held on the Ancient Farm include the Exmoor pony, comparable to the extinct Celtic horse, and equally strong as a pack animal. Prehistoric pigs were also exterminated completely, but a crossbreed between European wild boar and Tamworth sow has resulted in an animal whose bones resemble those of prehistoric pigs.

Archaeologists are not often involved in genetic experiments but one such project has created much interest. One of the dominant animals of the prehistoric forests in Europe was the aurochs (*Bos primigenius*), widely hunted until final extinction in Poland in 1627. The bulls were up to 2 metres high at the shoulders, and had extremely impressive horns. From their bones, from historical records, and from representations of the aurochs in prehistoric art, it was possible to gain some impression of the original beast, and in 1921 a series of cross breedings were initiated in Germany involving many breeds until the desired aurochs-look emerged. Herds were built up and survive today, presenting us with an impression, perhaps inaccurate in parts but nonetheless valuable, of a huge animal, fierce and extremely agile. It is satisfying to learn that some now run in the Polish forests where their ancestral form had its final stand against the onslaught of man (Zeuner, 1963). But the point must be emphasized that breeding back cannot recreate an extinct species; once it is extinct it is gone forever. These experiments can only give an approximation of the animals now lost. The necessity to preserve the few descendants of once-numerous indigenous animals, e.g. the tiger and the rhinoceros, is obvious.

Ancient forms of cattle were perhaps the most susceptible to human interference. Unlike sheep and goats, cattle could not retreat to rocky isolated terrain, but were restricted to lowland forests where in time they became exposed to the hunter and pioneer farmer. Several centres now exist where rare breeds of all sorts are maintained and carefully bred to protect the original strains. The work of most of these centres is outside the scope of this book except, however, the Historical-Archaeological Research Centre at Lejre in Denmark, where animals are included in the unit. Lejre serves as a base for a large series of experiments, and some of these are described in Chapter 4. It has managed to rescue certain breeds of Scandinavian animals, including Gotland and Faroes sheep, from possible extinction and has also attempted to breed back the Celtic pig. Lejre has sometimes been described as an Iron Age farm, but this is a misnomer. The Centre acts as a focal point for many different research subjects; for instance there is a fine set of houses of Iron Age character (p. 157). Lejre has a special position in the history of experimental archaeology. It is an example of a unit founded for research but now firmly in the educational field; it makes unique contributions to the whole field of experiments (Hansen, 1977).

We have so far seen attempts to experiment with the primary processes of food production, and have been able to see some of the vital and basic types of information obtained from the work. Experiments concerned with the harvesting, storage, preparation and the consumption of food have also been carried out.

Although there are many experiments concerned with the harvesting of crops, most have been limited to cereals and little has been attempted with other plants. This seems no great loss as many fruits and vegetables require merely hand-picking or digging, and presumably this was so in the past. With fields of cereals, however, it is of interest to consider how ancient man gathered the yield, how efficient his implements were in the absence of combine harvesters and other enormously effective machines. Ethnographic evidence and observations among many peasant communities in the world today provide useful guides to ancient practices, but archaeologists also have a wide range of blades and sickles, of flint, bronze and iron, many of which were used to harvest crops of grass, reeds and cereals. Tests have been carried out on some of these to discover how efficient they were.

The basic method is simple enough, and involves two-handed backbreaking work. A group of stalks is grasped in one hand, and the sickle is wielded by the other, cutting fairly low to the ground where the plants are held by the earth, with the blade sweeping towards the harvester. Depending upon the type of implement, and how it is hafted, the cutting action may be horizontal to the ground, or downwards or upwards; without doubt individual personal preferences determine the precise height and angle as well. The action of blade edge upon the grass or cereal stalk involves friction, and early experiments with sickle flints were concerned with the gloss which could be seen upon many prehistoric blades (p. 29). It was discovered that reaping siliceous grasses and corn caused the gloss, and other substances such as wood and bone left different traces on the blades. The recognition of the characteristic gloss on very early flint blades in the Near East was one indication that deliberate harvesting of grasses and indigenous cereals was underway by 8000 B.C., a beginning of agriculture as we understand it. The harvest is a culmination of the planting process, and has often been treated with particular respect and ceremony by farmers. Parts of cornfields may be left uncut, the final sheaf may remain standing for a time, the last row of corn may be beaten into the ground, all in order to preserve and protect the fertility of the field and the success of the subsequent crop. Occasionally this might involve the spilling of human blood, but more often a specific part of the field, or a particular row of corn, was held apart from the rest. The corn dolly represents the preservation of the last stalks of corn from a field, displayed during the

E

harvest festival and maintained until the sowing of seeds for the next crop. The harvesting of the crop was an organized operation, carried out to a strict timetable when the corn was ripe and before the ears fell to the ground; and the ancient implements used in the harvest were correspondingly efficient and doubtless of value, perhaps ceremonial value, to the communities. We cannot re-create these ritual actions in the harvesting of the corn, but we can test the implements.

The most extensive series of experiments took place in Denmark under the direction of Axel Steensberg, one of the pioneers of the subject (1943). He used copies of flint, bronze and iron sickles and scythes such as had been recovered from sites dated 2000 B.C. to A.D. 1000; the style of hafting was based on ancient wooden handles preserved in wet peats (Fig. 36a). The precise details of this careful experiment need not concern us here, but it involved harvesting of equal plots of barley and oats. Each plot was cut by a harvester who had had instruction and practice in the manipulation of the tool. A bunch of stalks was grasped and cut, and the operation was repeated four or five times until a handful of stalks was obtained. These were laid down and the procedure was then continued until the plot was cleared. Each tool had its own peculiar character which required a specific method of use; the bronze sickles worked best when held low and swung upwards, but flint blades were most effective if used in a vigorous horizontal sweep. Iron scythes required two hands to work, and therefore shook and scattered the corn; hence they were probably for cutting grass and not corn crops in Iron Age and Viking times. A measure of the efficiency of each tool was its ability to cut cleanly through the straw without uprooting stalks; the actual time taken was perhaps not as useful an indicator as we will see. In cutting efficiency, iron tools were clearly the best. Sharp flint blades and bronze sickles were less effective and many of the other flints were not particularly successful. It is possible that the experimenters were more accustomed to using metal sickles and their own lack of efficiency with unfamiliar flints may have affected the results. Recent observations in Turkey have shown that wheat could be cleanly cut with flint sickles, with a yield of 1 kg per hour. Four persons, therefore, working a 10-hour day for three weeks could harvest 1 tonne—sufficient for a year's supply for a family in the short time when the corn was ripe and ears still firmly attached. The obvious may be stated again: ancient tools were just as efficient as they had to be, and Neolithic, Bronze Age and Iron Age man was well equipped here as in other areas of his agricultural work.

Less is known about subsequent stages of the harvest. If the corn was cut just below the ear, it would be gathered in buckets and taken to the barn for separation by beating and winnowing. The stalks would provide the straw for thatch, animal food and bedding. Little survives in the archaeological record to provide more detail, but a wooden spade recently found in north Germany has been shown by experiment to represent a

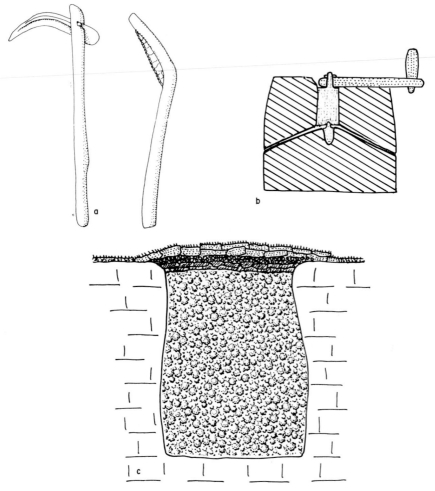

Fig. 36. (a) Sickles of Bronze Age and Neolithic types in modern handles: *left*, a bronze knobbed sickle; *right*, a serrated flint sickle deeply set in its haft. Length of tools *c*. 40 cm. In tests, these sickles were less effective than iron blades, but with slow and careful handling they could cut successfully through barley stalks. (After Steensberg, 1943.)

(b) Section through a rotary quern found at The Trundle, Sussex, England. Diameter of quern *c*. 30 cm. (After Curwen, 1941.)

(b) Section through a storage pit in chalk. The pit, *c*. 1·5 m deep, is filled with cereal, and is sealed with layers of clay, then chalk rubble, and finally turves. (After Reynolds, 1974.)

winnowing tool (Steensberg, 1973). The heart-shaped flat blade of this ash implement was attached to a long thin handle (Fig. 30, lower). A replica was used for shovelling sand and cutting turf, but it was found neither well enough balanced nor sufficiently heavy for these tasks. It was no more efficient for shovelling wheat than bare hands, but it seemed light enough to use in tossing up grain to separate, by wind, the heavier kernels from the lighter straw and chaff. Afterwards the replica was lacquered and used again in winnowing; the traces of wear which developed on the blade exactly matched the wear on the original object. In this way it is suggested that this object, 6000 years old, can be interpreted as an agricultural implement in use at a time when farming was only just introduced into northern Europe.

Although archaeological evidence for initial preparation of grain is sparse, much more information is available about its storage and grinding into meal. The work on corn storage pits and containers has been underway for years, and demonstrates as well as anything the value of repeated experiments and alternative theories. Preservation of food for future consumption was probably not a major concern of hunting and gathering groups; but as soon as agriculture became established the need arose to conserve parts of the harvest for future consumption and sowing back into the soil. Throughout the world various storage containers for harvested crops are known to be in use, and these provide guides to the experimental work. In central Africa, for example, underground pits store corn successfully for many months if they are well sealed by clay, termite mound, or dung (Cooke, 1953). Chambers excavated in prehistoric times from the rock, generally in limestone areas of central America, have sometimes been interpreted correctly as water cisterns. Others, in Maya territory, were situated in positions unsuitable for water catchment and storage; instead, they were considered to be for food storage, for burials, as sweat baths and latrines—not all at the same time of course (Puleston, 1971). An experimental pit or *chultun* was dug through the limestone and marl, and in it were placed maize, beans, squash and sweet potato; similar supplies were put above ground. Within a few weeks all the food above ground was eaten by animals or decayed by damp, and all the food in the *chultun* was also ruined by dampness; the humidity in the pit was almost 100 per cent. However, archaeological work on Mayan sites suggested that ramon seeds, the product of the *Brosimum* tree, might have been an important food of high nutritional value. These seeds have a very low water content, and in subsequent experiments they were stored in a *chultun* for over a year without decay, although the baskets holding them had perished. The work suggested that the ramon may have been intensively cultivated by the Maya, and stored in rock-cut pits.

Similar experiments have been carried out elsewhere, and they include work on a large number of storage pits dug and filled in the limestone and chalk of southern England (Reynolds, 1974). Many settlements of the Iron Age contain pits filled with debris, and these have generally been interpreted as storage pits for grain which were subsequently put to use as rubbish dumps. Experiments carried out over several years have shown that pits could be dug with antler picks and bone shovels and that an average size pit would hold 1600 litres (44 bushels). The pits could be lined with basketry or clay, or left without lining. Firing of pits destroys algae and bacteria as well as drying the walls. So long as the pits were sealed, by clay or dung, then storage of grain for several months was possible, and germination rates upon release were high (Fig. 36c). What is important is the realization that such pits had to be kept sealed, and could not therefore be used for everyday collection of corn for consumption. They must have been used for seed corn for the planting season. Food corn would be stored elsewhere, probably in unfired leather-hard or pottery vessels within the houses. Underground pits have also been shown to store grain successfully over many seasons, and the reason why they were abandoned and filled with debris remains uncertain. It is interesting to speculate that the heaping of domestic or farmyard debris over and around a pit, in order to seal it, might lead to a gradual filling with the debris when the pit had been emptied of its corn and lay open to the wind and rain. These experiments form an extremely valuable source of information, as well as of questions for the future.

Corn for consumption was traditionally prepared by grinding, and the earliest evidence for this practice as a definite process is from the Near East where the wild grain of 8000 B.C. was pounded by pestles in rock-cut mortars; the glume clings particularly tenaciously to the grain in wild wheat and therefore needs pounding to release it. In Mexico, seeds of the grass *Setaria* were recovered in coprolites from sites dated 5000 B.C. These seeds had been crushed in a manner unlike that used in later times; and experiments with mortars and pestles produced seeds of exactly the same character. Later communities in the area had ground the seeds on a stone metate with a roller, according to further experiments (Callen, 1967). The standard grinding tool from early periods was the saddle quern, a smoothed lower slab with an upper smaller stone which was rubbed back and forth, crushing the grain and requiring much hand work in retrieving the seeds from the front and the sides of the grinding stone in order to place them back in position for crushing. In central Africa, observations suggest that fully an hour's work was necessary to prepare corn for one family's daily needs.

A much more efficient method of grinding corn involves the rotary quern, basically two stone discs, the upper rotating on the lower (Fig. 36b). A central hole in the upper disc serves as a chute for the corn which then is ground between the stones, gradually working its way out to the edge before falling on to the surface prepared to receive the flour (Moritz, 1958; Moritz and Jones, 1959). Many varieties of rotary querns exist, and experiments have shown that the corn was probably roasted before grinding, as otherwise the soft grain would clog the grinding surfaces. There are still disputes about the methods of turning the upper stone. It might be rotated by hand, but many upper stones have holes for handle attachments, probably wooden sticks. These sticks would allow much more rapid turning, but whether complete revolutions or a back-and-forward motion of perhaps 120° were accomplished is not certain. The upper and lower stones generally touch at their outer edges, with a small gap between them near the centre to accumulate the corn. With a rotary action, the grain moves outwards, lifting the upper stone and thereby taking its full weight. Experiments suggest that a further grinding was probably necessary to complete the process, as some grain escapes the first grinding. In one experiment, 450 g undried wheat was ground and sieved eight times in about 35 minutes, with a yield of 396 g wholewheat flour, 28 g bran and 28 g lost. Roasted grain lost a lower proportion of fine meal in much the same time; there seems little doubt that grain in ancient times was heated before grinding, just as it is today in many regions. Oats and barley also require drying, especially to loosen the husks, and experiments show that these could be ground quite easily in rotary querns. Before leaving this subject, however, we might reflect on the work itself. Biblical references, and ethnographic sources, suggest that the grinding of corn was difficult and fit only for persons of low rank, and slaves were often so employed. Samson was made to operate the quern when he fell into disgrace.

Cooking of food, both plants and animals, is a subject which has had relatively few experiments, although there are a number of quite interesting pieces of work which throw light on some of the peculiar things ancient people ate. Baking and boiling of food is self-evident: pottery vessels often contain carbonized remnants of burnt cooking; traces of ovens and boiling pits are widespread. Clay ovens often existed within the houses (Fig. 37), and a Danish experiment was based on the discovery of circular clay structures, lacking their upper parts of course, which suggested a low, domed oven about one metre across and perhaps a metre high with a small entrance at floor level. Copies of these were made and were then tested to see if they functioned as smoke ovens. Fresh wood was placed within and then set alight, producing considerable heat and much smoke which filled the oven (Nielsen, 1966). Meat and fish could have been cured in the oven, and bread could have been baked. In a thatched wooden house, a fire contained in this way would be a safer prospect than an open fire, and it consumed far less fuel. Ovens of this character are known from many ancient sites, and some prehistoric houses contained batteries of such structures, like a modern soup-kitchen. We do not have much evidence for prehistoric soup-kitchens where communal meals were prepared, but a recent find at Zwammerdam in Holland suggests the existence of Roman soup-kitchens (Van Mensch, 1974). Here the chopped leg-bones of cattle were heaped in ditches, and they have been interpreted as showing a method of extraction of marrow for soup-making. The adjacent Roman buildings may have been where the bones were boiled to get out the marrow, and where the broth was prepared for hungry soldiers.

Apicius' cookery book of Roman foods provides far more elaborate recipes for dishes and meals than any other ancient records, but experiments with the animals he describes, such as the dormouse, have not been abundant in recent times. Fattening of these animals in special enclosures, and then in large pottery vessels to restrict exercise (Fig. 38), was accom-

FIG. 37. Reconstructed ovens of clay in a simulated Iron Age house at Asparn-an-der-Zaya, Austria. The thatched roof is protected from the heat by shields of skin and wood. (Drawn by R. Walker; after Hampl, 1970.)

plished by feeding with walnuts, acorns and chestnuts. Once the desired weight and tenderness was achieved, the dormouse was killed, stuffed with minced pork and dormouse steak, pepper, pine-kernels, and other exotica, then cooked in an oven. It was apparently delicious. Experiments with other Roman recipes have been successful, and two are provided here as an inducement to further testing:

HONEY-GLAZED HAM IN PASTRY. Boil the ham with dried figs and bay-leaves; remove the skin and incise in a criss-cross design; spread with honey; make a thick paste with flour and oil, and spread it over the ham; bake in the oven, then remove pastry and serve.
STUFFED HARE. Clean the hare and truss. Grind up pepper, lovage, origan, moisten with liquamen, then add cooked chicken liver and brains, chopped liver and lights of the hare, 3 raw eggs, blending all with liquamen. Stuff the hare with this mix; wrap in sausage skin and paper, tie and roast over a slow fire. Serve with a sauce of pepper, lovage, wine and cornflour.

FIG. 38. A dormouse fattener of Roman type (after Woodman, 1976).

In contrast to these dishes, which were served to the most affluent members of Roman society, the food of Iron Age man in northern Europe, and that of early settlers in Canada, seems poor indeed. All have been the subject of experiments hence their inclusion here. The whole subject of ancient foodstuffs, fascinating as it is, cannot be considered in this book.

Food in pioneer Canada was often limited and poor. Salt pork might be eaten three times a day, supplemented with potatoes cooked in the same greasy frypan. The sensation of such a diet can only be appreciated, or not appreciated, by those who have been subjected to it. Apple pie, of course, was another matter and the pioneer method was to dry apple slices in order to maintain a constant supply through the year. The "recipe" for this was as follows:

First they don't take half the peeling off,
Then on a dirty cord they're strung,
Then from some chamber window hung.
Where they serve as roosts for flies
Until they're ready to make pies.

Apple pie still tasted good, and for those able to experiment there is nothing sweeter than maple sugar made in the traditional manner. Gash your tree with a tomahawk, insert a wood chip which will draw and carry the sap into a birchbark container. Boil the sap in a clay pot, or drop hot stones into a wooden trough, pack the coarse maple sugar into *mokuks* (bark baskets) and consume at leisure. And the sweetest thing "this side of heaven" was supposed to be half-boiled maple sap poured hot on to new-fallen snow, to make maple taffy, guaranteed to remove fillings, and any loose teeth as well. Personal testing of this agrees in every respect.

Perhaps the most famous prehistoric meal is that consumed by Tollund man shortly before his execution in Denmark in the first century A.D. Tollund man was found in 1950, buried beneath the peat in a former marshland (Glob, 1969). Because of the waterlogging conditions, he had been preserved for 2000 years; he lay naked except for a hide belt, a skin cap and a rope tightly drawn around his neck. His hair had been cropped short, and he had a stubble on his chin, cheeks and upper lip. His eyes were lightly closed and the discoverers recalled the *Gilgamesh* epic "the dead and the sleeping, how they resemble one another . . ." The man had not been strangled: he had been hanged. Many of his internal organs had been well preserved, and in his stomach and intestines were the remains of his last meal. Only a few kilometres away, at Grauballe, another man was found, not hanged but with his throat cut (Fig. 39). He too was well preserved, and analysis showed that his last meal had been closely similar to that of Tollund man.

Tollund man's meal had consisted of a soup or gruel, made of barley, linseed, camelina (gold-of-pleasure), persicaria (knot-weed), with some corn spurrey, white goosefoot, wild pansy and turnip seeds. There were traces of *Sphagnum* moss and a teaspoon of fine sand, the former perhaps drunk with water from a bog pool, the latter brought in on ill-cleaned plants. The last meal had been consumed 12–24 hours before execution. There was no trace of meat or fish, and none of the plants had been roasted or baked. Without cooking of some sort, the linseed would have been strongly laxative, and it seems likely that all of the seeds would have been heated in a soup or gruel. Classical authors recall that contemporary peasants ate a gruel of barley, linseed, coriander and salt. In 1954, the Tollund man's meal was assembled, having been obtained from botanical gardens and a bird-food shop in London. Mixed well and cooked over an open fire, the resulting soup was grey-purple with orange and black flecks floating in it. Nutritionally it was suitable for the maintenance of life; in flavour, it apparently was terrible, and the two experimenters (Sir Mortimer Wheeler and Professor Glyn Daniel) felt obliged to wash it down with Danish brandy. Wheeler is said to have remarked that if the soup was really the standard food of the time, then he thought that Tollund man had probably committed suicide.

FIG. 39. Grauballe man, preserved in waterlogged peat. His last meal, still resting in his stomach, had consisted of a soup or gruel of many varieties of plants (Forhistorisk Museum, Moesgård, Denmark).

We do not, of course, know if this meal was a normal one for the period in Denmark. The circumstances of death make it likely that we will never know if the soup was as traditional for the living as it was for the soon-to-be-dead. Grauballe man's meal had been made from the same plants plus many others (63 in all). Other finds have also been made confirming that the meals were almost exclusively vegetarian and that the men and women were killed in winter or early spring, perhaps as sacrifices to hasten the coming of the warmth. Before we leave this particular set of experiments it might be added that experimenting with even ordinary foodstuffs can often yield quite delicious meals, and the equipment required is remarkably simple (Fig. 40).

Archaeologists have also experimented with even more unusual foods. At the Danger Cave, Utah, many small pads of matted fibre were found in layers dated from 8000 to 2000 B.C.; these were identified as desert bulrush stalks (*Scirpus americanus*) and they appeared to represent quids chewed and then spat out. Similar stalks were duly chewed by the excavators to see if the bulrush had served for a thirst-quencher, narcotic, stimulant or other purpose (Jennings, 1957). A slightly sweet taste, a refreshing flavour, was noted; but it is also possible that the stalks had been chewed as part of a rope-making exercise. At Salts Cave, Kentucky, the mineral mirabilite ($Na_2 SO_4 10H_2O$) was recovered from an occupation deposit. A sample was solemnly taken by the excavators to see what effect it had on them in an attempt to discover why the mineral was there (Watson and Yarnell, 1966). Four table-spoonsful apparently created a definite laxative effect, and if this was needed at the site in 500 B.C. then it is the earliest evidence for constipation in the world. There are perhaps few archaeologists who will automatically swallow any strange substances encountered, although many will readily taste bits of rock or soil or pottery to determine its texture

FIG. 40. Baking *chapattis* of wheat on a hot stone at the "Neolithic" settlement in the Ijsselmeer polder, the Netherlands. (Photo: R. Horreus de Haas).

and character. Canon W. Greenwell, a nineteenth-century antiquarian, is reputed to have tasted anything he got his hands on, and a presumably apocryphal story asserts that upon being shown the dried heart of Robert the Bruce, a precious relic in a sacred place, he unconsciously put it to his mouth, realized his error, gulped and that was that. There are few others who have carried their enthusiasm so far, and most archaeologists today are probably too cautious to suffer potential indignities by eating mysterious or ill-prepared foods.

Experiments concerned with meat have involved its preparation and cooking, and have not had to rely upon attempts to gather the unusual plants consumed in ancient times. Many different methods of cooking meat were practised in the past, and most of them were simple and highly successful; moreover refinements of these are in normal use today. Experiments with boiling and roasting of meat have generally been successful, if the evident satisfaction expressed by the archaeologists concerned is a guide; most have managed to consume all the results. One experiment was designed to test a sixteenth-century Irish record, which depicted the cooking of meat in an animal hide suspended over a fire (Fig. 41): "... after

Fig. 41. Cooking in a skin at an Irish feast *c.* A.D. 1600 (after Ryder, 1966).

the Countrie fashion, they did cut a piece of the hide, and pricked it upon four stakes which they set about the fire, and therein they set a piece of cow for themselves ..." And an earlier record describes how an army of retreating Scots left behind "more than four hundred cauldrons made of hide with the hair left on, full of meat and water hung over the fire to boil". Experiments to examine this method have generally proved unsuccessful. The evaporation of surface water is great and thus the depth of water round the meat too slight; furthermore, the skin and hair seem to insulate the water against the heat unless the fire is applied directly on to the skin, but then it cracks or burns (Ryder, 1966). Further tests have been more successful when sheep stomachs were used to contain water, but not meat. By adding hot stones to one paunch, and grain to another, temperatures of 95° C were achieved after three hours in an air temperature of 10° (Ryder, 1969). Nonetheless, that meat can be cooked in this way has yet to be demonstrated. Herodotus describes how easy it should be: "[The Scythians] cast all the flesh into the victims' stomachs, adding water thereto, and making a fire beneath of bones which burn finely; the stomachs easily hold the flesh when it is stripped from the bones; thus an ox serves to cook itself." There is room here for new attempts.

Cooking with hot stones has already been mentioned, and the boiling of water or maple sap by the use of hot stones plunged into the clay pot, rock basin, bark trough or buffalo hide was a method widely used in many parts of the world. Writing *c*. 1635, a French Jesuit in Canada described the procedure:

... they put their meat and water into these [bark] dishes, then they place five or six stones in the fire; and when one is burning hot, they throw it into this fine soup, and, withdrawing it ... put another which is red-hot in its place, and thus continue until their meat is cooked.

Related methods of cooking include steaming and baking with hot stones. One American Indian example, still practised today, should suffice to convince all of its effectiveness, and the experiment is well worth while. Upon a bed of hot stones place layers of wet seaweed alternating with clams, crabs, fish and sweet corn; cover the edifice and leave to steam until the unique flavours have been released in all of the food; then enjoy the Rhode Island clam bake (Russell, 1963).

Another historic description, from Ireland, relates to the *fulacht fiadha* or deer roast. These are places in the forest where hunters established fires and troughs for the cooking of the day's kill. Several sites of the Bronze Age in southern Ireland have been interpreted as deer roasts, and one was reconstructed and tested (O'Kelly, 1954). The evidence consisted of a series of post-holes, stone slabs, heaps of burnt stones and charcoal, and a wooden trough dug into the peat and filled with water. Wooden poles were set into the post-holes to form a tent frame, rack or table, for butchering the animals. The trough held 450 litres of water and was set into the ground beneath the water table, with plenty of cracks to allow it to fill from below. Hearths beside the trough were lit, and hot stones were dropped into the trough; within 30 minutes the water was boiling. A leg of mutton weighing 5 kg was placed in the water and cooked for 3 hours 40 minutes, using the recipe 20 minutes per old-fashioned pound plus 20 minutes for the cook; the mutton was excellent and was consumed by the experimenters. Beside the trough was a slab-lined pit which was interpreted as an oven; meat placed in the pit and covered by hot stones was also cooked well. In view of these results and the abundant historical information for the existence and functioning of deer roasts, it would seem that the experimental work on this 4000-year-old site demonstrated the existence of Bronze Age *fullacht fiadha*.

These experiments with cooking involved the workers in a certain amount of inconvenience; but no one depended upon the success of the experiments for his or her survival. Several other sets of experiments have been based upon the need to find and cook food upon which to live. Some of this work, which has the benefit of urgency, and which includes the killing and consumption of delicacies such as rattlesnake, are described in Chapter 6 where we look at experiments on humans. It will be more appropriate then to consider how diet has affected the attempts to live a different kind of life.

4 Settlement

There houses be fyttely made and close of wood, sett upright
and covered with reed, the most part of them after the fashion
of a pavillion, but there was one amonges the rest verry great,
long and broode, with settelles round abowte made of reedes,
tremly couched together, which serve them bothe for beddes
and seates.

Ribauld, 1563

Next to food, shelter from the elements is one of the basic
requirements of man and one which he shares with many other
animals. The way in which this need was satisfied depended
partly on the habitat, notably on the climate, and on the
availability of natural shelter or of raw materials for artificial
ones, but to a very great extent on the kind of society in which
he lived.

Clark, 1957, p. 196

ANCIENT SETTLEMENTS were of many different kinds: caves and rock
shelters, river terraces and hill tops, lakesides and sea shores, all these and
more were chosen by early man as sites for his settlements. Proximity to
water, the availability of wild foods, timber, desirable rocks and metals,
and the suitability of the land for agriculture and stock-rearing were some
of the reasons for his selection; but there were others too, including the
need for contact and communication with other human groups. Archaeological excavations of settlement sites have not been as numerous or as
extensive as have been the investigations of burial monuments; therefore
to a great extent we lack the quality and the quantity of information about
the size, scale and character of ancient settlements. Many of these occupation sites were extensively built of wood, which has in almost all cases
decayed completely, leaving only the traces of posts and walls where they
were placed in holes or foundation trenches in the ground. Where clay was
also used rather more may remain to be detected by the archaeologist's
trowel, although this material too has its problems for accurate detection as
we shall see. Where stone was used in foundations or walls it has generally

remained on the site although often in a disorganized tumble requiring careful investigation. The picture of an abandoned and decayed settlement contrasts strongly with that of a burial monument, because the latter was built to last forever and was not subject to the erosive activities of humans, except tomb robbers and archaeologists.

In seeking to reconstruct settlements, archaeologists have to rely upon the surviving traces which represent the plan of the structures as they were built upon the original ground; the pits, holes and trenches cannot be directly related to the upper parts of the structures, although they may give hints. Hence it is axiomatic that reconstructions are based on the lowest parts of the original, and the greater are the problems and the less certain the facts as the structure is built upwards (Fig. 42). For relatively recent

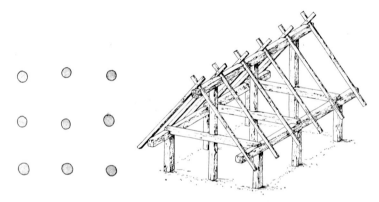

Fig. 42. Reconstruction of the framework for a building based upon the archaeological evidence of nine post-holes found at Kirchheim, near Munich, Germany. The proposed model becomes more and more uncertain with height. (From Dannheimer, 1976.)

periods, archaeologists can study historic records, ethnohistories in some areas of the world. They can also inspect examples of traditional regional structures or fragments of very ancient buildings. These can provide clear guides to reconstructions (e.g. Andersen, 1951; Trier, 1969; Randolph, 1973). However, even with evidence such as this—and it is restricted to quite recent periods of course—there is no guarantee that all houses in a settlement were built in exactly the same way. In fact it is likely that they were not, because they were probably intended to perform quite different functions in the life of the community as dwellings, stables, storerooms etc. Experimental archaeology can provide some hints about how structures might have been built, but this should not be the main reason for the work. It is the significance of the building to society that is important: why it was built and what role it had in the whole settlement. To understand this it is essential that the entire settlement is examined, the chronology of its development understood, and the function of all its parts ascertained. This has proved impossible for any single settlement so far examined in either the Old or the New Worlds. Archaeological studies are not yet sufficiently advanced to allow any complete picture to emerge, and this of course is one of the fascinations as well as the frustrations of the subject itself.

What part can experiment play in this effort? Its importance lies in several different directions, best seen by a brief examination of some of the work already done. At a primary level, reconstructions of ancient houses, even if they are highly conjectural, allow both archaeologists and public to appreciate the size and scale of the object and the work that went into it, and many replicas or simulations have been built for this purpose. Often these displays have been successfully combined with open-air museums of old buildings, particularly in Europe where foresight and dedication have allowed the preservation of many old structures. The Avoncroft Museum of Buildings in Worcestershire is an excellent example (Avoncroft, 1976), as is the museum at Hjerl Hede in Jutland. Museums such as these attempt to transport houses and barns from their original sites to the museum, where they are put together again with a minimum of new material added. At both the museums mentioned, activities have also included the erection of even earlier structures, based upon excavation plans of prehistoric settlements. The simulated Iron Age houses at Avon-croft have now decayed, but the Danish structures are being actively conserved and form an important part of the complex; they are spaced well apart and positioned with appropriate surroundings. The project here has been underway since 1938.

The reconstructed Neolithic houses at Hjerl Hede are based upon the excavated site at Barkaer, a site now considered to be rather atypical of the Danish Neolithic; reconstructed as dwellings, the houses are long and low, and used quantities of turf, reed, withies and oak timbers (Fig. 11). An attempt has also been made to build a Bronze Age house at Hjerl Hede, based upon an excavated plan at Hemmed Søgn; recent work in Denmark suggests that Bronze Age houses were rather similar to the well-known Iron Age houses (p. 156), but few reconstructions have been attempted. The structure put up at this centre for ancient buildings is formed of short upright posts slotted to hold split horizontal timbers, but there is no foundation trench. There are 17 of these plank panels, 4 each at the curved ends, 5 along the straight back wall, and 4 at the front wall where the single inturned doorway is positioned (Fig. 43, lower). As it stands, the house fits the excavated plan, but it is relatively easy to think of alternative

Fig. 43. *Upper.* A Roman granary at The Lunt, near Coventry, England, constructed of elm. (Photo: J. M. Coles.)

Lower. Reconstructed framework of a Bronze Age house at Hjerl Hede, Denmark, based upon excavation plans. No wattle and daub walling has been used, in contrast to most reconstructions. (Photo: J. M. Coles.)

ways of forming and placing the wall timbers which would also leave no archaeological slot on the ground.

Observations in northern Europe, and particularly in Eastern Canada in the eighteenth and nineteenth centuries, have demonstrated the ease with which farmers could build log cabins, consisting almost entirely of horizontal timbers easily dismantled and leaving little or no trace on the ground. Short stakes or small posts prevent the timbers from slipping away from the line of the walls, and a small cabin could be built of long complete logs rather than panels of split logs. A log cabin, 6 × 4 m and without any foundation trench, could be made from start to finish in 4 man-days (Guillet, 1963).

On occasion, reconstructions have been made not for a permanent museum but for a particular event or television programme; but this is surely only a legitimate exercise if it is admitted that the materials and the building techniques are modern, and that the appearance is highly conjectural. We need not expect many to make such damning admissions about their fairy-tale concoctions, but more responsible authorities have sometimes been careful to set out their procedures for comment. An early experiment by the BBC, for instance, produced a version of a Neolithic house at Lough Gur in Co. Limerick. The plan of the house was based upon the original excavation, and a few pieces of the lashings used to tie the wooden rafters and beams to the upright posts were made of twisted rushes. The rest of the house was put together by whatever modern methods and materials were necessary; but the aim was to give a general impression only, not show the technology of construction or use of the house (Johnstone, 1957).

More carefully considered, and a masterpiece in its own way visually, technically and politically, is the recent simulation of a Roman granary at The Lunt, Coventry (Fig. 43, upper). The Lunt was apparently built c. A.D. 60 to house a cavalry unit of the Roman army; it was abandoned c. A.D. 80. The defences consisted of a turf rampart with wooden palisade, and a wooden tower gateway, and among its many buildings was a granary. Parts of the rampart, the gateway and the granary have all been reconstructed as an open air museum (Hobley, 1967, 1971, 1973, 1974, 1975). The granary was 21 m long and 9 m wide, and its evidence on the ground consisted of transverse foundation slots set 1·5 m apart, each with postholes at 1·5 m intervals. The building sat upon 105 posts, but neither their height nor the height of the building was known. Within the fort, a Roman well had produced fragments of elm and oak, which determined the type of wood to be used in the reconstruction. The director of the exercise, Brian Hobley, had already persuaded the Royal Engineers to build a Roman gateway (p. 37) and they accepted the challenge to erect the granary. The supply of timber came from an enormous quantity of elm stricken with Dutch elm disease. The infected bark was stripped off, and tree trunks were cut into sections to make the foundation posts, and sawn into planks and boards for the walls and roof. It was thus possible to build the granary at a small fraction of the cost, and there is no doubt that without free labour and free materials the experiment could not have taken place.

The building was raised almost 1·0 m above the ground, just as surviving granaries are. No archaeological evidence existed for construction beyond floor level, and so multiples of Roman units were chosen. The walls were made about 3 m high, and loading bays for carts were put at the ends of the building. The walls were built up with overlapping plank tiles nailed on to the framework, and the roof had elm shingles. Although the materials were prepared by modern methods, the actual building operation was conducted in appropriate "Roman" fashion so far as could be deduced. The officer in charge of the Engineers arranged for a crane to assist, but the men preferred to haul the timber by ropes and the crane soon became redundant. Simple wooden joints were employed, such as were found at a waterlogged Roman site in Holland. The whole operation took about two weeks.

The granary forms only part of the display at The Lunt. Designed to demonstrate the appearance and strength of a Roman fort, part of the earthen rampart and the wooden gateway have also been rebuilt (Fig. 11). The gateway, of pine rather than of oak or elm, was prefabricated; it was erected as time trial by 25 Royal Engineers in only three days. A short stretch of rampart, 11 m long, was the first to be tested experimentally; this was put up by volunteers from Her Majesty's Prison at Leicester. The width of rampart at its base was 5·4 m, and with acceptable slopes at front and back, and a platform at the top, it was 3·6 m high. The body of the bank was one-third earth and two-thirds turf, each turf cut to Roman size (45 × 30 × 15 cm, weight 32–34 kg). About 5500 turves were needed to build 11 m of rampart, and so the rather small fort required about 140 000 turves for its 283 m rampart. Turves were cut in the experiment at a rate of 4·5–6·5 per man-hour, and the 11 m were built in just over 1000 man-hours. At this rate, the whole fort could have been put up in 9–12 days by 200–300 men; the estimated garrison size at The Lunt is 300 men. Estimates such as this are valuable, not because they pretend to be precise and wholly accurate, but because they provide a guide to the archaeologist in his attempt to postulate the rates of movement of, in this case, Roman armies, and the length of undefended time in a newly occupied territory. They are less accurate if extrapolated to much larger monuments such as Hadrian's Wall where the manpower could have

wildly fluctuated. The experiments at The Lunt have been in part duplicated alongside Hadrian's Wall, at Vindolanda, where rampart reconstructions have been attempted with varying success. Small sections of
various parts of the wall have been tested in order to understand the
acquisition and manipulation of 40 million turves, each weighing 25–30
kg, and many tonnes of local rock for facings, towers and gateways (Birley,
1977). These experiments suggest that the Wall could have been built in
only a few years, perhaps starting in A.D. 122 and finishing in A.D. 125. The
work, impressive to all who can see and walk along it, is smaller in scale
than, for instance, the London to Birmingham Victoria railway cutting,
also over 160 km long, built by hand by 20 000 navvies in only five years.

One of the important contributions that experimental archaeology can
make to both public and students (in the broadest sense) is an appreciation
of time and effort and the work-rates of earlier communities. Although
absolute precision in this cannot be achieved, nonetheless it is valuable to
provide some scale of endeavour to which we can relate in our own terms.
This is why work at The Lunt and Vindolanda, and other reconstructions,
is valuable. Scale models of such monuments cannot provide this information, and if only small parts of the monuments are rebuilt, the extrapolation of work-rates and quantities of materials are less likely to be near the
truth than if the whole monument, or a major part of it, is reconstructed.
The 3-metre sections of earthen rampart at Bindon Hill, Dorset (Wheeler,
1953), and of limestone walling at Stanwick, Yorkshire (Wheeler, 1954),
provide a hint, but no more, of the appearance and the work-load of
these extensive fortifications. The experimental firing of a Scottish timber-
laced rampart 4 m long to see if vitrified material would be produced
(Childe and Thorneycroft, 1938; Nisbet, 1974–75) was certainly helped
by the strong wind (a reasonable natural event in Scotland), but perhaps
the ease with which the fire entered into the core of the wall through the
artificially exposed ends also contributed to the success of the operation.
Such reconstructions, whether for display or for testing in some way,
should be extensive in scale and effort; moreover, the procedure is particularly effective when carried out upon the exact site, with posts re-erected
in the original holes or slots. In this way, the full environmental or geographical effect is clearly seen, as it was at the Bronze Age palisaded site of
"Motta Vallac", Switzerland (Fig. 44).

It is perhaps worth emphasizing that very few experiments concerned
with earthworks have been extensive in scale, and therefore that information on primitive work-rates, supplies and essential encouragements or
coercions are totally unknown. Whether or not we can ever know of these
things is debatable. Modern observations of quite unsophisticated methods
of moving and piling earth demonstrate a few of these points. In Nigeria,

FIG. 44. Reconstruction of a Bronze Age palisade, with timbers set in original post-holes, at "Motta Vallac", Savognin, Switzerland, 1977. Actual displays such as these provide a dramatic impression of the scale of materials, work and efficiency of the finished product. (Photo: Schweizerisches Landesmuseum.)

an earthen bank, 50 m long, 4 m high and about 4 m wide (volume 800 cubic metres) was created in less than a single day by a large gang of men using short-handled hoes, without any earth being lifted and carried (Shaw, 1970). The earth was loosened by one man and scraped between his legs to the next man behind him, and rows of 8–10 men moved the earth rapidly over the ground and up the ever-increasing bank. Much noise and encouragement was given, and informal competition developed, to ensure a high work-rate; there is no reason to assume anything less in more ancient times.

A very useful series of experiments at Uxmal in Mexico managed to bring together many of the operations involved with the construction of the Maya ceremonial centre (Erasmus, 1965). The centre covers 1200 × 600 m, and is believed to contain 850 000 cubic metres of earth and filler. The work of construction included excavation and transport of earth, quarrying and carriage of small blocks of stone. Metal crowbars and shovels were tested and found to be 2–3 times as effective as wooden levers and digging sticks. The experimental results of small-scale digging and carrying, when applied to the whole site, suggested that 4·5 million man-days were needed to obtain and transport earth and stone to the site, at a rate of 500 kg per man-day, with journeys averaging 750 m. Stone masonry was also examined by experiment, and 1 m³ of wall was built in 4 days, with 1400 kg of rock, 100 kg of lime and 300 kg of sandy material. At Uxmal, 0·4 million m³ of masonry therefore represented 0·5 million man-days. The sculpturing of the masonry walls was tested (cf. Fig. 45),

Fig. 45. Dressing a megalith with mallet and chisel, a hafted pick, and a hand-held pick (from Holmes, 1919, Fig. 196).

with 3 man-days to plain veneer 1000 cm²; the 0·075 million m² of cut stone thus represented 2·5 million man-days. The sum total was 7·5 million man-days for the building of the whole site. As it was occupied by the Maya for about 250 years, this represented 30 000 man-days per year for the continuing construction over the entire period. This estimate in itself was of some interest, but particularly when applied to other evidence about the site and its territory. The region around Uxmal could have supported about 1200 families, given certain land constraints for agriculture, and each family would have had to release one adult male for the building operations of the ceremonial site on only 40 days each year. If the buildings were constructed in a series of more intensive bursts of religious fervour, the largest structure would have required only seven years' work, quite within the capabilities of the population. Although there are dangers in extrapolating small-scale results to an immense site in the above manner, the demonstration of techniques for the various tasks, and the suggestions about the society's contributions to the site, are well worth the archaeological effort, if only to give us a measure, an impression, of the organization and skills required.

Observations such as these, together with small experiments, can provide useful hints about possible techniques and practices in the past; but longer experimental reconstructions allow more controlled and extensive recordings, and also provide permanent or long-term displays for study and education. The linking of technological experiments and visual displays is an easy combination. Some of the permanent institutions dedicated to these aims include the museums at Asparn-an-der-Zaya in Austria and at Moesgård in Jutland (p. 150). The Austrian experimental centre has particular interest because it has deliberately set out to provide experimental copies of a wide range of ancient structures, from Paleolithic tents to late Iron Age houses, thus spanning 25 000 years of Central European prehistoric dwellings (Hampl, 1968, 1970). Based upon archaeologically detectable groundplans, with appropriate and technologically acceptable materials, the replicas provide a most vivid impression of both exteriors and interiors of Neolithic, Bronze Age and Iron Age houses. The Early Bronze Age houses (c. 1800 B.C.) are based on plans recovered from Röschitz in Lower Austria; both are oval, about 6 m long, and have low wattle and daub walls with thatched roofs (Fig. 46). The Early Iron Age structures consist of a log cabin from Roggendorf and a potter's hut from Grossweikersdorf; the latter has a thatch extending right down to the ground and, to our eyes at least, looks most peculiar. Inside it is furnished with an array of clay ovens and kilns, the heat from which is diverted from the inflammable roof by square shields of leather. Some experimental cooking of bread has taken place in these ovens. Two Late Iron Age houses have also been built, dating to the closing centuries B.C.; these are based upon excavated plans from Roggendorf in Austria and Mšecké Žehrovice in Bohemia, the former furnished as a dwelling, the latter as a smithy with furnace pit and anvil.

The Neolithic long-house, based upon plans from Köln-Lindenthal, is 25 m long and 7 m wide, with a height to the ridge of 5·4 m. This type of house has been noted on many European sites of the fifth and fourth millennia B.C. (cf. Fig. 12), and has been the subject of much speculation. Their ground plans show external lines of wide post-holes or sleeper trenches, or more often both together in the same house. Pits scooped in the adjacent soil probably provided material for the wattle and daub walls. There are often three internal rows of post-holes for particularly massive uprights, which would have held the roof and perhaps other structural parts of the buildings which we cannot detect. Many settlements have yielded plans of this character, and only rarely has any site been fully excavated. At Köln-Lindenthal, the settlement was defined by ditches and it is suggested that the maximum size of the village was about 20 houses. The labour involved in building 20 longhouses must have been considerable, and it would almost certainly have been impossible to dismantle such structures if the settlement was abandoned and shifted elsewhere in a cycle of new land-take or reoccupation of old fallow ground. Definition of the cultivation practices of these Neolithic farmers has not yet been agreed by archaeologists who perhaps are seeking for a uniformity which did not exist; the house experiments can contribute a certain amount of information to these problems, but cannot solve them. Experimental versions of the longhouse have been attempted in several areas, most recently in central France at Cuiry-les-Chaudardes (Fig. 12) (Unité de Recherche Archéologique, 1977). The impressive house here was not

FIG. 46. Reconstructed round houses of the Early Bronze Age, *c.* 1800 B.C., at Asparn-an-der-Zaya, Austria. The house walls are of wattle and daub, and the roofing is thatched. (Drawing by R. Walker, after Hampl, 1970.)

built without modern technology, but some approximation of the materials for a rather small house, 12 m long and 6 m wide, was possible. The major uprights, holding walls and roof, totalled about 60, and over 200 poles went into the roofing members; 15 tonnes of clay and 1500 kg of reeds are other indications of quantities. The work occupied 6 persons for 6 months, but this figure cannot really be used to reflect upon Neolithic house-builders. Another longhouse has been reconstructed at Asparn-an-der-Zaya in Austria. Based upon excavated examples in Germany and Czecho-slovakia, the house has rather slender wall posts carrying wattle and daub walls, and the very heavy internal posts support transverse partitions to carry sleeping platforms, as well as the roofing members. The pits found beside the houses on Polish sites would yield enough material for daub walls 10 cm thick and 2 m high (Milisauskas, 1972). Other than these daub walls, the structures are, as we shall see, in essence not dissimilar to the Indian longhouses of central Canada. The reconstructions of these longhouses have provided indications of scale and quantities of materials used in the earliest Neolithic of central Europe; needless to say these opera-tions have been restricted because vast quantities of timber (not so easily found today) are necessary for such large structures. We still know little about the precise walling used in these houses, about the possibilities of a second storey or sleeping platforms, about roofing, or about the function of the houses. The use of one end as cattle byre has often been asserted, but equally the use of the houses for more than one family has been suggested. In these problems, experiment could play a part but it cannot provide the solution; only increasingly careful excavation, and the good fortune of preservation, will provide further hints. Both theoretical reconstructions (e.g. Dannheimer, 1976; Startin, 1978) and actual physical reconstructions are needed to gain a full understanding of ancient building operations. Without them we are left with only rows of post-holes, trenches and pits, the meaning of which is almost wholly lost.

Precisely this same point can be made for another quite impressive experimental reconstruction project, at Port Elgin in Ontario, Canada (Wright, 1974). In 1969 a salvage excavation was carried out at a site known as Nodwell, a fourteenth-century A.D. palisaded Iroquois village on the edge of Lake Huron (cf. Fig. 47). The settlement consisted of 12 longhouses, of which all but one were surrounded by a double stockade. The houses were 13–42 m in length, and were occupied by a community of about 500 people who were the predecessors of the Huron and Petun Indians. The settlement lasted for only 10–20 years. After the excavations in 1969–71, the Nodwell site was partly rebuilt before its loss to "develop-ment". A comparable settlement is now being built at London, Ontario (Pearce, 1979). Three of the Nodwell houses, the two palisades and various shooting platforms were reconstructed upon the original sites, using the existing post-holes (Fig. 48, upper). Cedar posts and holes were selected to fit each individual hole; for example, a 12·5 cm post-hole would be cleaned out and fitted with a pole of 11·5 cm. Post packing of gravel, potsherds and stone helped to keep these in place. Vertical poles and posts posed little problem, but as usual, the higher the structure the more uncertain the details became. Ethnographic records of the Huron Indians suggested that the houses were as high as they were wide, and this indicated heights overall of 6–8 m. A historic (A.D. 1740) scale-drawing of a longhouse indicated that the ratio of wall to roof height was 4:1. The outer wall poles of the houses, however, were only 7·5 cm diameter, far too slender to carry the height and weight, and this indicated that the two rows of heavier internal posts must have carried the rafters and joists, as well as supporting the walls, through a series of horizontal beams. When these internal posts were set up it was at once apparent that they also had acted as the bearers of bunk-line poles which were pinched in place by the slightly staggered line of uprights (Fig. 48, lower). The bunks were 1·5 m wide in most of the houses, and ethnographic evidence suggested

C.W. JEFFERYS

FIG. 47. An Indian village in Huronia, based upon descriptions by early explorers and settlers (from Jeffries, 1942). "Their lodges are constructed like garden arbours covered with tree-bark, 25 to 30 fathoms long, and 6 in breadth, with a passage down the middle 10 to 12 feet wide. At the 2 sides there is a bench 4 or 5 feet high on which they sleep in summer, and in winter they sleep below on mats near the fire. . . . In one lodge there are many fires, and at each fire are 2 families, one on each side." (G. M. Wrong (ed.) Sagard's *Long Journey to the Country of the Hurons.*)

Fig. 48. *Upper*. Reconstruction of an Iroquois longhouse at the Nodwell site, Ontario, Canada; the timber framing has been set in the original fourteenth-century post-holes.

Lower. Interior view of reconstructed longhouse, looking beneath the sleeping platform with structural posts interlocking with the inner bunkline poles.

(From Wright, 1974.)

that they should be set 1·2 m above the ground. The largest house in the village had wider bunk platforms, probably to conform to ancient records that during ceremonies the old men sat here while the young men stood below. These observations came from the reconstruction of the framing alone, and doubtless further suggestions would arise from the attachment of cedar bark shingles to form the walls and roofs.

In all such reconstructions there is an inherent danger that the visual result may become accepted as the standard for all sites of the same general pattern. Although one attempted replica may seem to fit the archaeological evidence, this is no justification for asserting that the ancient tradition was exactly as this, or was the only tradition in use. The Nodwell site has provided an impressive visual effect of an Iroquois fortified village, and conforms to the evidence we have, but the project directors make no claim that this is the complete answer to such settlements, and other experimenters would do well to heed their example. Many years ago one of the Viking barracks at the fortress of Trelleborg in Denmark was reconstructed as a very large and massive structure, with an external porch on all sides held by upright posts. After some years of increasing dissatisfaction, it has now been suggested that the building is unnecessarily high, that the porch probably did not exist, and that the posts were angled inwards to prop the walls (Schmidt, 1973). The building, put up in 1942, is still standing and clearly is successful as a structure; the current criticism, however, is entirely appropriate as it is based upon continuing excavation and research, new theories and suggestions for future experiment. We might suspect that because the Trelleborg building has stood for 35 years, it has been a constant reminder to specialists of a particular viewpoint, and has acted as a stimulus for critical examination and, now, alternative theories. This is precisely what experimental archaeology attempts to do.

An outstanding example of this is the current work at the Anglo-Saxon settlement of West Stow in Suffolk (Fig. 49, upper). The settlement was placed on a sandy knoll beside the River Lark in the fifth century A.D., the same century as the birth of Saint Brendan. Occupation took place for over 200 years, with many of the houses repaired or rebuilt from time to time. The entire settlement was excavated during the period 1965–72; it was the first such village to be completely examined (West, 1973). Over 70 buildings were discovered, most consisting of post-holes and large pits, the so-called *grubenhauser*, as well as six large post-built houses or halls. The basic settlement unit was a group of about six huts surrounding a hall. The pit houses have puzzled archaeologists for decades, and have helped the wholly unjustified impression that the Anglo-Saxons were "barbarian" and several stages lower in civilized nature, whatever that is, than the

FIG. 49. *Upper*. The reconstructed Anglo-Saxon houses at West Stow, Suffolk, England, placed upon the original Anglo-Saxon site. Three varieties of house have been attempted here: *left*, a tall house utilizing only two post-holes; *centre*, a house with six upright posts; *right*, a sunken house with roof extending to ground level. Behind the centre house, a hall is being constructed. (Photo: R. J. Darrah, West Stow Anglo-Saxon Trust.)

Lower. Thatching one of the houses at West Stow. Note the dense interwoven hazel rods beneath the straw bundles which are being stitched together with a wooden needle and rawhide. (Photo: J.M. Coles.)

Romans whom they overwhelmed in parts of Britain: "The bulk of the people, we can now be assured, were content with something that hardly deserves a better title than a hovel." (Leeds, 1926.) The evidence for Anglo-Saxon dwellings was not, however, restricted to a multitude of pits and post-holes; there existed as well some documentary evidence from manuscripts and inscriptions, and the surviving traces of medieval buildings in England also provided some guidance.

Then I gathered for myself staves and props and bars and handles for all the tools I knew how to use, and crossbars and beams for all the structures that I knew how to build, the fairest pieces of timber as many as I could carry. I neither came home with a single load, nor did it suit me to bring home all the wood even if I could have carried it. In each tree I saw something that I required at home. For I advise each of thou who art strong and has many wagons, to plan to go to the same wood where I cut these as props, and fetch for himself more there, and load his wagons with fair rods, so that he can plait many a fine wall, and put up many a peerless building, and build a fair enclosure with them . . .

King Alfred's preface to his translation of the
Soliloquies of St Augustine, W. Endter edition, 1864

Although this description is in fact a "figure of speech" referring to a library and not a dwelling house, it nonetheless suggests that the picture of Anglo-Saxon hovels may not have been entirely accurate, and in 1973 a project was initiated at West Stow to test some of the theoretical reconstructions of Anglo-Saxon houses and huts (West Stow 1974). One of the building complexes, consisting of a hall and associated pit houses, is now in process of experimental rebuilding, using the original Anglo-Saxon features and restoring the original contours of the landscape. One of the huts was built to the traditional view of *grubenhaus*, the hollow (*c.* 3·5 × 2·5 m in area and 70 cm deep) forming the actual living place. A heavy post at each end supported the ridge pole, and other poles rested on the ground around the edges, holding the thatched roof which extended down to the ground. The dwelling had little floor space, was damp and dark, and to some at least it seemed wholly unsatisfactory as a permanent house. A comparable sunken hut was built at the West Dean open air museum in Sussex in 1970.

The excavations had yielded evidence, however, that suggested rather more substantial buildings placed over at least some of the hollows. Two of the houses had burned down, and the stratigraphy showed floor planking covered by remains of a thatched roof with fallen wall timbers on top. This evidence led to the reconstruction of one of the houses as a heavy timbered building, supported on six posts standing within the original Anglo-Saxon hollow. The larger central posts, one at each end of the hollow, hold the ridge pole. The other four posts, at the corners, support tiebeams and purlins, allowing the roof to extend out well beyond the edges of the hollow which, cut in soft sand, must have been protected in some way to retain its quite sharp edges. The timber floor was supported by beams set 15 cm away from the edges of the hollow. The walls and the flooring are of split half-round oak from trees 15–25 cm in diameter, and all the timber was worked with Anglo-Saxon types of tools, such as axes, adzes, chisels, wedges and mallets. The rafters are ash poles from coppiced woodland, and the thatch is straw, sewn on to hazel rods and rafters with a hazel "needle" and rawhide thread (Fig. 49, lower). The entire task was completed by about six people in three months, including clearing the site, acquiring materials and learning skills. Doubtless the original builders would have been more efficient if less dedicated.

A third house has also been reconstructed, to a different experimental theory. The hollow held only two post-holes, as did the *grubenhaus* hollow, and a large building has been constructed over it. The two heavy posts hold the ridge pole, as well as cross-beams part way up, and the walls stand upon beams laid along the ground in order to leave no archaeological trace, as none was found. The height of the walls has been increased so that the cross-beams tied to the posts do not create head-bumping problems inside the house. The roof is rather steeper than the optimum angle of 50–55° for the climate. This structure has fallen out of true in strong winds, and is probably an example of experimental over-building. Nonetheless, the West Stow project has already demonstrated that a careful association between excavation evidence and experimental testing of theories can yield information essential to any understanding of the original site. The aim at West Stow is to recreate the Anglo-Saxon landscape and environment, and to use the village as a base for working the land at Anglo-Saxon levels of technology.

In contrast to plank-built rectangular houses such as these, the reconstruction of round houses involves different materials and techniques and problems. Many excavations of Bronze Age and Iron Age settlements in Britain have yielded the remains of houses surviving only as circular gullies containing stake holes, with larger post-holes at presumed entrances and sometimes within the structure itself. Although much variety in detail has been recorded the basic building seems to have had wattle and daub walls supporting a ring-beam which held roofing poles for the thatch (e.g. Fig. 46). Several of these round houses have been reconstructed, based upon specific plans from well-excavated sites, and they have posed few problems except in the attachment of the roof poles to the ring-beams, and the potential clogging of the roof apex by the poles. Experiments have solved these minor difficulties by double-notching the poles to transfer weight on to the stakes of the walls, and by employing a roof ring-beam to keep the poles well spread in the apex (Reynolds, 1979). Among other reconstructions are the two houses which form part of the working complex at the Butser Ancient Farm in Hampshire (Reynolds, 1977). One of these, based upon an Iron Age house plan from Maiden Castle (Dorset), is only 6 m in diameter yet required 7 tonnes of daub, up to one tonne of thatch, and over 30 trees (p. 114). When we consider the very large numbers of such houses on major settlements of the Iron Age, we can appreciate the impact upon forests and fields that house- as well as fort-building must have had. The central features of the demonstration area at the Butser Ancient Farm is a very large circular house based upon an excavation at Pimperne Down in Dorset. This house was *c.* 13 m diameter and it survived only as a series of post-holes cut into the chalk. There were two outer rings of small posts or stakes, and an inner circle (10 m diameter) of much heavier posts which must have carried the weight of the roof. As reconstructed, the wall of the house consists of oak stakes with hazel rods woven between them, then daubed with clay, chalk, straw and hair. The heavy posts inside are linked by horizontal poles, pegged and morticed in place. The rafters rest upon this ring, as well as upon the outer wall, and some of them reach down to the ground outside the house. A slender ring-beam near the top holds the rafters in place and prevents sagging. The purlins are tied in notches in the rafters, and the straw thatch completes the massive structure (Reynolds, 1979).

It is perhaps hard to recognize and appreciate that almost all ancient houses were made of wood, and not brick or concrete or glass. What archaeologists rarely find in their excavations are quantities of wood; traces and fragments, yes, but planks, posts and beams, no. Only in particular situations, where waterlogged muds and peats have protected wood, do we find huge quantities of this material. In the Swiss and north Italian lakes, for example, vast timber platforms and house remains show that here, in the Neolithic and Bronze Age, settlements were built almost entirely of wood. The reconstruction of these lakeside villages point to the careful management of woodlands and the sophisticated carpentry practised by prehistoric communities (e.g. Drack, 1969, 1971; Vogt, 1954).

A series of experiments in Tennessee has highlighted the question of wood supplies yet again (Nash, 1968). Along the banks of the Duck River, many mounds mark the sites of former houses occupied *c.* A.D. 1000–1600. The mounds consist of charred poles and posts, burnt clay, fragments of thatch, and beneath this collapsed debris are multiple sets of post-holes. The houses were of various types, mostly square in plan, and in size from 4 × 4 m to 6 × 6 m approximately. Several of these were rebuilt in order to see how much wood was required, how the walls and roofs could be constructed, and how easily these houses could have been erected. The

F

earlier type of house on the site had multiple post-holes set close together
in a foundation trench; to reconstruct, slender poles were set in place and
packed with stones, earth or wood. The poles from the four sides were then
bent over and woven into one another, to form a huge upside-down
basket. Thin rods were woven along the walls, and plastered with clay, and
thatch was tied to the curved roof. The later house type on Duck River
had heavier and fewer post-holes (about 40). Logs were set in these to
extend 1·5–2·0 m upwards; to these were attached horizontal poles which
supported the rafters of the peaked roof. Panels of thin rods plastered with
clay made the walls, and thatch completed the roof. Although quite small,
the quantities and standard sizes of wood required for these buildings make
an impressive total for the whole settlement.

All of the experimental reconstructions have been designed to present
an impression of the appearance, or possible appearance, of ancient houses.
Some have also attempted to yield information about quantities of material,
and the technology required to prepare and to fit the elements together.
A very impressive building, based upon an Iron Age house plan from
Tofting, has recently been constructed in the open air museum at Moesgård, Jutland (Fig. 50, upper). The excavated plan suggested a house
about 20 m long with stout uprights along the walls, two rows of heavy
posts inside, wattle and daub walls and thatched roof. The reconstruction
has been carefully contrived to record the exact quantities and character
of the materials going into the house, the methods and time required to collect and prepare them, and the time needed to construct the house. Green
oak was used for the heavy timber uprights and posts; split with wedges,
allowed to dry and then resplit to remove warped edges, these formed a
solid base for woven hazel rods subsequently packed with clay and straw
daub. The upper parts of the building were devised by the carpenters and
archaeologists as there are few clues surviving on prehistoric sites. Each of
the internal posts was joined by tree-nails to horizontal beams extending
across to the wall posts at a height of about 1·5 m. The two rows of inner
posts were joined at the top by other horizontal beams running across the
framework, and the centre of these beams held king posts extending up to
hold the ridge pole. A finely finished reed thatch roof was tied to the
purlins and rafters. Inside the completed house, woven partitions divide
the structure into a cattle byre at one end, and a dwelling at the other. The
house is a particularly fine example of combining experimental archaeology with the requirement of a museum display, and its subsequent
weathering and settling into the landscape will be observed with interest.

Without doubt, however, the finest series of experiments dealing with
the erosion of houses over measured periods of time is the product of the
Historical-Archaeological Research Centre at Lejre in Denmark (pp. 116,

FIG. 50. *Upper*. Reconstructed Iron Age house at Moesgård, Denmark. Based upon an excavated structure at Tofting, this substantial house has split oak uprights, wattle and daub walling and a heavy thatch. (Photo: J. M. Coles.)

Lower. Reconstructed Iron Age house at Lejre, Denmark, based upon a structure at Norre Fjand, and built with wattle and daub walls (house 4 in Fig. 52) (photo: J. M. Coles).

Fig. 51. Experimental destruction by fire of an Iron Age house at Lejre. All of the wooden posts, beams and rafters have been labelled, thermocouples placed on floor and in roof, and timing and photographic mechanisms positioned to record the stages of collapse. (Historical–Archaeological Research Centre, Lejre.)

by intruders, the interior of the house would very soon be wholly intolerable for any living thing. If set alight there would be only 2–3 minutes to rescue elderly humans and babies, then precious objects of metal, then clay pots and the mass of other domestic equipment. If the house began burning while the able-bodied adults were out working, perhaps there would be no time to rescue anything. Single doors, perhaps no windows, would not permit mass evacuation. Yet from parts of northern Europe, a majority of Iron Age houses upon excavation have yielded very little in the way even of ordinary domestic pots and pans, tools and equipment. Why should this be? A possible reason is that these houses were deliberately burnt by their original occupants, after abandonment for any of several reasons—moving to new agricultural lands, infestation of the house, death in the family, or pressures from other groups. All movable pieces would be taken out and the shell burnt upon departure. We cannot know the precise reasons and can only suggest some possibilities.

What seems likely, however, is that an abandoned house would soon be stripped of its portable elements, if not by its former tenants, then by others. A very few experiments have been carried out on this problem, where recently abandoned houses in rural areas have been recorded and interpreted before the last occupants were interviewed for their official versions of what went on, what was taken away, and what was left for others (e.g. Lange and Rydberg, 1972). These experiments suggest that abandoned settlements are likely to be stripped of their movable assets either by the departing group or by subsequent scavengers both human and non-human, and that the traces of major living habits may be totally distorted or removed. The outcome of such observations as these indicates the need for vigilance on the part of archaeologists in retrieving and assessing all of the available evidence, and not merely that which suits preconceived ideas.

The experiments dealing with house destruction have all concentrated upon wooden and wattle and daub structures such as are found in north-western Europe. In south-eastern Europe and south-west Asia, mud brick was commonly used in prehistoric times; and it is used today in some areas. The modern houses can be observed as they erode and are replaced, and their lifespan seems to be on average about 15–20 years. Upon collapse they yield anything from 10 to 40 cm of deposit, which can serve as a foundation for a succeeding house, or can be partly cleared away; but this deposit is in any case more or less indestructible. In west Africa, similar observations have been made of the decay of mud huts, the spread of the deposits, and the likelihood of recognition of structural and domestic features (Shaw, 1966; McIntosh, 1974). Many of these observations on decay and collapse of mud brick or wattle and daub walls suggest that rates of accumulation can suggest wall heights and thicknesses; one cautionary tale may be enough. During the excavation of a heavy building of stone and peat in northern Scotland, about 50 cm of peat ash was recorded from the decayed structure (Calder, 1956). In an attempt to determine the height of the wall, some peat was burned and carefully measured for volume. The peat was reduced to a volume of only 3 per cent of the original, which therefore suggested an original wall height of 15 m, quite ridiculous as the experimenters were quick to point out.

The stonework of such structures survives, of course, and although in many cases it is not easy to reconstruct the original positions, sometimes it seems possible. The careful attempt to recreate the enormous burial monument at Matignons, France, using only material believed to be collapsed, is a good example (Burnez and Case, 1966). A well-built stone structure has an advantage over a timber structure in that it is far more decay and fire resistant, but its individual components are less likely to be identifiable, slab upon slab, compared with, for a building, posts and wall panels. The destruction of stone houses generally begins with the decay of wooden floors and roofs, with the stone shell remaining to be gradually pulled apart by water and plants over a very long period of time. Deliberate destruction of stone buildings was likely to be more difficult than the firing of wooden houses. The organized demolition by the British Army of villages in the Afghanistan–Pakistan border region many years ago serves to demonstrate this. For reasons now less apparent than they originally were, certain native settlements had to be cleared; the buildings were made of rubble with few windows, and mud and brushwood roofs held on beams (Gordon, 1953). A simple torch flung into the house would do nothing but burn out, and the British army ingeniously devised the appropriate method: stack brushwood inside the house, bash holes in the walls or roof, blow up the roofing beams, pour kerosene on the brushwood, then light and stand back. The officer in charge, Colonel D. H. Gordon, concluded that mud-walled and mud-roofed houses of the great tells of south-west Asia were far more likely to have fallen down through rain than to have been destroyed by fire. He also made the point, simple yet often ignored by archaeologists, that any deliberate destruction of a settlement was not likely to have been received calmly and passively by the occupants; his engineers required protection.

At the present time the major experimental work on ancient houses is carried on at the Historical-Archaeological Research Centre at Lejre in Denmark (p. 244). The Centre was effectively founded in 1968 by Hans-Ole Hansen and initially financed by the Carlsberg Foundation, now by governmental funds through the Ministry of Education, with much local support. The Centre occupies 50 acres leased from the Ledreborg estate for a century; the land is lake, marsh, hills and flat fields, and within this a large number of experiments are carried out. Cattle, sheep and pigs of old breeds are kept; much pottery, weaving and iron work are produced; various crops are grown; and other activities relating to historic times are carried out. Some of these experiments are discussed in Chapter 5. Central to the whole enterprise is the Iron Age village, a group of 9–10 houses huddled behind a stockade (Hansen, 1977). Each one is different from the others, because they are based upon excavated Iron Age houses from all over Denmark, as well as representing different stages in the life of a building or different theories about particular structures (Fig. 52). The idea is one of an evolving display and research complex; in both aspects it is successful.

The Grøntoft settlement in Jutland provided the plans for three houses (one now destroyed), and another three plans came from the Nørre Fjand village in Jutland (Fig. 50, lower; one dismantled); three others are experimental buildings to test particular theories and house-elements. Of the many comparisons and contrasts seen here, only one or two can be discussed. Two houses were made with closely similar walls, but one had cross-beams and king posts for the roof while the other was made without these roofing members and had to be dismantled as it was on the point of collapse. Two other houses were similar except for the walls, one with daub plastered on vertical planks, the other without any daub. Another house was burned in 1967 as a controlled experiment; part of the remains were excavated, the rest left to erode for future investigation. Most of the buildings still standing are used to house experiments, demonstrations and exhibits, because the Centre has a strong educational and museum role to play. About half a million visitors have passed through the Iron Age village since it was opened over a decade ago. Occasionally, trial occupation of the houses takes place, mostly as a public display of a "life in the past" character; but these trials can only contribute to scientific knowledge if they are done specifically to determine if features built-in experimentally

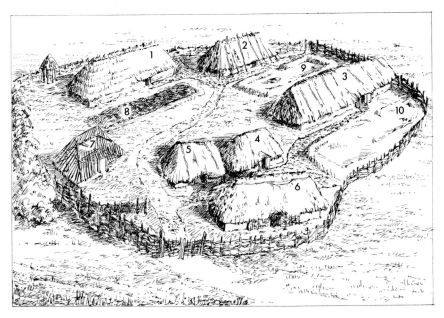

Fig. 52. The reconstructed Iron Age village at Lejre, Denmark. Six houses were built by volunteers in 1965–66, to form the nucleus of the Research Centre. Subsequently, additional houses have been built, and several of the originals removed. At 1977, the village consisted of six houses (1–6), a framework (7), a burnt house (8), and traces of two dismantled houses (9–10). Houses 2, 6 and 9 were exact copies (on ground plans) of the Grontoft Iron Age site, including the palisade. Houses 3, 4 and 10 were copied from Norre Fjand site. Houses 1, 5 and 7 are not based upon named sites, but test various structural principles. Houses 1, 2 and 6 are currently occupied by humans and/or animals. Houses 3 and 10 were built at the same time to contrast different methods of construction; house 10 was dismantled as it appeared likely to collapse. Houses 2 and 9 were similar except for walling of either wattle and daub or timber alone. House 8 was destroyed by fire (Fig. 51) and part of the site was subsequently excavated. (Drawn by R. Walker.)

(e.g. screens, smoke holes, windows, sleeping platforms) perform useful functions. Most of the occupations have been for other reasons—a "whiff of the past" in all senses of those words. Some careful experiments have been carried out on heating the houses at Lejre. Most of the houses have a central door with the living quarters to one side, and cattle stalling on the other. The hearths, in the centre of the living area, produce heat only in a narrow ring around the fire itself, and only when the hot air begins to settle down the walls does any appreciable temperature rise occur away from the hearth. Against this, a vigorous fire creates draughts, pulling in cold air through cracks in the daub walls. Cattle stalled in other parts of the house can produce a considerable temperature rise as they compress the layers of dung, but again this is a localized heat. Any partition, reasonably dense, such as a blanket or a skin placed between the two sections of the house, acts as a reflector and helps seal in the localized heat. These observations are not the result of single one-off experiments, but represent a few of the results from many hundreds of tests. The value of the whole enterprise at Lejre lies in the opportunity to give time to experiments, to allow natural processes to act upon full-scale reconstructions, and to patiently record data not at once relevant to current problems but which may be of value to future research. The operation of the Centre as a focus for experimental research in other fields and regions of Europe is an aim deserving full encouragement.

5   Arts and Crafts

... considering the want of such meanes as we have, they seeme
very ingenious; for although they have no such tooles, nor any
such craftes, sciences and artes as weé; yet in those things they
doe, they shew excellencie of wit.

Harriot, 1588

If I would study any old, lost art ... I must make myself the
artisan of it—must, by examining its products, learn both to see
and to feel as much as may be the conditions under which they
were produced and the needs they supplied or satisfied; then,
rigidly adhering to those conditions and constrained by their
resources alone, as ignorantly and anxiously strive with my own
hands to reproduce, not imitate, these things as ever strove
primitive man to produce them.

Cushing, 1895, p. 310

IN THE ARTS AND CRAFTS of primitive man we seek to gain understanding
of the materials he chose, the techniques he used to work them, and the
purposes for which they were made. The wide range of materials available
to early man, the variety of ways they could be obtained and prepared,
and the multitude of uses to which they were put, make the task of
archaeologists virtually impossible to fulfil. Even a relatively simple form
may tax the ingenuity of archaeologists to deduce a precise use in the unrecorded past, whether prehistoric or historic. For perhaps the most abundant implement of all time, the Stone Age "axe", the recent comment still
applies: "we do not know how, or for what, handaxes and cleavers were
used" (Kleindienst and Keller, 1976). Archaeologists have tried for over
a century to understand the ancient technologies of working stone and
flint, bone and antler, copper and iron, hides and wood, and the ways by
which pottery and textiles were produced from natural materials. In these
studies, and there are hundreds of them, experiments have played a
considerable and increasing part as one of the important ways of
appreciating the achievements of the past.

The commonest materials of early man were those naturally available to his hand through simple collection, such as stone and wood, and perhaps clay too. Other materials, such as bone, antler, hides and shell needed only a little more organization. Yet other materials, however, required more complex processes, such as quarrying or mining to obtain obsidian, flint and amber, the smelting of ores to yield metals, and the mixing and firing of clays to make pottery. For many regions, some desirable commodities could only be acquired through lengthy travel or exchange or seizure. Archaeologists are concerned with all these events, or presumed events, and experiments have been carried out with almost all the materials mentioned. The value of this work can be very great, but far too many experiments have involved operations with modern materials and tools, metal punches instead of stone or antler, bottle glass instead of flint or obsidian, mechanically propelled pumps instead of foot or hand bellows, and many other lazy aids. The necessity of maintaining standards of materials and technologies has already been stressed (p. 38). Many other experiments, however, have been adequately documented, and have illuminated aspects of ancient behaviour over a wide range of subjects, none more so than those in the field of lithic technology which we examine below.

There are three sources of evidence which archaeologists use in trying to emulate ancient processes of manufacture and use. The first is the surviving artifacts themselves, those objects of organic or, more often, inorganic materials which have survived and been recovered. These can provide essential information about the composition of the artifacts, deduced by various forms of analysis, as well as signs of manufacture through scars, seams, polish and other traces. In addition, the possible function of the object can be sought from traces of wear on the equipment if its shape alone does not indicate its use. As examples, analysis of a metal axe may show it to be of copper or bronze; its seams and surfaces will indicate the method of casting and hammering, and marks on the blade may suggest its use for cutting or wedging. A flint flake will bear the scars of its previous place on the core, the retouch which turned it into a tool, and the striations or polish produced during use. A pottery vessel may be analysed for its clay composition and its firing procedure, may show its method of manufacture through body sherds and surface texture and may even preserve traces of the substances it held.

The second source of evidence is obtained from historic records of the seventeenth to nineteenth centuries when many communities existing as hunters and gatherers, primitive farmers or pastoralists were encountered by European explorers, missionaries and settlers. Written descriptions of the native patterns of existence have served to guide archaeologists in their explanations of territory, settlement, industry and beliefs of many societies now extinguished but which may have represented some aspects of more ancient peoples. How valid it is to extrapolate from observed behaviour back to unrecorded activities through these records is a difficult problem. For the arts and crafts of recent and ancient societies, it is surely reasonable to assume a relationship between artifacts of similar physical material and character if other evidence suggests continuity of population, but it is unreasonable to assert exact identities in either manufacture and function. In the use of these early histories and records, archaeologists must rely upon the accuracy and honesty of the first observers, assuming that they were influenced neither by ideas of "the noble savage" nor by the belief in the superiority of "the white man".

In more recent times, archaeologists and anthropologists have been able to observe and record for themselves (e.g. Gould, 1977), but of course their subjects have become increasingly more divorced from the original conditions of isolation and uncontamination by other societies' ideas and technologies. This subject cannot be pursued here in more detail, but it is perhaps useful to note that a majority of the interest shown in such pre-industrial societies has been directed to hunting and gathering communities and not to farming and herding groups (Lee and De Vore, 1968). Throughout almost all of human prehistory, man was a hunter and a gatherer, and therefore many archaeologists have directed all their attention to the recovery of the traces of this immensely ancient episode, perhaps covering three million years. Today there remain only the Congo Pygmies, the Kalahari Bushmen and the Australian aborigines as modern representatives of this behaviour, and the cultures of all three are altered by contact with other populations, and influenced by enforced occupation of marginal lands probably well outside their ancient traditional territories (Elkin, 1964; Turnbull, 1968; Lee and De Vore, 1976).

The third source of evidence about arts and crafts of early times is experimental archaeology itself, the attempts to simulate, replicate and duplicate ancient technologies, artifacts and uses. Of the huge number of attempts to copy and thereby understand original processes, many have been failures, and few have been unqualified successes; nevertheless, the contributions remain considerable. Some of these are mentioned here, a few are described in detail, and the references provided will lead to a multitude of further experiments which often duplicate those discussed here, expand our knowledge, or open new fields. The experiments have been grouped rather loosely into those concerned with the working of raw materials (stone, flint, wood, bone, antler, shell and the metals copper and iron), some "home industries" (pottery, textiles, hides and leathers), and the arts (ornaments, paint, paper and music).

Of the raw materials regularly used by early man, only flint and other stones have survived the processes of decay and erosion. Wood and bone must also have formed important segments of primitive equipment, either as tools in themselves or as handles for stone artifacts. Because stone (including flint) survives so well in many geographical situations, it provides about 99 per cent of the surviving equipment of Paleolithic man; as the episode of Paleothic hunting and gathering occupies about 99 per cent of human presence on earth, it is no wonder that archaeologists devote so much time and energy in studying stone tools. The interest began early in the nineteenth century as we have seen, and it has continued with little abate in America, Europe and Asia ever since. The history of experimentation with flintwork is less continuous, but American participation in the last 50 years has been extensive as a recent history of the subject makes clear (Johnson, 1978). Over 350 papers have appeared on the subject, of which 200 were published between 1960 and 1975. Many of these are remarkable publications, particularly the early contributions; they set out the highly personal views of flint-knappers attempting in various ingenious ways to duplicate ancient artifacts.

> It is necessary that the artisan know just the amount and quality of force that is required in working the different materials, and for successful accomplishment he must concentrate to the limit. In his hands the materials, the tools, and he himself become one, isolated from all surroundings and noises. In working he continually watches what he has done, studies for position for the next blow or pressure and has in mind the finished product of his labor.
>
> Barbieri, 1937, p. 101

There were several subjects of particular interest to experimental flint-knappers in the decades from about 1920. One was obviously the replication of the traditional Paleolithic tools being recovered in abundance from French, German and English river gravels and caves. A pioneer in this was L. Coutier who succeeded in manufacturing hand axes, Mousterian flake-tools and Upper Paleolithic blades in attempts to understand the ancient technologies (Coutier, 1929); he also experimented with heat and found that flint could be worked more easily if its moisture was partly removed. In this use of heat he had been preceded by a peculiar experiment on the shaping of a flint arrowhead by heat and water (Eames, 1915); in this, a flake was heated and then water was dripped on to it from the end of a feather: "... I frequently became much discouraged with the results obtained. Persistence won at last, however, and I succeeded in forming a very large specimen of arrow-tip. ..." Unfortunately the successful object was never illustrated.

A major interest for experimental flint-knappers, and for many Paleolithic archaeologists, was the problem of eoliths, those flaked flints found in enormously ancient geological deposits which to some demonstrated the presence of humans but indicated to others nothing more than entirely natural processes of fracturing of stone. The conflicts between Reid Moir (1919, for human activity) and Warren (1914, for natural activity) involved experimental work in crushing and fracturing flints, but Wen Chung Pei's review was a notable contribution to the problem (1936) and rightly ignored the rather hysterical utterances of the conflicting parties as well as the subjective opinions of others: "A careful study of the edges and points of these so-called tools will convince anyone who has used flint tools than an extremely small percentage could ever have cut or penetrated any solid substance more resistant than soft butter" (Pond, 1930, p. 132). The eolith controversy died about 20 years ago, with almost universal acceptance of the natural origin of these objects found in Europe, Asia, Africa and America.

Experimental work on flint tools has generally been concerned with the replication of ancient implements, and the numerous practitioners have often commented on the difficulties of describing in prose the precise procedures to be carried out in the production of artifacts; even in 1895 one of the pioneers of experimental archaeology (p. 23) admitted as much in describing the removal of flakes "by a most dexterous motion, which I can exhibit, but not adequately describe or illustrate" (Cushing, 1895, p. 318). This is why films of flint-knapping are so useful for students and others, but there are also several published accounts of experimental work which set out, step by step, the procedures to be used. The first do-it-yourself guide was probably Knowles on flint arrowheads (1944). More recent contributions are those of Bordes (1968), Crabtree (1972) and Tixier (1974), who are certainly among the three leading specialists in the world, and a reading of these texts is essential for any real attempt to comprehend the multitude of variables involved in manufacturing replicas of ancient implements. Each of these men was self-taught by constant experiment, and one vitally important feature has emerged from a study of their individual techniques: there are likely to be several different ways of producing a replica. The flint-knapper may be able to dismiss certain techniques in making an implement, but more often than not two or three procedures remain as possible methods used in the past (Crabtree, 1970, p. 148). And experimental styles also exist now; Bordes has said:

I myself—I know that Crabtree, Tixier, Bradley, Callahan and others will agree—am absolutely unable to describe exactly what I am doing when I work a tool by pressure. Moreover, we do not do it in exactly the same way: the position of the hands, the knees, and the shoulder and the way the pressure is applied to the stone vary from one to the other ... most of the time I can tell whether a stone has been worked by Crabtree, Tixier or myself. Our styles are different, but do not ask me to say what the differences are!

Bordes *in* Johnson, 1978, p. 359

Some experiments recently conducted have investigated subjects of quite basic interest and importance to those many archaeologists who are concerned with the stone industries of prehistoric man; it is surprising that these investigations were not made sooner. As an example, Newcomer examined the well-known series of "Clactonian" flakes from Swanscombe, England, and by experiment demonstrated that the famous block-on-block or anvil technique for detaching these from the cores was unnecessary, and perhaps not used at all. He could produce similar flakes with a quartzite hammerstone (Newcomer, 1970). Bradley experimented with bifacially worked tools from the Casper site, a bison-kill in Wyoming, America (Bradley, 1974), and demonstrated by a very careful set of experiments how these implements were made, hafted, used and resharpened. Work on earlier bifaces, the Acheulean handaxes, has also yielded basic data for Paleolithic specialists: in making a handaxe with stone and antler hammers, 51 flakes and 4618 chips of flint were removed, the flakes in particular being easily divisible into those struck with the hard hammer, those with a large soft hammer, and those with a small soft hammer (Newcomer, 1971). The original nodule of flint weighed 2948 g, and the handaxe weighed 230 g (9 per cent). In contrast, an obsidian core weighing 820 g yielded 83 blades suitable for use, weighing 750 g or 91 per cent of the original weight of the core (Sheets and Muto, 1972); of course, some of the flakes detached in the making of the handaxe could have been used as tools as well. It is interesting, nonetheless, to learn that the obsidian blades yielded by one core alone totalled 31 m of cutting edge.

The Stone Age artifact upon which many experiments have been directed over the past century is the flint or obsidian projectile point, often described as an arrowhead. Such objects occur in bewildering variation over wide areas of the world, but most work has been concentrated upon slender North American points of the earliest phases of human occupation, and some work has also been done on the smaller European arrowheads of flint. The production of these involves percussion and pressure flaking, using a relatively simple set of tools including antler, bone and wooden punches and points, pads of hide or leather, and little else other than hours of experience and attention to detail. Some of the American projectile points have a characteristic fluting extending from the base towards the tip. The successful replication of this was first reported by Crabtree, who stated that either indirect percussion or pressure flaking with a chest crutch could be used (1966); since this breakthrough, many others have followed and enhanced the explanations of these techniques (Swanson, 1975). The establishment of new publications devoted to flintwork is a welcome development in the field of experimental archaeology, and one that could be emulated in other aspects of the subject (*Lithic Technology and Flint-knappers' Exchange:* addresses in References).

Among the many contributions made by experimental work on flint and stone tools and techniques, two remain of potentially the greatest importance. The fact that experimenters themselves can now see individual variations in their own work, and can recognize the design and hands of others in the work of replication, opens up the possibility, not yet realized, of identifying the workmanship of single persons in ancient industries. Knowledge of this character would open up new avenues of research and under standing about past human activities and behaviour.

The second experimental subject concerns the traces of wear and usage which may remain on the edges of ancient flint and stone implements. The pioneer in this approach is Semenov who has studied wear marks on Russian Paleolithic and later materials (1964). Striations, scratches and polish on flints can be observed under conditions of high magnification, and these may be identified by comparison with experimentally produced markings. In theory this sounds simple; in practice however it is more difficult and problematical (e.g. Brose, 1975). Flints may receive damage by other mechanisms, after abandonment for example, and many archaeological excavations and storage procedures will allow scratches to develop by careless digging, or by the finds rattling in bags or shuffling about on sorting trays. However, given better circumstances than these, the wear marks on flint tools can be observed, recorded and compared with known actions. Semenov has identified the precise use of "end scrapers" in cleaning animal skins, of long blades in whittling wood, and of many more objects. More recently, a valuable series of experiments between a flint-knapper and a microwear specialist allowed a fair test of the latter's ability to identify traces of ancient activities (Keeley and Newcomer, 1977). Fresh flakes were used in a variety of ways and on a variety of substances such as wood, bone, antler, skin and meat, and then submitted blind to the specialist for identifications; most of these were correct, a powerful argument in favour of the study and a strong recommendation to excavators to observe the necessary care in recovery of the raw materials.

Experiments with stone tools such as polished axes, adzes and hoes have not been extensive since the work of Evans and others in the nineteenth century, but a careful experiment at greenschist, slate and amphibolite quarries near Brno, Czechoslovakia, has provided a useful guide to the processes possibly employed by Neolithic communities in central Europe (Malina, 1973). Stone hammers, wooden wedges and crowbars were used by a group of students to extract the materials; one person's yield was 25 kg of stone in 5 hours. Suitable pieces of split stone were then cut up by stone and wooden "saws", with wet quartz sand poured into the cracks; once the stones were sawn a third through they were snapped by percussion with a stone boulder. Holes were drilled through some of the objects with a wooden stick, quartzite sand and bow-drill; a hole of 25 mm diameter and 2·4–3·0 mm depth took about one hour. The slate and amphilobite implements were also ground with quartz sand poured between the object and the grindstone, and a final polishing with hide and fur completed the work. Simple stone axes similar to those from a Neolithic settlement at Holásky took 3–9 hours to produce, not an excessive time and rather less than is sometimes postulated. The attempted perforation of a wide hole through a thick stone axe of diorite, however, involved one experimenter in 2 hours' work for the net result of a hole only 0·3 mm deep (Evans, 1897). Working with nephrite in New Zealand, a Maori *hei tiki* only 6 cm high was produced by drilling, shaving and smoothing in 350 hours (Barrow, 1962), a result that must compare in time with the presumed shaping of a flint point by dropping water from a feather! The perforation of a green-stone pebble 14 mm thick, with a form of pump-drill, wore out 27 drill points of quartzite, jasper, basalt, sandstone, obsidian and finally wood-with-sand, which was the best of all (Steele, 1930). These and many other experiments indicate that the manufacture of stone axes, adzes and hoes in Neolithic Europe and elsewhere may not have been a major task, but particular rocks would require special techniques and effort; sawing and drilling were likely to be the most time-consuming operations, and many unfinished specimens occur (e.g. Rieth, 1958, see Fig. 8).

In work on stone tools, a combination of experiments, including microwear analysis and ethnographic records can provide quite conclusive evidence. As an example, recent experimental work with quartzite scrapers based on those from a Late Glacial reindeer hunters' camp at Borneck, near Hamburg, Germany, show that some had been used on a soft material, probably skins. From modern historical observations in northern latitudes, and in Africa as well, it is apparent that the use of heavy hafted scrapers for skin preparation would result in characteristic wear, resharpening, damage and eventual working-out of numerous scrapers. Such aspects can be detected in prehistoric hunting camps such as Borneck, a site occupied in autumn some 10 000 years ago, when the hunters were killing reindeer in order to obtain sufficient hides for tents and clothing; the hides would be roughly cleaned of fat and laid aside for further preparation when the killing season ended (Knutsson, 1975–77).

Potentially of even greater significance is a recent experiment with elephant bone and stone hammers in Canada. The date of the first entry into the New World by man, crossing the Bering Strait land-bridge, is currently 40 000 years ago, but at the Old Crow site in Yukon, fossil mammoth bones have now been dated to 50 000 years, and the problem was to determine if these bones showed signs of human workmanship, rather than natural breakage. Spiral fractures on the bones, possibly caused by stone hammers, suggested breakage while the bone was fresh, perhaps in order to allow the marrow to be extracted. Experiments on horse and cow bones suggested that deliberate and controlled smashing of leg bones would yield the characteristic fracture marks, but the experiment could only be conducted on entirely appropriate raw material when an elephant called Ginsberg, a star of Hollywood movies, conveniently died and made its bones available to the researchers. The tests duplicated the fossil mammoth evidence, and help to indicate a presence of man in the New World 50 000 years ago (Stanford *et al.*, 1979).

Stone and flint assume a great importance to prehistorians concerned with the earliest traces of man; as in almost all such sites only inorganic materials have survived. Yet ethnographic records suggest quite clearly that a majority of pre-industrial societies use wood far more extensively than any other substance, and stone tools can often be seen as the primary equipment in making tools of wood and bone, and not as normal everyday implements themselves:

> It would seem probable that prehistoric man, from the earliest times, utilized wood for making into implements and weapons, but it is only under exceptional geological conditions that any examples of this material would be preserved till the present day. The experiments I have carried out have demonstrated to me that very many of the ancient stone implements, referable to every phase of the Stone Age, which have been found, are admirably adapted for the shaping of wood and similar material, and I feel that these practically indestructible flint implements represent, as it were, merely the "insoluble residue" of prehistoric industries, of which the other and more friable artifacts have disintegrated and disappeared during the great periods of time that have elapsed since they were made.
>
> Moir, 1926, p. 656

Wood provided early man with material for tools, buildings, heat, light, boats and other essentials, and it is perhaps the greatest loss suffered by archaeologists that so little wood has survived from prehistoric times. Where it has survived, it demonstrates man's understanding of this material, and the skill with which he could control and work it. Few archaeologists have felt the need to experiment with wood itself, although many choose wood as the material for testing the capabilities of stone, bronze or iron tools. The felling of trees, however, in the early establishment of farming communities has often been the subject for experiment

(p. 102), as has the timber necessary for house and boat-building (pp. 150 and 76). Spears and clubs were made by L. S. B. Leakey, using only retouched flint flakes (1954), and Crabtree and Davis made wooden pegs and paddles with obsidian flakes (1968); a simple willow peg took 30 minutes to make including fire-hardening of the point, but an oak paddle, split, adzed, scraped and ground, occupied two hours. The firing of wooden points, to harden them, has been shown to be an erroneous belief, as tests demonstrate either no change or the reverse (Cosner, 1956; Clarke and Boswell, 1976); more work needs to be done.

Many other small experiments with wood have been carried out, but there has been no real attempt to understand the differing capabilities and qualities of ancient trees, the reasons for their selection for specific purposes, or the various methods used to work the timber into equipment and structures. Comparisons between stone, bronze and iron axes, in felling trees, in cutting mortices and in general carpentry, have only begun to be made, at Cambridge; and comparisons between stone and steel axes are of some interest although the choice was not available to Neolithic or Bronze Age man (Saraydar and Shimada, 1971; Leechman, 1950). The chopping of a single tree by stone and bronze axes, half cut through with each axe, demonstrates the differences of attack. The stone axe, with thicker blade, requires a wider cut in the tree to avoid jamming, and can knock off large chips only with difficulty and with great accuracy; the debris consists mostly of small fragments and pulverized wood powder. The flat bronze axe, in contrast, can bite more deeply, and detach large chips; it was about twice as efficient as the stone axe in cutting through the same tree with the same operator. The more interesting task of splitting the trunk into planks requires only wooden wedges and a mallet (Fig. 53), and experimental work on oak, ash and other woods demonstrates the ease with which Neolithic builders could shape enormously long planks for their structures. In mortice work, metal axes, of bronze (Fig. 53) or iron, are far superior to stone axes, and this can help to explain the differences in Neolithic and Bronze Age planks with pegged holes such as are known from Switzerland and England (Coles et al., 1978). Soft wood, of alder, is also easily perforated with bone chisels, but seasoned wood is too resistant for such tools and requires metal blades (Becker, 1962). The varying characters of fresh green and seasoned timber, for ease of working, has not yet been thoroughly investigated.

One group of experiments combining wood and flint, as well as feathers and linen, concerns the production and function of bows and arrows, atlatls and spears. The literature on archery is enormous, and a recent compilation lists about 5000 papers, books and films (Lake and Wright, 1977). Bows and arrows have an immense prehistory and history (e.g.

Clark, 1963; Korfmann, 1972), and the subject lends itself to experiment; however no one has yet surpassed the work of Saxton T. Pope (1923). Pope was a surgeon in the medical school of the University of California when Ishi, the last survivor of the Yahi tribe, was brought in a derelict (Kroeber, 1961, illustrated edition, 1976). Under Ishi's guidance (Fig. 54), Pope learned, and then published, a comprehensive account of Ishi's archery in 1918. He followed this with a more extensive study of bows and arrows from both New and Old Worlds in 1923, in which he reported on the many experiments he had devised to test the capabilities of bows, bow-strings, arrowshafts, arrowheads, and feathers. Some of the bows were originals and others reproductions, but each was tested for its cast (the capacity to throw an arrow) and its weight (the force needed to draw the bowstring 71 cm from the back of the bow). Both the Sioux and the English release were used in the experiments; the Sioux release has all fingers and thumb on the string, the arrow nock being held by thumb and

Fig. 53. *Left.* Splitting an oak trunk into halves, using only wooden wedges and mallet. The trunk has been lightly adzed before splitting, to form one of the required plank edges.

Right. Mortice work with a small bronze axe; the timber is ready for corner drilling and final splitting out of intervening wood to make a squared mortice. (Photos: J. M. Coles.)

first finger, while the English release has the string drawn by the first three fingers, the arrow being held by the first two fingers and not the thumb.

The bows tested by Pope included a range of American Indian, African, Asian and European weapons; they were made of ash, hickory, yew and ironwood, as well as several horn–wood–sinew composites. Linen, silk, catgut and cotton threads were wound to make bowstrings, with 60-strand Irish linen the best. In the experimental tests, the maximum cast was 257 m

FIG. 54. Ishi demonstrating the techniques of archery. Here he is calling rabbits by making a "kissing sound", with bow and arrow at the ready. (Lowie Museum of Anthropology, University of California, Berkeley.)

with a replica of a Turkish bow of cow-horn strips, hickory wood, catgut and rawhide, using an arrow of bamboo tipped with a rifle bullet jacket. Another composite bow was an original Tartar weapon over a century old; its bowstring was rawhide rope, and it required two men to brace and string it. In use, the archer had to lie on his back, brace his feet against the bow and draw with both hands. Its cast was only 82 metres but its original owner was said to have braced it single handed and to have shot arrows 400 m; but perhaps like a fisherman's tale the claims grew with time and telling. The English yew longbow was an efficient weapon in comparison with some others, throwing arrows about 200 m; the first English longbow, of Neolithic age, precedes the famous medieval weapon by 4000 years (Clark, 1963).

The arrows used in the experiments were of bamboo, hickory, birch, ash, pine and willow, and a variety of different arrowheads were used; these were of obsidian, metal and wood. The arrows were fired at first into pinewood planks, and simulated animal bodies of hide-covered boxes filled with animal livers. The obsidian points penetrated better than the metal points because of the slightly serrated obsidian edges which acted as one-stroke saws. A test was made of a historical reference to an encounter between Spanish explorers and Florida natives. This account described how the chain-mail clad Spaniards were nervous about the prospect of receiving the sharp end of a stone-tipped arrow, and they bribed a native to shoot at an unoccupied suit of armour. He did so, and shot almost completely through it; the Spaniards promptly abandoned their heavy armour and adopted felt padding instead. To test this tale, Pope borrowed a set of sixteenth-century chain mail from a museum, dressed a dummy body with it, and shot a steel-tipped arrow from 7 m; the arrow struck with a shower of sparks, passed through the front, through the body, and stopped against the back of the armour. The views of the museum curator are not recorded, but Pope's plan to next shoot an English broadhead arrow (*c.* 9 cm long and 5 cm wide) was abandoned.

Final experiments were carried out in the field, and included the killing of a running buck deer with a single arrow from 75 m, and two adult bears from 60 and 40 m. A female grizzly, charging as her cubs were being taken, was shot five times by two hunters, before a rifle bullet finally stopped her a few metres away. Pope commented: "These bears were wild and taken at great risk", which seems rather laconic in the circumstances. He was positive in his claims that hunting with bow and arrow is a more humane method than with rifle and bullet: the bullet tears the tissue and prevents healing, but the arrow cuts cleanly and spills more blood, killing quickly yet allowing an escaped animal to heal more easily.

An example of the power of the bow and arrow to kill humans was provided by Pope, not of course by experiment. An Indian skull found in San Joaquin valley bore various fractures, and part of an arrow shaft of wood and reed lay within the skull; no arrowhead was found but it appeared that originally a stone point had been attached. Pope's medical training allowed him to suggest that the Indian had been struck in or near the right eye by the arrow which passed with considerable force down and out through the lower jaw, the man fell and fractured his upper jaw, whereupon he was clubbed in the back of the head and abandoned—a sorry tale.

Modern experiments have to rely upon inanimate targets, and therefore lack the immediacy and "drama" of the actual hunt. A recent series of tests on slate arrowheads of the Neolithic in Sweden (3000–2000 B.C.) used a sheep's body, a large but dead fish, and a styrofoam block, the last providing a control for the degrees of penetration of different arrowheads (Johansson, 1975–77). These series of experiments on bow and arrows are excellent examples of the careful organization of materials, procedures, tests and publication. Several smaller and more restricted experiments dealing with spearthrowers or atlatls have complemented the archery work by comparing the range, penetration and accuracy of arrows, and spears as well as harpoons, although it seems likely that inexperience with the atlatl reduced its performance (Fig. 55, lower) (see Spencer, 1974). Other weapons of the ancient world include Roman artillery, made of wood, metal and gut (Fig. 55). In the war cemetery at Maiden Castle, Dorset, an iron projectile head embedded in a defender's vertebra suggested the manner of bombardment by the Romans in A.D. 44. The defenders' slings could hurl stones about 100 m but the Roman ballista could pump iron darts two or three times this distance. The inhabitants of the fort were presumably defenceless against this long-range attack, and reduced to despair before the final assault and slaughter. Reconstructions of Roman artillery have often taken place (Johnstone, 1957), and the range of instruments tested, sometimes inadvertently. In several cases, bolts have been released prematurely to the alarm of the experimenters, but other than the loss of a few plateglass windows and a broken arm, no major damage has been done. But intending experimenters should be warned.

A final comment on ancient wood technology must relate to the quantities of timber required for certain structures and equipment. Observation of surviving woodwork, and experiments, have demonstrated the immense amount of timber needed for buildings, fences, mines, kilns, boats, ramparts and many other artifacts of early man. As an example of a single group, the Danish Viking fleet was reputedly 1100 ships of an average life of 25 years; hence 44 new ships had to be built each year. As good quality

Fig. 55. *Upper*. Replica of a Roman ballista, the equivalent of a cross-bow on a stand, and capable of pumping iron darts 200 m or more. (Photo: L. P. Morley).

Lower. Throwing a spear with an *atlatl* (spear thrower); the effect is to extend the arm and therefore increase the speed of the spear (from Browne, 1940).

oak timber was very important, each ship may have required 12 good trees, and 44 ships each year would result in the clearance of 10 ha of oak woodland. A Viking fortress of Trelleborg character would need about 8000 large oak trees, from 85 ha of woodland, and defensive systems of piles and booms such as existed in Rødby fjord probably required over 15 000 piles. To these totals we can add the timber required for houses, docks and fences, that consumed in pottery kilns and metal furnaces, and that employed for implements and equipment such as wagons and sledges. The quantities were immense at all periods of human history and many phases of pre-history, and experiments can only hint at what archaeology has lost by decay of organic materials.

Although stone and wood formed the bulk of materials used by ancient man, bone and antler were also prized for their hardness, their ability to take and keep a sharp point, and for the variety of shapes which were sometimes put to unusual use.

If we go back to the dawn of human tool-making, we find Man surrounded by animals whom Nature has armed more efficiently than him . . . Carnivores had their teeth and claws, grass-eaters their horns and antlers; what more natural than to rob them of these weapons to use against them.

Breuil, 1939, p. 4

Archaeologists are particularly interested in bones because they show man's dependence on hunting or herding, and his control over herds of wild or domesticated animals. Experimental archaeologists are concerned, however, that clear indications of industrial work on bone, its use for points, scrapers, hammers and the like are being ignored:

Diagnostic criteria of bone-tool manufacture and bone-tool use should be employed . . . in studying this massive category of potential technological information, traditionally labelled "faunal remains", "kitchen refuse", and "unidentified bone", before it is dropped into paper bags and shipped off to zoologists and paleontologists. Fractured bone, like fractured stone, is cultural data for archaeologists.

Sadek-Kooros, 1972, p. 381

Although many tonnes of animal remains have been recovered from sites, there is still little understanding of the patterns of bone fracture, of how natural breakage can occur, and, more important, how it cannot occur. Some experimental work has been carried out, but the results have been variable. From the great cave at Niah, Borneo, many broken bones were recovered, some of which appeared to be functional tools such as points; experimental smashing of fresh pig and deer bones suggested that these points were accidentally produced when a bone was broken to extract the marrow (Harrison and Medway, 1962). At the middle Pleistocene kill-sites of Torralba and Ambrona in Spain, elephant bones had also been broken open for marrow, but some were then flaked to make tools. Experiments demonstrated that only deliberate flaking at these sites could have produced the shapes and edges needed (Biberson and Aguirre, 1965). A well-constructed investigation of bonework from Jaguar cave, Idaho, also suggested that long bones of bighorn sheep were systematically broken by fracturing the bone shaft with a hammer, then twisting it to yield two pieces, each with a sharp point (Sadek-Kooros, 1972). Some 400 leg bones of lamb, obtained from Boston butchers and meatpackers, were used and the experiments involved different conditions of cold and damp, different bashing or grooving before the twisting or snapping of the bones. The results suggested that at Jaguar Cave most of the sheep leg bones had been broken at random to extract marrow, but that over 10 per cent of the bones had been broken systematically to yield certain bone shapes suitable for further preparation before use as tools. Ethnographic observations suggest that bone, and antler, could be softened by boiling and soaking in various natural organic acids which would ease grinding and polishing of the projected implement, and experiments with sour milk and brine-pickled plants such as sorrel have yielded the same results (Zurowski, 1974).

Bone points from the Pleistocene rock-shelter at Ksar Akil, Lebanon, were more clearly shaped and polished for use, and recent experiments have been concerned to show how such implements have been made (Newcomer, 1974). The bonework showed striations running along the length of the points, and chattermarks (corrugations) at right angles. The experimental work was carried out on sheep and cattle bone (raw and cooked), red deer antler (soaked and dry), elephant ivory and hippo tooth; the originals were of bone and antler from gazelle, deer and sheep or goat. Stone tools such as those from contemporary levels at Ksar Akil were used, including burins, blades and scrapers, and every tool reproduced the original striations and chattermarks—striations from irregularities in the tool edge, chattermarks by the bouncing of the tool edge as it was swept down the bone. Similar results were obtained by experiments on French bone tools although more precise identification of the individual stone tools used were made (Rigaud, 1972). This seems an unhappy conflict of results. No such problems seem to exist for the working of antler into points or harpoon heads; the groove and splinter technique of detaching blanks for further work is well documented (Clark and Thompson, 1953), and the production of barbed points and harpoon heads has also been demonstrated (Fig. 56, left) (Dauvois, 1974). Tests of these Pleistocene weapons have not been extensive (Thompson, 1954), and here ethnographic comparisons would seem particularly relevant and useful (e.g. Nelson, 1969).

Several more unusual experiments and reconstructions may help to show the range of potential uses for bone. In excavations of Basket Maker sites in Colorado, notched ribs and scapulae of large animals were consistently encountered. A major industry carried on by the Indians was the production of cordage from leaves of the yucca plant. The two items were brought together in an experiment (Morris and Burgh, 1954). Yucca leaves were gathered and after their edges were stripped off, they were pounded, both smooth and notched bones being used to scrape away the pulp from the fibres, leaving a clean hank ready for twisting into cord. An ancient rib recovered from a nearby site still retained a smear of fibres and dried yucca sap; an ethnographic record also suggested the same association for notched bone and yucca fibres. In this experiment the result seems certain.

Bone is particularly useful to the archaeologist as it acquires and retains the wear marks of scratching, grinding, rubbing and polishing. Much work has been carried out on this functional aspect (e.g. Semenov, 1964). One particular problem concerns the bone skates of northern Europe dated from 1000 B.C. up to recent times. Long bones of horse and ox were

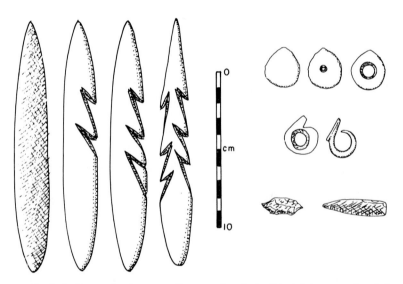

FIG. 56. *Left.* Stages in the manufacture of a Late Glacial harpoon-head from antler, by cutting and splitting out wedges of antler (after Dauvois, 1974).

Right. Stages in the manufacture of abalone and mussel shell fishhooks, using chert drill (lower left) and stone file (lower right). The elegant shape of the hook was designed by the Chumash Indians of California in order to catch bottom feeders such as bass and halibut. (After Robinson, 1942.)

trimmed and ground on one face to produce an even surface; sometimes there was bruising and scratching on the other (upper) face. Using modern skating pressures and movements as a guide, the bone skates were found to be totally inconsistent in their wear patterns, and were dismissed therefore as skates for ice (Semenov, 1964, 193). However, other experimental work with reconstructions show that bone skates were not laced on to the foot, the foot was not lifted from the ice, and propulsion was by stick; the skates are really slides, like sledge runners (MacGregor, 1975). Several hours of sliding on ice created wear patterns like the originals. The recent recognition of medieval jaw-sledges from the Netherlands is precisely similar, the jaw of a horse, or two of them (catamarran sledge), furnished with a board (Fig. 57, upper), and serving as a seat for a child who propels himself along the ice with a pair of pointed sticks. Peter Bruegel the Elder painted such an event at Antwerp in 1555 (Ijzereef, 1974) (Fig. 57, lower).

Another material readily available to early man was shell from major rivers, estuaries and coastlands in most parts of the world. From shell, ornamental pendants and beads were often made, as well as musical horns and small pieces of equipment. One experiment has been carried out on shell fishhooks of the Chumash Indians of California (Robinson, 1942). These fishermen caught tunny and sea bass from canoes with hook and line, the hooks being made of abalone and mussel shells. Stone tools resembling those found in Chumash middens along the coast were used to make replicas of the shell hooks (Fig. 56, right), and experimental fishing with them resulted in bottom-feeders such as bass and halibut being caught. Every fish caught had worked the thin soft tissues in its mouth through the narrow clearance between hook point and hook shank, the steady pull (not the European strike) on the line causing the hook to rotate and its point to slide sideways into the mouth. Versions of this type of hook are found throughout the Pacific islands where European metal barbed hooks are considered worthless.

The metals most commonly worked by ancient man were copper, tin, gold, silver and iron. The earliest of these was copper, which was used in parts of the Old World and the New where native copper or outcrops of ores were recognizable. Just as lithic specialists exist for research into Paleolithic technologies, so do metallurgical experts in later prehistoric and early historic fields of research; but here the comparison ends because most of the studies of early metal technology have been conducted by metallurgists with an interest in archaeology, whereas lithic experiments are the concern of archaeologists and not geologists. The differences in approach and in publication of results is quite noticeable.

A large number of metallurgical experiments have been concerned with the smelting of copper ores in simple furnaces. Oxide ores from weathered

upon the originals suggested a prestige product, not used in actual battle, and this was demonstrated by slashing a replica with a Bronze Age sword; the shield was cut almost in two by one blow (Fig. 58, lower). The magnificent replicas of Roman armour, recently made on the basis of surviving fragments and artistic representations, were more heavy and undoubtedly functional in physical terms (Fig. 59), but experimental destruction has not taken place (Robinson, 1972, 1975).

FIG. 58. Experimental testing of the defensive qualities of replicas of Bronze Age shields of leather (left) and sheet metal (right). The author has prudently armed himself with the entirely functional leather shield, but the metal shield has been sliced by a single blow. (Photo: Ralph Crane © 1963 Time Inc.)

Experiments in casting by the lost-wax process are far more complex than any other casting procedures so far attempted. One of these attempted to reproduce a gold bell of prehistoric Mexican character and was based upon a sixteenth-century account (Long, 1965). Copper was used instead of gold for obvious reasons: most experiments lack adequate finance. A wax model of the bell and its handle was shaped over a clay and charcoal core with embedded pebble; outer clay and charcoal skins were placed around the wax model, with airvents left in places, and the mould was gradually built up. A crucible containing copper lumps was attached to the top of the mould. The whole object was placed in a draught furnace filled with charcoal, and heating began; the wax model and its

reservoir melted out, the copper flowed at 1200°C into the space to form
the metal bell. Later, the clay core was broken up and extracted, leaving
the pebble clapper in place, and the bell tinkled. A rather similar experiment using a wax model attempted to reproduce the terminal of one of the
first-century B.C. gold torcs from Suffolk, England (Brailsford and Stapley,
1972). The body of the torc was swaged from a cast rod into an octagonal
section, then bent in to a hairpin shape before twisting to form the torc.
The same general processes of beating and twisting were used in earlier
times to produce gold torcs and neck-rings, as other experiments have
shown (e.g. Taylor, 1968); and these reflect the historic beginnings of
experiments in metal work in America, with Cushing (1894) and
Willoughby (1903) working on copper plates and sheet metal.

Iron working involves quite different techniques from copper and
bronze. As a substance it was much more readily available to communities

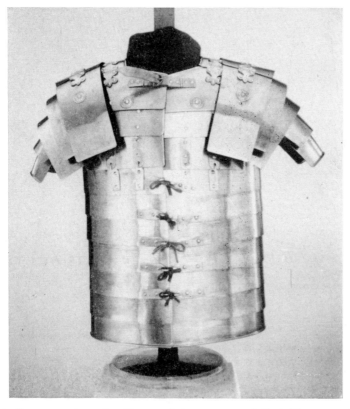

FIG. 59. Reconstruction of a Roman *lorica segmenta* of Corbridge type (photo:
courtesy of H. R. Robinson; see Robinson, 1975).

in Africa, Europe and Asia, and relatively simple yet efficient methods of reducing iron ore, and forging iron were devised. Many experiments have recently been conducted in the reduction process, and only one or two can be noted here. The formula for reduction of iron ore to iron is $FeO + CO = Fe + CO_2$, so a simple bowl furnace prepacked with charcoal and calcined ore lumps could yield some compacted iron, much slag and some reduced iron ore (Wynne and Tylecote, 1958); an alternative method involved alternate layers of ore and charcoal added during the firing. More complex shaft furnaces have also been tested in England, Denmark and elsewhere (Voss, 1962; Tylecote and Owles, 1960; Jasiuk, 1969; Tylecote, 1969; Cleere, 1971); these have the advantage of provision for the removal of the molten slag, either collected in a pit beneath the hearth, or flowing in a channel out of the furnace (Fig. 60). The shaft

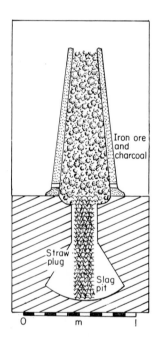

FIG. 60. *Left.* Cross-section through a shaft furnace for smelting iron, based on excavated finds of the Iron Age in northern Germany and Denmark. The slag pit is beneath the ground level, and entry to the pit is blocked by a straw plug; the clay shaft above ground has four vents near its base for draught. The shaft is packed with charcoal and, higher up, with iron ore; the smelt lasts 24 hours, and at 1200°C the slag runs off the iron particles and either flows into the pit or sticks to the sides of the shaft. (After Hansen, 1977.)

Right. A shaft furnace in operation at Lejre, Denmark (Historical–Archaeological Research Centre, Lejre).

furnace consists of a lower portion or pit dug into the ground and sur-
mounted by a slightly tapering shaft of clay, vented at its base to allow the
flow of air. In a Danish experiment the pit was closed by a straw plug
held by sticks. Ore and charcoal layers were placed in the shaft, fired to
1200°C until eventually the iron slag burnt through the plug and flowed
into the pit. The spongy metal would then be extracted and hammered to
remove the slag. The quantities of materials required for this process were
132 kg of bog iron ore, 150 kg of charcoal, and the yield was 15 kg of
iron. Another experiment with a Norfolk furnace and a continuous slag
run had a potential yield of 13 kg of raw bloom from 45 kg of charcoal
and 35 kg of iron ore.

The reconstruction of a Roman furnace from Holbean wood, Sussex,
has carried these experiments further (Cleere, 1971). A cylindrical clay
furnace one metre high was built, dried and fired in order to reveal any
cracks for patching. Charcoal and then iron ore were stacked within the
furnace, which had an aperture at the base for the forced air draught, for
loading and unloading, and for the flow of slag. The aperture was sealed
as necessary with a turf plug. Temperatures of 1200°C were achieved, the
slag was easily removed, and the bloom was collected. The best trial
yielded 9 kg of iron from 91 kg of iron ore and 120 kg of charcoal. The
bloom was hammered and heated to expel slag and to weld the particles
of metal. This work set out to examine many principles of iron smelting
and it is a useful example of an experiment which attempted to solve problems arising during the work; it also yielded results worthy of further
experimental studies. The reconstructed iron foundry at Nowa Słupia in
Poland is another notable experimental centre (Fig. 61).

Throughout these experiments dealing with stone, flint, wood, bone,
antler, copper and iron, the basic raw materials used by man, there are
several common themes. The first is that experimental archaeology can be
entertaining, but it is hard work; the second is that ethnography cannot
be ignored, as it provides guides to experienced use of materials; the third
is that much remains to be done, with some areas of interest scarcely or
badly explored. These points will be made again.

Pottery was first made by prehistoric man over 20 000 years ago when
small figurines modelled in clay were hardened by heating in a camp fire.
Pottery vessels began to be made about 10 000 years ago (Fig. 62), and
subsequently the practice of firing clay to make many varieties of both
figurines and containers became widespread over most of the world, with
independent invention in various places. As pottery fragments are often
the most abundantly represented artifacts on archaeological sites, they
have always formed an important material for study (e.g. van der Leeuw,
1976) and in recent years experiments in the manufacture of pottery have

added to our understanding of ancient techniques. Although a considerable number of experimental kilns for firing the pots have been constructed, there has been a surprising absence of uniformity in the work, and many basic procedures have been repeated because of the lack of detail provided in some publications. In these aspects, the experimental work on metallurgy, for example, is well in advance. Nonetheless, there have been some notable experiments with pot-making, and only a few can be noted here as examples of the procedures and results.

One of the major activities of the Historical-Archaeological Research Centre at Lejre, Denmark, is experimental work on pottery, and a very large series of kilns and firings have been undertaken (Fig. 63, upper) (Bjørn, 1969; Hansen, 1977). Most of these kilns are based upon excavated examples from Denmark and north Germany, but others are entirely experimental and devised from the pottery vessels themselves. The colour,

FIG. 61. Reconstructed shelter and furnaces on original metallurgical site of the first millennium A.D. at Nowa Słupia, Poland (photo: M. Radwan Museum of Ancient Metallurgy).

texture, decoration and fabric of pots obviously provide clues about the manufacturing process, and it should be possible to deduce the firing temperature and general type of kiln by analytical work alone; some experiments have tested these possibilities (e.g. Hodges, 1962). However, experiments designed to reproduce pottery with particular characteristics are a better method of investigation as they yield data not only about the vessels but also about kiln construction and firing techniques. The earliest known pottery in northern Europe is of Ertebølle type, that is, conical-based thick-walled vessels made by coiling. We do not know how these were fired, but it seems likely that a simple open fire was used. Experiments at Lejre suggest that these very heavy coarse vessels would require air-drying for about one month before they could be placed near an open fire; also they would have to be turned regularly to complete the drying process. The vessels would then be placed in a low fire which was gradually

Fig. 62. Pottery manufacture (drawn by R. Walker).

built up to cover the vessels. The success rate in the experiments is not high, about 50 per cent. Even so, the procedure, involving some care and much time, adds something to our knowledge of coastal dwellers whose

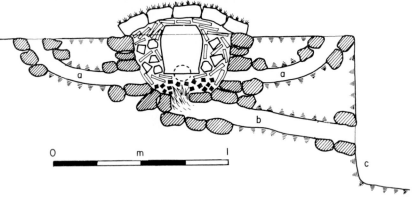

FIG. 63. *Upper.* Experimental firing of a clay-walled pottery kiln at Lejre, Denmark. Kilns such as these generally improve in their production of well-fired pottery as successive repairs and firings achieve increasingly stable conditions within the kiln. (Historical–Archaeological Research Centre, Lejre.)

Lower. Section through an open-pit pottery kiln, based upon a site at Limhamn, Sweden. The dried pots are placed upside down on straw in the pit, which is ringed with stones; wood fuel is piled around and over the pots, and a turf cover is placed over the hollow once the straw and wood are alight. a, Air vents (4 in number); b, firing canal; c, clay pit. (After Bjørn, 1969.)

middens of shell and bone represent almost all of the surviving evidence about their existence.

The firing of pottery in a shallow pit is a more efficient procedure, although temperatures can reach only about 1000°C. Both at Lejre and at Butser, Hampshire, experiments in open-pit firing have yielded new information about prehistoric pottery (Bjørn, 1969; Reynolds, 1976). The pits are 10–25 cm deep, about 45–75 cm in diameter, perhaps dug into a shallow slope. This pit-clamp, as it is known, is lined with straw, and dried pots are placed upside down within the hollow and covered with dry and green wood. After lighting, the whole heap is immediately covered with turf, as otherwise the pots will burst. A few holes or cracks allow the smoke to escape, and cracks near the base let air into the pit. Cracks and collapses of the mound must be repaired, and after 4–5 hours all visible cracks and holes are covered, and the pit abandoned for 12–24 hours. Opening requires care to prevent too rapid cooling, and the pots should be completely black; experimental pots are often mottled red and black. The pits can be used again and again, and it has been noted that with continual scraping out to prepare for the next load, the pit is enlarged. At Butser, pits 15 cm deep and of 45 cm diameter become one metre deep and 1·5 m wide. With normal weathering all visible traces of burning disappear and the pit is then available for a wide variety of archaeological, non-experimental interpretation, as many reports will concede.

A more developed type of pottery firing was used about 4000 years ago in Scandinavia, and experimental reconstruction of one of these "pit-kilns" from Limhamn in Scania, Sweden, showed its efficiency (Fig. 63, lower). The pit, only 40 cm wide, was lined with stone and had four narrow air vents dug through the surrounding ground, partially lined with stone where the vents had become too wide; a firing canal was made in the same way. The procedures used in the experiments were otherwise identical to the open pit method, but the vent holes allowed far greater control over the firing; the firing canal was sealed after lighting, and two vents were covered at first, then opened and the kiln left for a day. Although the disadvantage of any pit firing is that charcoal touches the pots, and may crack them, the Limhamn kiln experiments achieved up to 90 per cent success of unbroken hard-fired pots.

Pottery kilns as such were designed to separate the fuel from the pots, and this could be done in several ways as surviving Iron Age and Romano-British kilns clearly demonstrate. All of these are structures raised in part above the ground, with an opening at ground level leading into the firebox, and either a shelf or a clay tray placed above the fire (Fig. 64, upper). The construction of these kilns is relatively easy, and most of the experiments have been rightly concerned with reproducing the exact quality of pottery

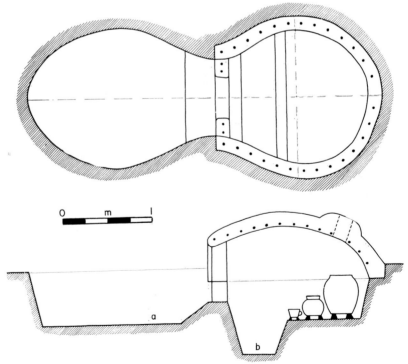

of the relevant period. In this work experiment has built upon the experience of the preceding test, and many new variables have been inserted
for investigation. This is not exactly the "series testing" already mentioned,
but by publication and consultation among those working with Romano-
British kilns, the procedures carried out 1500 years ago are now quite well
understood, although no one would argue that the experiments have completely succeeded in answering all the problems.

In Highgate Wood, London, Romano-British kilns were producing a
range of domestic wares, including jars, beakers, bowls and dishes, in the
first century A.D. Experiments were devised to investigate the clays, kiln
construction, pottery-making and firing (Brightwell *et al.*, 1972). Three
kilns were built, modelled on the surviving furnace walls, central pedestal
and tiled flue of one of the ancient kilns. Puddled clay formed the central
pedestal for each kiln *c.* 40 cm high and 60 cm diameter. Kiln walling of
clay slabs and puddled clay was placed around the pedestals, and brick
firebars bridged the pedestals and the walls. The upper domed parts of the
kiln were made of puddled clay or wattles and daub, leaving a central
hole at the top of each kiln. The flues were covered with clay blocks or
wattle and daub. The building of the three kilns involved three or four
people for 5–9 hours per kiln. The clay was dug from the site itself, and
prepared for potting by mixing with water and puddling with bare feet, a
messy but doubtless eminently satisfying job as most experimenters have
remarked. The clay was then kneaded on wooden planks and thrown on
direct-drive kick wheels; beakers took 8·5 minutes and jars 12·5 minutes to
produce by an experienced potter but one unaccustomed to this particular
method. After drying to leather hard for about three days, the vessels were
shaved, and some were decorated by dipping into a white slip, dotting by
clay slip and wooden comb, scratching or cordoning; but some were left
plain. Drying for 4–5 days preceded the kiln loading, and 75 per cent of
thrown vessels were judged suitable for firing. The kilns were loaded
through the tops of the almost completed domes, stacked rim-to-rim and

---

FIG. 64. *Upper.* Experimental kilns of Romano-British type from Barton-on-Humber,
Lincolnshire, England, prior to loading, covering and firing. The oven and flue are
below ground level, and the walls are of clay blocks, with cracks sealed. The kilns
hold up to 100 pots, covered by a layer of tiles and a layer of turf during the early
firing. By stoking up the flue and pushing fuel and embers into the stoke pit, temperatures of over 800°C can be achieved, and reduced wares are produced in emulation
of Romano-British potters. (Photo: courtesy of G. F. Bryant.)

Lower. Plan and section of an experimental kiln of the fifth century A.D. from
Hasseris, Denmark, built of clay, sand, wattle and daub. Temperatures up to
1400°C were achieved in this kiln. a, Ash pit; b, fire box. (After Bjørn, 1969.)

base-to-base in several layers with the lowest layer resting on the pedestal and firebars of each kiln. The kilns could each have received about 180–200 vessels, but only 170 vessels were fired in the three kilns together. Hornbeam, birch and oak wood were used as fuel, first to pre-fire the kilns, then for the firing of the pottery. The first kiln cracked severely in a test firing, but this allowed refinements for the other two. A major problem was the bridging of the flue at its entry to the kiln, and this was solved by clay blocks, by a pillar holding up the clay arch, and most successfully by a corbelled arch. The firing was relatively uneventful, with repairs to dome walls and attempts to improve the draught and maintain the maximum temperature of 900°C; after the cooling the dome caps were removed and the vessels unstacked. Of 170 vessels fired in four attempts (one kiln fired twice), 144 emerged, the remainder presumably having been blown up during the firing; about half were cracked, and all vessels were oxidized, unlike the grey reduced ware produced by the Romano-British potters on this site. The circulation of air during the cooling probably caused oxidation. A further experimental firing, with pots packed in the kiln with humus and with the kiln thickly covered during the cooling period, yielded vessels suitable reduced and appropriately coloured.

This experiment tried to recreate the original conditions of pottery-making, and did so in the knowledge of a near-complete excavation of the site, thereby allowing some suggestions to be made about the working of the ancient pottery, and its yield of vessels to the local markets of London. About 25 000 vessels may have been produced here, occupying one skilled potter for perhaps half a year; this in itself can lead to further considerations about the role of small-scale industries and marketing procedures.

Similar experiments have yielded more evidence about kiln construction (Bryant, 1973). A valuable series of tests at Barton-on-Humber, Lincolnshire, achieved temperatures of over 1000°C and the production of reduced wares, particularly from kilns previously fired (Bryant, 1970, 1971); the first firing usually resulted in cracks and holes, and only when these were patched and the whole structure baked hard could a sealed kiln be assured. Further work on kiln domes, however, has suggested that permanent clay-built domes may not have been necessary; clay plates, tiles, turf and clay have been successfully employed to form a temporary dome, and again the wares were reduced, with very few "wasters" (Fig. 64, upper). All of this work is continuing, and provides increasingly detailed knowledge of Romano-British pottery production (Bryant, 1977).

An experiment based on a fifth-century A.D. kiln at Hasseris, Denmark, but of a type known in northern Europe both a thousand years earlier as well as later, has also contributed to this series of tests on small domed structures for local products (Bjørn, 1969). It was built in 6–7 hours by five people, using clay and sand, willow twigs, straw and turf blocks. The chamber had a simple ledge to support the back of the dome and a wider ledge for the clay vessels (Fig. 64, lower). The dome was made of inter-laced twigs and withies, lined with straw and plastered with clay. After air drying and patching cracks, it was fired with intense heat (1400°C) to create a solid dome, which was covered by turf in the later stages of this pre-firing. The firing of the pottery itself was not difficult. For red wares the pots were air dried inside a building for a month, then placed in the kiln, the entry to which was partially closed; after a slow start, with low heat, the kiln was stoked with fuel and the stoke hole was closed, leaving only a couple of narrow vents for air. Temperatures up to 1400°C were reached, after which the stoke hole was opened and the fire allowed to die down. For reduced black wares the kiln was loaded with the vessels, dry wood and charcoal, and the stoke hole closed. Lighting by straw through one of the air vents allowed the firing to start, and then the air vents were almost totally closed. After five hours the fire box was filled with green wood, and then the stoke hole was closed while the air vents were opened to raise the temperature. After 7–10 hours all entries were closed and temperatures reached 1200–1400°C. The entire front of the kiln was sealed with sand and clay, and after a day the kiln could be emptied of its hard-fired black reduced wares.

Although much of this pottery is of a high quality, it inevitably suffers by comparison with wares from Greek and Roman civilizations, and from Egypt as well. Glossy but unglazed red pottery from Etruria has been experimentally produced by rubbing vessels with red ochre, burnishing with a pebble, and firing in a pit (MacIver, 1921). Egyptian black-topped ware was also produced by using iron-rich clay rubbed with red ochre and burnished. After drying, the pot was placed upside down with its rim buried in sawdust. After firing in oxidizing conditions, the red-bodied black-topped vessel emerged (MacIver, 1921; Lucas, 1962). Greek red and black wares, highly decorated with classical scenes, are also the result of firing in either oxidizing or reducing conditions, with black iron oxide colouring altering to red if oxidized, remaining black if reduced, and with illite clays producing the characteristic gloss and shine (Bimson, 1956).

These experiments do not by any means exhaust the range of work done on ancient pottery through analysis and replication, but they represent a sample of the quality and the care put into the investigations. It is not merely a question of an ability to reproduce wares of equivalent composi-tion and character, although this is important. The problem faced by many archaeologists over production yields and schedules, the distribution of wares, and the small-scale pottery and the major factory, cannot be answered by experiments alone but they do provide some clear hints and guides to these problems as well as suggesting further lines of pursuit. The fact that wares can be produced by particular methods today cannot be taken to signify that ancient wares were made in the same ways. Both ethnography and experimental archaeology demonstrate the range of possibilities.

In many parts of the world containers made of wood and bark supplemented or replaced vessels made of clay. In eastern North America, Indian containers made of birch bark were popular where the paper birch (*Betula papyrifera*) grew; by observation and by experiment, a simple container may be made in the following manner (Fig. 65, upper). Select clean white bark growing above the normal snow line, avoiding bark with black eyes (knots); following Indian tradition, do not eat the lumps in your corn mash on the day of the bark collection, as otherwise all the bark you find will have black eyes. Slice and peel the bark from the tree, then press it flat for several days; choose a single piece *c*. 90 cm long and 65 cm wide, fold 20 cm of the ends and sides upwards to leave a base 50 cm $\times$ 25 cm, turning the V-flaps of the corners inside the container at the ends; use a wooden pin or root to stitch the flaps to the ends of the container. The result of this extremely simple operation is a seamless and therefore waterproof vessel suitable for gathering maple sap during the season (p. 125); if a sugar camp had 900 "taps" in the trees, and each tap had two containers, one filling as the other was laid down ready for emptying, the camp would have nearly 2000 of these bark vessels, easily made and perfectly functional. Such containers could be used to cook food by dropping hot stones in the water, and even the flames of an open fire would not burn through the bark so long as the liquid level of the vessel lay above the top of the flames.

Bark objects such as these have only rarely survived from early times either in America or in Europe, although there are a few complete bark boxes of the Bronze Age from the tree-trunk coffins of Denmark (Thomsen, 1929). From the same coffins come the first collection of prehistoric clothing in all of Europe, consisting of both male and female costumes, preserved by the waterlogging conditions within the coffins and their mounds (Broholm and Hald, 1935, 1948). One of the garments was a short woollen jacket from Skrydstrup, Jutland, worn by a young woman; unlike the Tollund and Grauballe men (p. 125), she had not met death by execution; her long ash-blonde hair was held in place by a horse-hair neck, and she had gold rings at each ear. She was wrapped in a woollen cloth from waist to foot, held by a belt, and had cloth ankle-bindings and leather shoes. Beneath her body was a cow's hide, and the coffin contained plant remains of grass and wild chervil, showing that the burial of this 18-year-old took place in the early summer, about 3500 years ago. The jacket was made from a single piece of cloth cut on each side (Fig. 66); the lower part was folded and stitched together to make the tubular body of the garment. The upper part was folded back and the edges were joined to make the sleeves. A horizontal cut opened a space for the head. Of particular interest was the embroidery at the neck and the sleeves, and

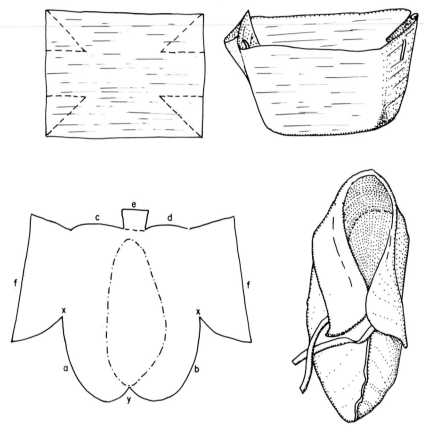

FIG. 65. *Upper.* A seamless waterproof birchbark container, 50 cm long, stitched at each end by a root, cord or twig pin. "A woman in good circumstances might have as many as 1200 to 1500 birchbark vessels, all of which would be in constant use during the season of sugar making." (W. J. Hoffman, *The Menomini Indians*, 1892–93.) Easily made in 5 minutes or so, these bark containers must have been in widespread use. (After Schneider, 1972.)

Lower. A Woodland Indian one-piece soft-soled moccasin (plan on left with imprint of foot). x – x = circumference of instep. The leather pattern is turned upside down, and edges a and b are stitched together, starting at x and ending at y. Edges c and d are stitched, e is folded inside and the moccasin is then turned inside out. A thong tie slips beneath the flaps f. (After Schneider, 1972.)

Hald's careful reconstructions, and experimental versions of the jacket made at Lejre, demonstrate the care and precision of this work. The outside parts of each sleeve were ornamented by a three-ply cord edging rectangular panels decorated with ribs raised by two-ply thread. The neck border was made by double stitching, the first a scallop stitch forming a network through which the second, a three-ply cord, was passed.

Each leather shoe consisted of a single square cut at the toe into narrow

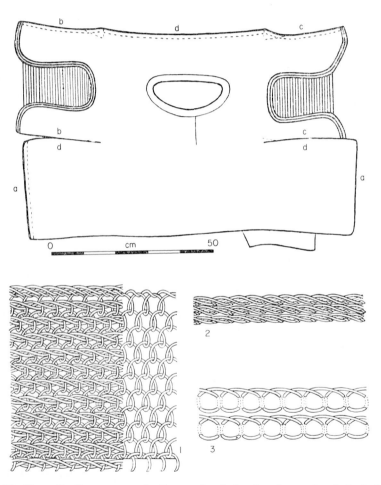

FIG. 66. *Upper.* Outline pattern of a Bronze Age jacket found on a female body in a tree-trunk coffin at Skrydstrup, Denmark; the garment was stitched together as indicated (a—d).

Lower. Detail of the embroidery at the neck (1), on the sleeve (2) and stitching of ribs on the sleeve (3).

(From Broholm and Hald, 1948.)

strips and held together by a shoelace laced on the instep after passing around the foot, the whole resembling a soft moccasin or ballet-shoe. Reconstructions of this shoe, and of North American Indian moccasins, demonstrate the simplicity and efficiency of the designs. As a comparison, a soft-soled shoe of Iroquois character was also made of a single piece of leather cut in a more detailed pattern (Fig. 65, lower), folded up and stitched along the instep and the heel, then turned inside out, and completed by thong laces under the flaps, crossing to tie at the heel (Schneider, 1972, p. 113).

Probably the leading centre for experimental work on ancient textiles is housed at Lejre, where over a decade of research has taken place (Fig. 67, left) (Hansen, 1977). Numbers of different weaving appliances have been made or imported, and investigations of plant colours and dyes have been particularly intensive. One of the major experiments concerned

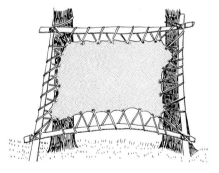

Fig. 67. *Left*. Experimental reconstruction of an Iron Age loom. The weft thread can be pushed up with fingers, comb or sword, to make varying degrees of tightness which match ancient cloths. The vertical loom, with its loom weights, must in fact have been slanted slightly to allow speed in weaving. (Historical–Archaeological Research Centre, Lejre.)

Right. A drying frame for preparing skins by fleshing with flint scrapers and notched bone tools (after Schneider, 1972).

a replica of a medieval gown found in a Norse cemetery in western Greenland, made on an upright warp-weighted loom. Other work has included
Bronze Age jackets of Skrydstrup type, although based upon another
find from Egtved in Jutland. A recent experiment has investigated the
methods of weaving a poncho of the Iron Age of Rønbjerg, Jutland. Many
Iron Age fragments have survived in wet graves in the north (e.g. Schlabow, 1976), but the poncho posed various problems, particularly in the
choice of loom. Both a horizontal loom and a round two-beamed loom
were tried, and both created difficulties in the weave of the garment. One
of the difficulties was the oblique character of the fabric, perhaps produced
when threads were inserted, as these pressed the weft aside and created
uneven tension when the fabric was released from the tension of the loom.
The insertion of extra threads, in the widening of the garment, was accomplished by pulling out certain loops of thread at the sides, and weaving
new threads into these for about 5 cm at both top and bottom. An irregu-
larity in the original cloth could not be copied at first, and upon further
examination of the poncho it could be seen that before the new threads
were inserted the weft had turned several times. All of these problems
have now been solved by three aspects of the work, the precise description
and drawn reconstruction of the garment, the experiment which brought
to light new items and queries, and the re-examination of the garment for
answers to new questions (Fig. 68).

Although other experiments with looms and weaving appliances have
taken place (e.g. Reynolds, 1972), and much is known about ancient textiles and the appliances used to produce cloth (e.g. Henshall, 1950; Wild,
1970), relatively little work has been carried out on plant colours except
at Lejre. For about ten years plant dyes have been investigated here; both
the identification of suitable plants and the methods of extracting, dying
and fixing the colours have been covered. Experiments have shown that
freshly cut plants are best, in weight about 3–4 times the weight of the
yarn to be dyed. Layers of yarns and plants are put in a clay pot with
water and boiled for about one hour; if the desired colour is achieved
before the hour is up, the yarn is removed and boiled for the remaining time in clear water. The soupy dye left in the original pot can be
strained and reused. The dyed yarn is cooled slowly and is not perfectly
fast, but the colours can range from browns, purples and greens to reds,
oranges and yellows. The use of alum (obtained from shale clays and loams
by roasting) is recommended for dying with most plants, which include
not only flowers and grasses, but also leaves and seeds.

The soft shoes on the young woman from Skrydstrup are not the only
surviving pieces of leather from prehistoric Europe. Skins and hides must
always have been valuable sources of material, and the earliest presumed

uses for which there is any evidence are as tents and windbreaks in late glacial Europe and Asia (e.g. Klein, 1969). Unfortunately, relatively few pieces of hide have actually survived, and of these only a few have been examined in detail and reconstructed experimentally. That hides were tanned with oak bark is now not in doubt, and possible tan-pits in Neolithic settlements have been identified (van de Velde, 1973). The processes of preparing and tanning skins and hides have been tested on various occasions. The skin is stretched on a frame and fleshed with a flint scraper or a toothed bone implement (Fig. 67, right). The hair is also removed; soaking and rinsing or burial in earth for several days will loosen it, and rubbing over a beam will work the hair out. Thereafter, curing of the skin with urine is supposed to have beneficial effects, but this is a debatable action according to recent trials. Tanning of the hide has been attempted in several ways. A North American Indian method involved deer brain, substituted by sheep brain in experiments, simmered in a pan of water and then mashed with fat added; the skin is dipped in this cooled mixture and

FIG. 68. Replica of a Danish Iron Age gown (A.D. 1–400), based upon burial finds of Denmark and iconographic and textual references. Tacitus' description: "The dress of the women differs from that of the men in two respects only: women often wear outer garments of linen ornamented with a purple pattern, and the upper part of these is sleeveless, leaving their whole arms and indeed the part of their breasts nearest the shoulder exposed." Precise details of the garments and the manner of wearing are not known, and this is only one of a number of attempts. (Historical–Archaeological Research Centre, Lejre.)

rubbed firmly to allow penetration, then left to soak. After wringing out, the skin is stretched on a frame and laced tight by cord passed through holes around the edges. It is scraped and shaved to a uniform thickness and then evenly stretched with a wooden flat rod over all the surface until the skin is supple, soft and completely dry. Otherwise, re-braining is necessary. The next step is to smoke the skin; it is suspended over a pit filled with green wood and bark, cones or corncobs, producing smoke and not fire, so that the skin is permeated. Turning is essential to allow even absorption, and the length of time will determine the colour of the skin, 3–4 hours for dark, one hour for orange. This completes the process, and the skin will not rot, and will retain its softness even after it dries from a prolonged soaking in rain or river; its pungent aroma will gradually fade, although experimenters are warned not to leave the skin around: "The skin is really smoked animal tissue and may seem to a dog to be nothing more than a flat summer sausage." (Schneider, 1969, p. 82.) A more common method of tanning hides was to soak them in pits with layers of oak bark (Reed, 1973, pp. 72–85), and the practice is attested from many areas of the Old World, including Egypt, Mesopotamia, Greece and much of the Roman Empire. Skins were fleshed and dehaired by beating, treading, stretching and beaming. Tanning was with alum, oak galls, oak bark, nuts and berries. A defensive shield of the Bronze Age in Ireland was made of vegetable-tanned oxhide, and the earlier possible tan-pits in north western Europe have already been noted. Little experimental work has been done on ancient leather, partly because the processes of preparation and tanning were quite likely to be identical to those used today in some regions and historically known in others.

Several replicas of the Bronze Age Irish shield were made, not, however, to test the tanning process but to examine the manufacturing necessities, and to produce shields for defensive actions (Coles, 1962). The leathers were soaked to make them supple, then beaten into wooden formers copied from Bronze Age examples (Fig. 69); in this way, the central boss and strengthening ribs were easily shaped. Drying and slight shrinkage of the shield took place for about three days, with the ribs and boss beaten back into the mould every four hours. A stout handle of folded leather was stitched behind the boss, and the shield was complete. In tests against a bronze sword it resisted well, bending slightly to absorb each blow and stab. This was in contrast to the uselessness of a sheet copper shield tested in the same way (p. 180). However, in a rainstorm, the leather shield would have softened and slumped over the warrior's arm, a disconcerting event at the best of times, and in a fight probably disastrous. The Bronze Age shields must have been hardened somehow, and experiments with hot water dips, hot oven roasts, and hot wax baths showed that wet heat

Fig. 69. Manufacture of a leather shield of Bronze Age type.

Upper. After a cold water soak, the piece is scrubbed to remove excess tannin then beaten into a wooden mould or former in order to produce the central boss and ribs that strengthen the shield.

Lower. The imprinted pattern can be seen on the shield which is still soft and flexible. Drying on the mould, and then hardening with heat, completes the process.

(Photos: L. P. Morley.)

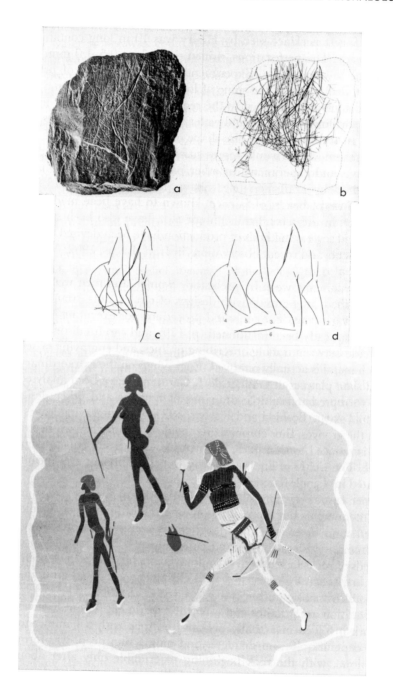

deep and 100 mm wide, pecked and then ground, and the much larger engravings of ships and animals clearly involved much effort. Some designs have only been outlined by pecking, while others have been deeply ground, the whole artistic tradition representing many man-hours of devotion to the concept.

The same can be said about the multitude of paintings on rock which, often associated with engravings, have been found and are still being discovered in many parts of the world. Among the most prominent groups of these rock paintings are the Late Glacial art of western Europe (e.g. Leroi-Gourhan, 1968), the Bushmen paintings of southern Africa (Fig. 70, lower) (e.g. Rudner and Rudner, 1970), the art of Australian aborigines (e.g. Berndt, 1964) and American Indian art (e.g. Grant, 1967). In most cases the paints used were broadly similar; they included iron oxides (ochres) for red, orange and brown, limmite or yellow ochre, gypsum white, blood red, burnt bone carbon black, copper ores for rare greens and blues. The medium used with these paints, to allow it to flow and spread, is generally considered to be animal fats, blood, egg white and vegetable oils. Analysis of some African paints has indicated that animal fats were not used in the samples tested, and that blood or blood serum was preferred to egg or vegetable liquids. In 1849, however, the explorer Thomas Baines viewed Bushmen paintings on the Baviaans river and was informed that the artists had been seen at work there:

they mix red, yellow and white clay or charcoal and a black stone finely powdered with fat, and with pencils formed of variously sized feathers imitate on the flat rocks about their dwellings the various animals of the country.

Kennedy, 1961

An experiment set out to test the nature of the pigments used in the art, and employed local pigments and various media of fat, plant juices, animal droppings, honey and egg tempera; only the egg allowed fine thin lines to be painted, as all the others created paste or patches of colour (Johnson, 1957). We do not know if this result can be applied to other areas in south Africa or elsewhere in the world. In other respects, experiments can do little to help us understand the meanings behind the art, and most other

---

FIG. 70. *Upper.* Engraving on a slate plaque of *c.* 10000 B.C. at Gönnersdorf, Germany. a, The plaque as found; b, all scratches drawn; c, major scratches extracted, interpreted as outlines of female humans on the basis of more complete representations elsewhere; d, designs separated. (From Bosinski and Fischer, 1974.)

Lower. The "White Lady" of Tsisab ravine, Brandberg, South Africa, a painting in browns, reds and white. The "lady" is actually a man. (From Rudner and Rudner, 1970.)

archaeological approaches are equally unsuitable in dealing with the belief, religion, dreams and hopes of the many prehistoric groups who have left their inward identities in paintings and engravings. The opportunities to observe and to maintain the rights of pre-industrial peoples to expressions of their own beliefs were lost long ago, before anthropologists and ethnographers were aware of the urgent need to record, to understand, and perhaps to help. The same can be said of ancient musical instruments.

It seems like a messenger from quite another culture, more developed, finer, as from a people whose taste for the beautiful was of such a pitch that it tried to realize it not only visually, but also audibly.

Hammerich, 1893

These words, describing the experimental results of tests on Bronze Age horns of Scandinavia, have often been dismissed as entirely too romantic and unscientific, but they reflected a genuine attempt to view prehistoric musical instruments as a distinct and separate class of artifact able to add a new dimension to our thoughts about extinct societies. Like ancient paintings and engravings, musical instruments can tell us of characteristics, materials and techniques, but they can go little further, as the ceremonies and occasions for which they were designed are lost as surely as sounds die today. What studies of musical instruments can do, however, is to point to the potential range, volume and character of the notes, and knowledge of these can go some way in our attempts to understand the reasons for their existence.

The most famous ancient musical instrument in the world, and perhaps the best known of any single instrument of any age, is the silver trumpet (one of a pair) of the pharoah Tutankamun who ruled Egypt in the fourteenth century B.C. (Fig. 71, left). The discovery of the pharaoh's tomb in 1926 was an unparalleled event in the world of archaeology, but it was not until 1939 that the first radio broadcast of the trumpets was arranged in Cairo. The trumpets, of copper and silver, are in reality rather feeble instruments, short and with poorly devised mouthpieces. For the broadcast, Bandsman James Tappern of the 11th Hussars was ordered to the museum to perform upon the trumpets; on arrival he realized at once that he would be able to produce much noise but little music. The publication of these finds had included the description "wrapped in reeds, . . . a silver trumpet, which, though tarnished with age, were it blown would still fill the Valley with a resounding blast" (Carter, 1923–33, vol. II, p. 30). Bandsman Tappern was resourceful enough to indeed fill the Valley, and households around the world, with a resounding blast, and his "trumpet voluntary" has perpetuated the myth of the young king's marvellous trumpets. What was not announced at the time, and never fully publicized (Kirby, 1946), was the fact that a modern metal trumpet mouthpiece had been inserted into the instrument, and this guaranteed a virtuoso performance even if Tappern had been playing a piece of brass pipe, or a garden hose. The contribution of this event was not therefore in its reliability and objectivity, but in its wide publicity for archaeology in general and experimental archaeology in particular. It seems a bit ironic that the first public expression of the experimental approach should have been so misleading.

VIII   *Altra Tromba piegata antica*

Fig. 71. *Left.* The trumpet of Tutankamun, of bronze or copper with gold overlay, the bell decorated with figures of the king and three gods. Length of instrument 49·4 cm. (From Carter, 1923–33, vol. II.)

Right. Representation of a Roman *cornu* with supporting crossbar which helps balance the instrument on the shoulder of the musician. The horn is over 3 m long. Modern copies of the *cornu* can yield over ten musical notes. (From Bonanni, 1723.)

Other ancient instruments had already been tested by this time, and some were quite well known. The Danish *lurer* had been blown from time to time for a century, and Dr Ball of Dublin had passed away from his exertions with the Irish horns 75 years previously (p. 14). Bone pipes of great antiquity, 30 000 years, were known (Megaw, 1960), and the stringed instruments of Ur, 4500 years old, had been miraculously recognized and their shapes retrieved by pouring plaster into the voids left by their decay (Woolley, 1934). The lyres found in the burial chambers at Ur were of wood cased or decorated with silver or gold, and precious stones. A Sumerian epic, describing a descent to the lower world, contains references to the lyre itself:

> O Father Nanna, let not thy daughter be put to death in the nether world,
> Let not thy good metal be covered with the dust of the nether world,
> Let not thy good lapis-lazuli be broken up into the stone of the stoneworker.
> Let not thy boxwood be cut up into the wood of the woodworker,
> Let not the maid Innana be put to death in the nether world.

Many other instruments, or fragments, were also recovered from Ur and from many other sites, so that today the range of musicological studies can encompass almost all of the types of instrument in the modern orchestra, drawing upon finds from the Old and New Worlds (e.g. Megaw, 1968; Rimmer, 1969; Salmen, 1970; Klar, 1971; Hammond, 1972; Lund, 1973). One of the early Spanish chronicles, Torquemada, said of Mexican societies: "Not in all the Kingdom of Christendom are there as many flutes, oboes, sackbuts, trumpets, horns and drums as in this land." And many other early communities, probably possessed numbers and varieties approaching this. Because all of these are instruments for music, almost all have been blown, struck, plucked, or whatever seems appropriate, and the experimental testing has continued in some cases with the manufacture of replicas. No one has yet copied, however, the legendary horn of Alexander the Great, 5 cubits across, transported by 60 men, and with a range of 100 stadia (111 km).

Although surviving instruments and copies can be made to yield notes, we cannot know their sequence, their volumes, or the occasions upon which they were played. In a prehistoric society this information is unrecorded, and even in societies with written records it may not be possible to recognize musical notation. The earliest known musical composition which has survived is a score for words and music on a clay tablet at Ugarit (Ras Shamra), Syria, about 3500 years old. This has been transcribed and played upon an 11-string lyre of Sumerian type, apparently producing a "monophonous melody with a delicate Oriental redolence", a description which perhaps sounds better than the tune. The Spanish chroniclers described some of the Postclassic Mayan music as "sad and horrible sounds, frightening just to hear", and Polybius, writing of Celtic and Roman conflicts, was equally unimpressed with the instruments of the Celtic adversaries which "made a clamour so terrible and so loud, that every surrounding echo was awakened, and all the adjacent country seemed to join in the horrible din". Perhaps fortunately, none of the Celtic *carnyx* has survived to assail our ears (p. 13), but other Celtic horns from Ireland have proved by experiment to be sonorous and responsive (Coles, 1973, p. 164).

Because they were made of bronze, the lip-reed instruments have often survived. Tutankamun's trumpet may be the best known, but the earliest discovered were Bronze Age and Iron Age horns from Denmark and Ireland, recovered and still surviving after 200 years of private and public collections (Coles, 1963). Quite remarkable. The early tests on these included the fatal experiment for Dr Ball, and public performances in Copenhagen (p. 13). The Irish bronze horns, both end-blow and side-blow types (Fig. 6), make little provision for assisted mouthpieces, and experiments have subsequently suffered because of the reluctance of the blowers to accept cut lips, but even so we can say that musically these instruments are quite restricted, and provide no evidence for deliberate tuning or playing in concert. The 24 horns and 48 metal rattles from one site, in central Ireland, would create a cacophony unacceptable even to most modern musicians.

Of the abundant evidence for horns and trumpets for other areas and times, the tragedy is that few have survived for testing. Roman and Greek instruments have rarely been preserved, although representations suggest that Roman horns such as the *cornu* (Fig. 71, right) and the *lituus* would have been powerful instruments; experimental copies, based on fragments and representations, have yielded the amazing total of 17 notes when blown by a highly competent lip-reed musician, and a few actual *litui* can produce up to six notes (Klar, 1971). Perhaps the most spectacular horns of all are the Bronze Age *lurer* from Denmark and neighbouring areas of northern Europe (Fig. 72); about 50 of these have survived (Broholm *et al.*, 1949). They represent the most complicated metal work technology in Bronze Age Europe, cast in segments and then joined together to make evenly conical instruments up to two metres long, curved and twisted in matching but opposed pairs, in emulation of their origin in paired animal horns. As musical instruments the *lurer* are very impressive, yielding up to 16 notes by professional musicians, but perhaps 7–9 notes by competent Bronze Age players. Of course we do not know how competent prehistoric musicians were, how they organized their music or their occasions, how venerated their instruments were, and why their skills eventually were discarded and the instruments abandoned. For many groups of instruments in the Old and New Worlds, we can see from the archaeological record that drums, horns and pipes were important in battles now forgotten, in ceremonies now unknown, and in the lives of communities now extinct. Experiments can demonstrate the devotion and skill of craftsmen and musicians in producing and playing the multitude of instruments that existed in almost all known societies in the world. By testing these products, through analysis and experiment, we can hear some of the voices of the past, but alas we cannot understand the language.

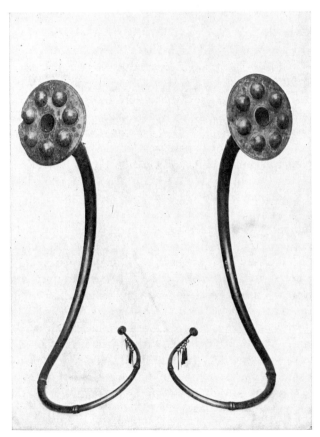

FIG. 72. Two matching *lurer* or horns from Brudevaelte, Denmark, *c.* 800 B.C.; a total of six *lurer* were recovered from this site, with their mouthpieces "killed". The instruments as restored are capable of yielding a wide range of musical notes, and presumably were played on ceremonial occasions. (National Museum, Copenhagen.)

6   Life and Death

...they retire themselves for three or foure moneths in the
yeere into the woods, where they make little cotages of Palme
boughes for their retraite and live there of Maste, of Fish which
they take, of Oisters, of Stagges, of Turkey cockes, and other
beasts which they take. They eate all their meate broyled on the
coales, and dressed in the smoake...

Laudonniere, 1586

Perhaps the ultimate step, the ultimate experiment in living
archaeology, is to become a prehistoric individual for a time and
live entirely on what you can get from the wilderness.

Pfeiffer, 1969, p. 367

ARCHAEOLOGISTS are always reaching for ways to obtain and study data
about early societies, societies now extinct whose "life-ways" may be
known only from the settlements, cemeteries and artifacts which have
survived. We know from ethnographic observations, and from ancient sites
that have been waterlogged or desiccated, that a large proportion of the
materials used by pre-industrial societies were of organic origin, plant and
animal, and that stone and metal probably formed only a small, but
important, part of the whole assemblages. We also know that neither
settlements and cemeteries nor tools made of stone, bone, wood and metal
represent all of the activities undertaken by communities; many actions
need no structures and no objects. Sleeping, eating, procreating, walking
are but four universal activities which require little artificial assistance,
and which can leave no trace at all. It is axiomatic that the habits, customs
and traditions of early people cannot be wholly recreated by studies of
material culture alone. Even so, efforts are constantly being made to gain
further insights into ancient behaviour through sophisticated analytical
and predictive techniques, and through physical experiments outside the
laboratories and libraries. It is these last that we will look at here, the
attempts to recreate conditions of the past and to experience some of the
activities and effects of behaviour. In this way, archaeologists hope to
glimpse some of the constraints and encouragements that influenced the

patterns of life of ancient man. This approach, experimental and conjectural, is often dismissed as non-scientific, non-useful, and a total waste
of time. It is clearly none of these, but it is not the ultimate step either.
There is no way on this earth that an archaeologist or anyone else can
become a prehistoric individual, and no amount of skill in primitive living,
in survival courses, and in ancient technologies can recreate the patterns of
behaviour now extinguished. It is not possible to "live in the past". The
serious attempts to simulate ancient activities make this point very clear:

> It is doubtful if accurate reconstruction of a sizeable portion of the way of
> life . . . can ever be effected. But light can be shed, with a greater or lesser degree
> of accuracy, on some aspects; from these, other aspects may be intelligently
> surmised, probably with a decreasing degree of accuracy.
>
> Callahan, 1974, p. 101

The aims, then, are not for total retrieval of information; instead they are
for a greater understanding of data already available, and for an insight
into other behaviour the traces of which may be too faint to decipher.
Greater aims, and claims, are beyond realization.

There have been numerous attempts to recreate ancient settlements and
factory sites, some short-lived and unstructured, others longer-termed and
highly organized. Many of these experiments have taken place in America,
often as student training courses from universities and colleges, but others
have been based in Europe and elsewhere. All have involved the participants in actually experiencing the indignities, real and imagined, of living
rough, working in unfamiliar ways, gathering and eating strange foods,
and being totally isolated from their own cultural environment; for some
experimenters, the last of these has posed the greatest problem of all.

In summer 1973 a group of students undertook what was at the time one
of the most ambitious experiments, to recreate a basalt and obsidian
quarry workshop and camp in Coconino county, Arizona (Callahan,
1974). The aims of the project were to locate and describe the prehistoric
quarries which had existed there over 2000 years ago, to make replicas of
the stone tools found at the sites, and to use these tools and others to establish and maintain a work camp under hunter–gatherer conditions. The
student participants were trained for six weeks in lithic technology, pot
making, basketry, plant recognition, and general experimental and camping procedures. Each prepared his or her own bedding, tools, dried food
and other appropriate equipment and carried it into the camping area.
Shelters were made from drooping juniper branches supplemented by
extra timbers and foliage, to create enclosed spaces each capable of housing
and sleeping 3–5 persons (Fig. 73). After quite severe problems at the
beginning, the surviving team of nine (14 had started the course) settled

into the routine of quarrying, collecting and flaking basalt (Fig. 74), gathering plants and testing other ideas or equipment. Meals often consisted of pounded jerky stew, fresh greens of *Rumex* (curly dock) and *Chenopodium* (lamb's quarters), rice or corn, pinole bread and nuts, berries and seeds. Cooking in rock pools with hot stones was easy and successful, and stone, wood and clay artifacts were manufactured and used in the variety of activities on and off site. The major problems encountered, and mostly overcome or ignored, were "culture shock" both on arrival at camp and on the return to "civilization", the heat, scarcity of drinking water, the consumption of unusual foods, flies, and the uneven terrain and low trees which necessitated unaccustomed muscle movements. Nonetheless, no participants suffered any lasting ill-effects, and most acknowledged that greater physical preparation, and understanding of

FIG. 73. A rough shelter made from juniper branches and low trees, to house student members of an expedition working at an obsidian and basalt quarry in Arizona (drawn by R. Walker, after a photo by E. Callahan, 1974).

FIG. 74. Detaching basalt lumps with antler picks and hammers, Arizona (photo: E. Callahan).

possible problems, would have helped in the adjustment to new conditions.

Subsequent experiments did not neglect these results, and in 1974 and 1975 a highly organized and well controlled project was again undertaken by E. Callahan on the Pamunkey River, near Richmond, Virginia (Callahan, 1976). Two archaeological sites of Middle Woodland character (c. A.D. 1000) were chosen as models for the experiment; one was the Island Field cemetery on Delaware Bay (Thomas and Warren, 1970) which has yielded 100 burials and quantities of associated lithic material. According to the evidence from this site, supplemented by that from many others, the original inhabitants were hunters and gatherers; corn, beans and squash may have been cultivated. Hunting with bow and arrow, as well as with *atlatl* and spear, yielded deer, beaver, fox and various birds. Harpooning and line fishing were practised, and fish nets and weirs may have been in use. Shells of oyster, clam and whelk were valuable exports, and perhaps helped bring in stone for an extensive lithic technology. Large bifacially flaked points were probably produced at the site, although some may have been received in fully finished state. The rarity of pottery at Island Field is a contrast to the other model site, Accokeek Creek, on the Potomac River, Maryland (Stephenson *et al.*, 1963). The site is now within Piscataway Park, named after one of the Indian tribes which occupied the Creek. One of the latest Indian settlements here, in a defended village, was recorded by Captain John Smith in 1608 (Arber, 1910). Susquehannock Indians occupied the site in historic times, and the eventual and seemingly inevitable betrayal of the Indians, and their extermination, is a sorry chapter in the continuous archaeological record of human activity. The Middle Woodland period here, c. A.D. 1000, is represented by abundant pottery from the settlement, although few traces of houses survived the later periods of occupation. The combination of the evidence from the Island Field and Accokeek Creek sites thus provided complementary views of the Middle Woodland episode, and this was the basis for the experiment in living archaeology in 1974 and 1975; that it did not continue beyond these dates is unfortunate.

The aims of the Pamunkey Project were to create and record a series of replicas of the material culture of the Middle Woodland period, using tools, supplies and technologies relevant to the time, as well as inferential equipment deduced by necessity. Single objects could of course be copied in the laboratory, but it was felt that variables introduced by field conditions might well affect even direct copies, and could suggest other forms of approach and other equipment which had not survived at all. These replications of known and inferred artifacts were then to be used in an environmental situation approximating as closely as possible to the original. A seasonal camp was to be established, the occupants working as hunters and gatherers, planting crops where possible, but in all cases depending upon the fabricated equipment for all facets of their existence. The suitability of the tools and weapons was to be under continuous assessment, both as individual pieces and as parts of a whole interrelated set of artifacts upon which the community depended. These aims seem entirely reasonable and appropriate, although they did not at first make provision for idiosyncratic behaviour on the part of individual makers and users. What is important is that interest extended beyond single technologies, artifact-types, or settlement components; instead, the relationship between artifacts, activities and environments was to be examined. What was not attempted is as important:

> We had no interest whatsoever in simply "playing Indian" or "survival" as some have accused us. Yes, we did live like Indians and yes, we did manage to survive, and rather well at that under Indian-like conditions. But we were careful not to allow ourselves to think that we really were living in the past or that we were ... resurrecting the past.
>
> Callahan, 1976, p. 4

The differences between experiments designed to test the methods of ancient seasonal or permanent subsistence and those testing survival practices are fundamental here. Survival signifies an impermanent situation, under stress through conflict, disability, starvation or abrupt cultural changes, and in the circumstances no effort is made to plan for the future, but only for an immediate solution to the problem. In most situations in the past, stress of this kind was unlikely, judged by the archaeological record, historic records, and ethnographic observations. Instead, communities were more interested in long-term problems and their solutions, in annual or seasonal rounds of gathering, hunting or farming, in acquiring bulks of raw material for future use, and in providing permanent shelters and social organizations that could allow them to develop and retain an identity. Experiments in survival have, of course, often taken place, sometimes under real emergency conditions, but in a real test of survival no living archaeologist can pretend to be other than what he is, a human being fighting for his life with whatever he can devise and use; in any other assumed circumstance, the theoretical base of the experiment is self-defeating.

The Pamunkey Project took place in two separate phases. The first of these, in the summer of 1974, involved the eight participants in a month-long occupation beside the Pamunkey river. The camp was placed in a beech wood within easy reach of ravines, open fields, swampland, and a wide river, with tidal waters rising about one metre several times a day. In a situation such as this, the plant and animal resources were quite remarkable as will be described. The team of students had undergone individual training for fitness for some time prior to an intensive two-week session when technologies for lithic material, wood, clay, plants and animals were absorbed. Supplies of all these were readily available at the site, other than silicified slate, a tonne of which was quarried in North Carolina and imported to Pamunkey. The original artifacts for the Island Field site were analysed for types and technology, and at Pamunkey copies of the original artifacts were made and used under field conditions. Food supplies were based, as far as possible, upon local resources and both plants and animals were consumed; many varieties of leafy plants, roots, tubers, inner bark, nuts, berries and flowers required only minor supplements from garden corn and squash. Shellfish were regularly collected, and frogs, turtles, eggs and several snakes were also put into the pot.

One of the major tasks was the construction of a substantial shelter about 6 m in diameter. This was made entirely of fallen or dead sweetgum and hickory, prepared with stone axes and flakes; the 74 poles used in the hut were fastened with over 700 metres of hickory and elm bark cordage into a domed solid structure thatched with 288 bundles of sweet flag rushes. Various openings were left to allow easy access and adequate light for working during the summer rains. Cooking was done in pointed base pots made of local clays, and in pit-ovens. During the month, almost 700 tools were made, and documented before, during and after use; wear patterns were a particular interest. The data cards devised for this record provided for records of size, shape, primary and secondary scars, edge angles, hafting, wear, efficiency, maker and user, time and motion notes; all these provided data for subsequent research reports, some of which pointed out the possible confusions about interpreting wear marks (p. 165), as well as agreeing with other experimenters that "no amount of numerical manipulation can produce the understanding of tool use which comes with the direct experience with manufacturing, handling and close examination of replicas" (Adovasio et al., 1974, p. 87). The gathering and hunting activities were also closely monitored and assessed. Bows and arrows of the Middle Woodland period are known to have existed, but only arrowheads of stone have survived, so the equipment was made to conform with general, not specific, Indian traditions. By much practice a measure of accuracy was achieved, and various hunting expeditions were held in order to test both weapons and techniques of stalking. No animal was killed at all, although many were sighted and approached. A woodchuck was ambushed and shot from only two metres but the arrow merely bounced off the back of the animal's skull; the necessity to fully draw the bow, and shoot for softer parts, was duly recorded. Another hunt resulted in a successful stalking of a rabbit from 20 m to less than one metre in gathering gloom; the final grasp with the hands found only air. Nonetheless, the experience gained in hunting methods was invaluable for the subsequent phase of the Pamunkey Project.

Pot-making and cooking were more domestic activities, and here some sexual division of the group was seen; although equal sharing of all tasks was intended, the men generally undertook the most strenuous tasks, chopping wood, digging holes, driving posts. The women took on some of the other work, including pot-making, not by design but by results, as their pots were more successful. Local clays were used for the vessels which were mostly made by the coil method, before drying and firing. Many pots were broken in use, through too-rapid alteration of heat or by inadequate handling when full. Cooking seems also to have been a woman's task on the site, and some surprising dishes were devised, including blacksnake steak, mussel stew, and sumac berry brew. "In addition, during work, some of our women tended to communicate verbally with one another without ceasing and to laugh a lot. Both are necessary to congenial social interaction, of course—at least among the participating group. But these very actions tended to reduce concentration and to lower the rate of production." There is no need to state the sex of the commentator.

After the first phase of the project had been completed, the site and its debris were recorded before abandonment. After 3, 6 and 9 months, the changes in the house, the midden and the tramped areas were carefully noted. One year after abandonment, phase 2 began. The team consisted of seven members, of whom two had already participated in phase 1. The training included the usual technologies for stone, clay, bone, shell, wood and basketry (e.g. Fig. 75); hundreds of tools were prepared for use and recorded on data cards. A careful analysis of the lithic material recovered from the Island Field site provided guides to the preparation of the stone tools. In addition, physical training was intensive, as one of the potential participants recorded enthusiastically:

I had no idea what it would be like, but looking back I think of it as something like an army training track. The beginning was charming: we had to float down a river sitting in inflated tubes. After disembarkation we were blindfolded and guided through forest and over hills until we came before a fence fifteen feet tall. It was intended as an exercise for the team to climb over. Behind the fence, nine tree trunks were dug into the earth perpendicularly, at different distances, and we had to jump from stem to stem like goats. It takes a tiger right behind you to do this exercise well. Then followed a test of individual's trapezist skills, through the tops of trees, creeping over swaying tyres, balancing over swinging beams, rushing down to a lower level, hanging on a pulley . . . Exhausted, you have to climb a 75 foot rock and go back the same way in ropes. If you have plowed your way through this mound of tortures you are allowed to go with your team to the land of Cockaigne, called Pamunkey. There is an Indian hut with a half-finished roof here, and when you've been lying on the soil during the first night of pouring rain wet as a drowned cat, you think: this is too much ...

The writer was aged 71, and the inspiration of a similar experiment in Holland (p. 223).

FIG. 75. Personal equipment for one of the participants in a "living archaeology" experiment, Arizona. Among the implements are flint blades and points, bone and horn picks and throwing sticks, cordage, and woven matting, all produced by the experimenters. (Photo: E. Callahan.)

The camp at Pamunkey was reoccupied, the roof of the hut repaired, and adaptation of routines made to overcome the difficulty caused by incessant rain. The emphasis was on maintaining the settlement rather than on a new construction. Hunting, trapping, fishing, mussel collecting, gathering of plants and animals, and gardening of gourds and corn formed the major activities. In addition a woven fish weir was built across a high-tide lagoon; poles were driven into the muds, and branches woven to create a barrier to large fish except through a narrow funnel opening at low tide, when the width of the lagoon was only one metre. At high tide, the fish could swim over the weir and the waters extended over 30 m across the lagoon.

The rainfall was excessive by any standards, with up to 10 cm per night. The fires were maintained except in the heaviest downpours, but wet wood, clothes and equipment gradually caused the decline and then abandonment of hunting, trapping and fishing; the fish weir was destroyed. When dampness began to penetrate the data cards and cameras, and when almost all activity on site had come to a standstill, the project was temporarily abandoned for 4 days to allow drying of gear and re-thinking of objectives. During this absence, the hut collapsed through the weight of water on the thatch because poles used in the construction were inadequate; the sweetgum poles were soft and had rotted in one year, whereas hickory or cedar would have lasted from 3–10 years. Upon returning to the site, the team put up a tipi and enjoyed dry weather until the end of the period. The various activities were resumed. Daily tasks consisted of maintaining the water supply, acquisition of food, general preparation of food, gathering of fuel, cooking the main meal, and dish-washing. Group activities, such as building the weir, making a path, repairing the hut roof, were suspended for the final part of the occupation. Individual projects included hunting with bow and arrow, manufacture and use of bone tools, trapping, fishing, working with shells, and potting. Gathering activities took up to 3 or 4 hours a day, using antler digging tools, reed baskets and stone knives to collect a large variety of foods from a 1-km radius around the camp. Berries, seeds, leaves and nuts were gathered. Crops of pumpkin, beans, squash, maize and gourds provided a major portion of the food. These had been planted earlier in the summer with antler digging "sticks", the traditional corn moulds being built up artificially. Under normal circumstances, corn tends to raise the soil around its roots and over a period will create a very humpy ground (p. 105). Due to a misunderstanding with the landowner, the field was subsequently fertilized commercially, effectively destroying all the plants except the maize but this yielded a successful crop.

Hunting of wild animals with bow and arrow was not successful in the number of kills (none) but stalking methods were devised and tested, and the quite important effects of dampness on arrow glue and binding were assessed; animal glue made of boiled rawhide, and cow gut bindings, tended to slacken when damp. Ishi, the Californian Indian (p. 169) used pine resin which is not soluble, although it is brittle, and he apparently rarely shot while there was dampness in the air. Trapping with snares yielded one animal, a ground hog, but another was run down and dis-patched with a wooden club. Mussels were abundant in the river, and were easily gathered. Blacksnakes were occasionally caught, one with delicious eggs inside. All of these animals provided valuable meat, but some others were lost due to careless handling or neglect; these losses were keenly felt. Fishing with line and bone hooks, harpoons and fish traps was in general unsuccessful but no real concerted effort was made in this potentially productive exercise; the failure of the fish weir was spectacular and regrettable. Basket fishing, in which shoals of minnows were directed by shadows and splashing to an exit guarded by a reed basket, was successful and seemed an easy way of acquiring "hors d'oeuvres". Overall, the potential yield of fish food was considerable, and would certainly have allowed a greater concentration of population here in a tidal area than would be possible elsewhere, either away from the river or adjacent to it upstream.

Most of the food cooked at Pamunkey was roasted in the hearth or boiled in clay pots, although much raw food was also eaten. The variety of foods prevented more boredom. Over the whole experiment, fresh corn formed about 25 per cent of the food, dried grains of corn, sunflower seeds, rice and nut meal made up another 25 per cent, and raw plants such as leaves, berries, roots were about 20 per cent. Cooked wild plants, rice, soft seeds and various herbs made another 20 per cent, leaving only 10 per cent for meat of all kinds. Some of the foodstuffs were imported, but these were reasonable alternatives to home-grown corn, squash and other crops, and to hunted and fished meat. Many of the dishes were improvised, but a typical dinner was roasted acorn squash, succotash of beans and corn, cooked apples, watermelon and pumpkin seed bread with walnuts, currants and blackberries. Alternative dishes included boiled blacksnake with its eggs, or roasted woodchuck, or a fish soup made of rice, grubworm, dried fish, mussels, lily roots, ears of corn, seeds, hog gut and poke weed.

Throughout all of the activities, emphasis was placed upon the utilization and wear of lithic tools, and the documentation of this must have occupied much time during the experiment and subsequently. Even with constant attention to these valuable relics, some were misplaced and lost, and a few subsequently reappeared in unexpected places. Of about 900 artifacts of all materials, over 100 were broken or lost. After the field experiment had ended, records were assessed and reports written on all of these aspects, as well as general reports on research projects, and overall statements on the project as a whole. The last are remarkably free of comments about the social organization, leadership and personal conflicts of opinion; lacking these, the publications of the Pamunkey Project doubtless leave much unsaid, and provide a welcome change from many "living archaeology" experiments which misguidedly set out to examine just these aspects.

A useful follow-up to the project's phase 1 had been the return to the site (for phase 2) after 12 months; the traces of activity were still much in evidence and could be interpreted correctly by non-participants. Following phase 2, further occupation was planned and the site was marked off to avoid accidental disturbance by local farmers. After 3 months, however, the garden had been ploughed again, and surveyor's marks signified impending destruction; within 6 months of the termination of phase 2, the whole site had been bulldozed, and soon afterwards the project's organizer reported:

> House erected over site...Front yard, formerly the heart of our camp, now levelled and ready to grow grass. Lumber, trash, and other "improvements" all about. But to the knowing eye, a few evidences of our occupation are seen: our shell midden, some pot sherds, our trail to the dishwashing area with sherds in the mud beneath, the remains of our fish weir in the lagoon, the spirit...All in all, the new owners have been quite successful at erasing any sign that we ever had been there. The wonder of modern technology.
>
> Callahan, 1976, p. 255

Perhaps the aboriginal peoples in America, Africa and Asia could have said the same thing, and it is surely ironic that the white man's attempt to recreate an Indian site, the ancestor of which he had destroyed in the first place, should itself have been destroyed by the same forces of "progress".

It will be clear from this very abbreviated account of the Pamunkey Project that important experimental concepts were at stake. The idea that we can recreate the life styles of the past is totally misguided, and the project made no attempt at this. Instead, it directed attention to subsistence technologies, and particularly to the tools used in the acquisition and preparation of land, shelter and food. The effect was a series of studies into different aspects of technology, which could have been conducted separately in either field or laboratory. With either of these approaches, however, the divorce of material from its place in a particular pattern of existence must give its subsequent interpretation one more variable, which it can ill afford to have; there are enough variables and uncertainties in experiments as it is. The Pamunkey Project was, in essence, not "living archaeology" at all, but was a well-constructed experiment in the technologies of a particular cultural group at a defined time and place in its life. As such, and even with the sequence of misfortunes beyond control, the project must be judged a success, both in its practical achievements and in its establishment of concepts for the future.

It is satisfying to know that after a year's delay, the Pamunkey Project was revived by the Catholic University of America and the Pamunkey Indian Nation in 1977; a site was offered in Tidewater, Virginia, on the Pamunkey Indian Reservation, for the construction of a late Woodland village.

The Pamunkey Tribe was the major tribe of the Powhatan Confederacy united by Chief Powhatan in the mid-fifteenth century. In 1607 contact with white settlers was made and the Powhatan were instrumental in saving the first colonists at Jamestown from starvation induced by a series of severe winters. Pocahontas, who saved the life of Captain John Smith, was the daughter of Powhatan. By 1640 the Confederacy had been destroyed by the settlers, and the Pamunkey Indian Reservation now occupies only *c*. 400 ha beside the Pamunkey river, with a very low population. The aims of the Pamunkey Research Center are to conduct archaeological and botanical studies, to collect evidence about Virginia Indian groups, to carry out experiments dealing with aboriginal equipment of all kinds, to help develop the Pamunkey Indian Museum, and to initiate research into the past history of the Powhatan. One of the major undertakings is the establishment of a Pamunkey Indian village, set at a specific phase in its development *c*. 1600 A.D. The village lies adjacent to the Research Center, sheltered by woods and hedgerows; the village will consist of a series of homesteads and associated garden plots, with a central assembly area and communal hearth. The first three houses have been built on different principles; all are longhouses, with maximum sizes of *c*. 9 × 3·7 m, the frames made of maple and cedar or black locust wood, but faced with panels of marsh grass (*Phragmites*) or cornstalk or cattail (Fig. 76). The first complete homestead consists of a thatched longhouse, work hut, garden plot, outside hearth, storage bins and pits, and a central work area; the house took *c*. 700 man-hours to build. Its marsh grass thatched walls should provide excellent insulation, described by Captain John White "as warme as stooves". The village itself has *c*. 30 garden plots, where Powhatan Indian crops are grown for analysis, for seed banking, and for consumption. The plants include varieties of corn, squash, and beans, as well as sunflower, tobacco, pumpkin and gourd. The unique character of this project lies in its close association with an existing population, and its interrelated studies, display and educational potential. Opportunities for long-term research, recording and publication should allow an expansion of the concept of "living archaeology" far beyond the original ideas.

The number of projects in "living archaeology" in America now exceeds 40, although most have been short-term single experiments. It is now evident that some measure of control is needed over the locations of these sites, as each is contributing the debris of its experiments to the environment, and may mislead future generations of archaeologists. Most important is the need for such projects to keep away from ancient sites, whether settlements or lithic quarries, in order to prevent mixing of modern and authentically old material. A particular danger, not restricted to "living archaeology" sites, concerns quarries of good-quality flint or obsidian. These are legitimate sources for experimental raw materials only if there

Fig. 76. *Upper.* A longhouse at Pamunkey, Virginia, length 7 m. The framework is of cedar and maple, lashed with jute; the house is thatched on roof and walls with marsh grass (*Phragmites* reed). Total time for erecting the frame was 376 man-hours, with thatching 300 man-hours.

Lower. Sorting cattails for the sewn matting walls of a longhouse at Pamunkey, with thatched house in background.

(Photos: E. Callahan.)

is no evidence of ancient exploitation, as otherwise the traces of previous work will be destroyed, obscured or altered. The experimental chipping of stone on ancient sites is totally irresponsible.

As we have seen, experiments in "living archaeology" such as the Pamunkey Project are legitimate only if acknowledgement is made that we cannot reconstitute ancient life-ways, extinct patterns of behaviour, and prehistoric traditions. Not all experiments have made this admission, but another exception is a project in the Netherlands, underway since 1975. This work was based upon a simple problem, a curiosity to see how an integrated group of people could exist under simulated Neolithic circumstances (de Haas, 1977, 1978). The site chosen was ten hectares of land in the Flevo polder, but before this was occupied the group undertook well over a year of preliminary work in learning some basic skills and experimenting with types of houses. Meetings were held every 2–3 months to learn new techniques of pottery making, stone work, weaving, basketry, bone work, fire making and working with skins; moreover between meetings each member was required to practise his or her skills. There was great variation in the individual skills developed, and some techniques were apparently never fully mastered by some. As the various pieces of equipment made during this period formed the basis of the field experiment, some members found themselves rather ill-prepared, if cheerful, when the time came to move to the site:

These differences had nothing to do with money, but were determined by diligence, skill, motivation, time available, fervent wish to be prepared for anything, or, on the contrary, light heartedness in those who thought they could trust to their own gift of improvization.

Particular attention went into spinning and weaving with various experimental looms, vertical, horizontal and inclined, as well as copies of traditional looms from Egypt, India and Japan. Plant colours, from root, bark and weeds, yielded red, yellow and browns for polychrome weaving. Woven clothing was made of simple shapes, but most of the participants decided to wear skin clothes (Fig. 77, upper); rabbit-skin was used for underclothes, sleeves or socks, and deerskin or goatskin for overcoats and trousers, with stitching for all of strips of gut, yarn or plaited rushes. The general inventory of equipment prepared for the field experiment included baskets and woven traps, sleeping mats and covers, stone and flint axes, scrapers, knives, adzes, hoes and saws, a variety of pots, antler and bone hammers and points, shell ladles, wooden handles and hafts.

Before the total occupation of the site, shelters had been constructed (Fig. 77, lower) as well as storehouses and a goatshed, and the land was

FIG. 77. Activities at the "Neolithic" settlement in the Netherlands.

Upper. Cutting skins with a hafted flint blade.

Lower. Building a house; the domed stakes form a strong framework for wattle walls and roof.

(Photos: R. Horreus de Haas.)

broken ready for planting. This preliminary work, particularly in preparing shelters ready for occupation, certainly reduced the initial impact of the experiment; when conditions were still new, surroundings had to be explored, and acclimatization and adaptation to weather, food and behaviour had to be rapidly made. Six huts were built, in different ways as there were few Neolithic models then known; one was circular with a central post, others were either rectangular or had several separate parts attached to form irregular structures (Fig. 78). Woven walls, some with clay daubing, and reed thatch roofs were logical and effective. Eventually a larger structure, "the Big House", was built to shelter the whole group; this was oval in plan, and took over 300 man-hours to build. The huts were built around a central area used for communal cooking; beyond were the goat enclosures, a well, clay pit, beehives and plots of cultivated land. The remainder of the 10 hectares consisted of an expanse of willows and reeds, the latter damaged severely by commercial plant spraying from the air.

FIG. 78. Reconstruction of a Neolithic settlement in the Netherlands, winter (drawn by R. Walker after a photo by de Haas.)

The team consisted of 10 adults and 4 children, in ages 4–72 years. Before the field experiment began, the participants were asked about their expectations; some felt unprepared through lack of training, but not one believed that he or she would miss the modern world. In the event, both expectations were realized. Activities included tending the goats, keeping the fire in, filling the jugs from the (artificial) well, grinding wheat for porridge, digging clay, cutting reeds and wood, digging in the garden plots, making pots and clothes, gathering plants and cooking. There was little time for total rest during the waking hours. The small fields around the settlement were hoed with wooden and flint-bladed tools, and wheat, Celtic beans and *Camelina* were planted. Because the experimental area lay within a region where hunting was prohibited by law, wild animals were abundant and consumed the sown cereals and beans three times. Eventually only the beans yielded a crop, as even wattle fencing did not dissuade rabbits, and certainly not pheasants. The animals kept were five goats, one dog and some bees; the goats yielded about 4–5 litres of milk each day.

Food was imported for the short 3-week period of occupation; it consisted entirely of plant foods. To start each day, porridge was eaten; it was made of coarsely ground wheat, honey, water and goatmilk. Lunch consisted of flat cakes baked of coarse meal and herbs, and nettle soup. Dinner generally comprised the same cakes, with beans, wild greens and other vegetables. Mushrooms, cheese, chestnuts and hips were eaten as special treats. This uniform diet over three weeks seemed to agree with almost all the members, although intestinal complaints were numerous at first. Hunting was not permitted by the authorities, but in any case some members did not want to kill any animals out of "respect for life". Some molluscs were gathered and provided the only animal food consumed, but again not by all the members.

The participants neither gained nor lost much weight over the period, but all their pulse-rates were lower at the end of the experiment, probably a tribute to the decrease in tension. The only problems encountered were injuries sustained by hands and feet, and occasional burns. One man was badly scalded when a pot full of hot porridge was dropped in front of him. Infection set in, and consideration about moving him to a doctor was only shelved when the patient refused to go. Instead the wounds were disinfected with soda-water after the scabs were taken off with a flint flake— a good compromise. *Sphagnum* moss was used for bandages on small cuts, and also provided useful nappies for the smallest child.

The project did not set out to provide scientific observations and records for others. Instead it was simply designed to provide a test and an experiment for the members, to see how they would enjoy, and react to, life under simulated Neolithic conditions. In the absence of detailed knowledge of Neolithic life 4000 years ago in this area, and in the short period of time of the experiment, of course it was not possible to recreate all aspects even had they been known. But for all members pleasure was found in creating new things, learning new ways to live, and in gaining more respect for ancient people. Because of these, the group has not disbanded and has built a substantial longhouse on the site to provide shelter for the whole team in future occupations.

This experiment was designed on a totally different basis from the Pamunkey Project, and provides a useful contrast in aims and achievements. It was much more a personal, human experiment, and was not so heavily directed towards recording utilization and wear on tool-kits. It could not build or operate close to a prehistoric model, and it did not have the undoubted benefits of a long-term occupation. The background support for documentation provided by bodies such as a university was also lacking from the Dutch work. It is therefore unreasonable and valueless to compare the two "living archaeology" projects. Instead, the Dutch work serves as an excellent example of a small experiment, asking no more than to see how things would work out, and how people would respond. That all found it satisfying, and that all gained some understanding of the past, and appreciation of the environment, is sufficient.

Experiments with death are another problem for the archaeologist, and one with the difficulties we might expect. Few, if any, will knowingly donate their bodies, alive or dead, for the type of experiments that some archaeologists would like to carry out, and there has therefore been much substitution of other animals for work on trephination, cremation, burial and mummification. Doubtless some specialists would dearly love to experiment with the real thing, and perhaps a few have dreamed of certain people who would make satisfying material.

The enormous number of human remains from almost all periods of the past create opportunities for detailed studies of physical characteristics, racial groups, diet, mortality rates, injuries, diseases and other valuable evidence for human populations. Associated experiments have sometimes made contributions to these studies, although the tests have often been directed at the methods of disposal of the dead rather than maintenance of the living. Bones and teeth preserve well in many soils, but the softer parts of the body do not, and conditions for their preservation are restricted to the extremes of cold, wet and dryness. The famous tattooed bodies in the frozen tombs at Pazyryk, Siberia (Rudenko, 1970) provide almost unique evidence for body decoration. Bodies preserved in peat bogs in Germany and Austria suggest that Neolithic and Bronze Age tattooing consisted of scarification of the skin (scratching and insertion of earth or ashes), and puncturing was only practised in the later Iron Age; some implements suitable for these cosmetic or ritual operations have been recognized (Dieck, 1976).

The numerous bodies from peat bogs in northern Europe, 100 B.C.–
A.D. 500, were not tattooed but have excited interest by the methods of
death; some were probably victims of murder but more were clearly put
to death by the societies in which they lived and which they had perhaps
displeased in one way or another. Tollund man and Grauballe man are
important finds for experimental archaeology because of the contents of
their stomachs (p. 125), but not all the bodies were complete; heads of
men and women have often been found, as well as feet and hands,
detached by knife of iron or stone. The body from Dätgen, Schleswig,
represents a particularly unpleasant ritual act; killed by a dagger thrust
in the heart, the adult male had been decapitated and skinned. The
body was pinned to the marsh by branches, his head placed nearby (Todd,
1975). The severing of heads and limbs with sharp knives or axes would
pose few problems, and examination can sometimes tell which implement
was used. A chopped body recovered from the presumed Neolithic occupation at Maiden Castle, Dorset, provided the only evidence for Neolithic
mutilation until experiments showed that the wounds had been inflicted
with a metal blade, hence the Neolithic association was unlikely; radiocarbon subsequently indicated a post-Roman date (Brothwell, 1971).
Marks on the elephant femur club from Piltdown, Sussex, also indicated
that a metal blade had been used—yet another revelation in the decipher-
ment of the notorious forgery (Weiner, 1955). Other experimental work
on the Piltdown material included staining and filing of a chimpanzee
molar, to demonstrate its resemblance to a Piltdown tooth, and Charles
Dawson, the "discoverer" of the site, stained bones and flints to determine
if they would resemble finds reputedly from the site.

Among the numerous well-preserved skeletons from the prehistoric Old
and New Worlds are a considerable number with holes in their skulls (Fig.
7) (e.g. Piggott, 1940; Stewart, 1958; Brongers, 1966; Brenot and Riquet,
1977). The practice of removing a roundel or disc from the head was
widespread, and is still a feature of some communities today. It is said to
relieve the patient of his obsession or illness, and occasionally does. In early
times, the operation was without doubt a difficult one, and the mastery of
"surgeons" in opening the cerebral cavity of a living person so carefully
that the wound healed thereafter is not to be dismissed lightly (Stewart,
1958; Wells, 1964). Experiments in the nineteenth century suggested that
adults could rarely survive (p. 15) but we know this conclusion was
wrong. Many did survive, their wound healing well, and some persons
continued to live after another, and another, of these operations. Two
main methods were used. In the shaving technique, the blade of the cutting
tool was moved in at a very shallow angle to the skull, slicing through the
tabula externa, diploe (spongy bone tissue) and tabula interna (the inside

surface of the skull), but not entering the *dura mater* (brain membrane); the result of this technique is a bevelled edge to the hole. In the other method, the cutting blade moved perpendicularly to the bone, cutting down through the *tabula externa* and *diploe*, after which the *tabula interna* was carefully broken and removed. Both methods are shown in Fig. 7.

There is great variation in the methods, and success of the operation; certain skulls have neat circular holes, with roundels surviving complete, but others have jagged perforations and the disc presumably was extracted in pieces. A recent study of five Anglo-Saxon skulls from Watton, England, suggests that one surgeon was responsible for the quite uniform and successful operation. His implement was apparently a gouge with blade 18 mm wide (Wells, 1974). More sophisticated tools existed, however, and some Late Iron Age skulls from Guntramsdorf in Austria suggest the use of a trephine, a cutting tool with central guide (Wimmer, 1930). The grave of a physician of *c.* 200 B.C. from Obermenzing, Germany, contained a delicate iron saw, perhaps a trepanning saw (de Navarro, 1955), and a Roman doctor's grave at Bingen-am-Rhein, Germany, had a bronze trephine which was centred on the skull and rotated to cut a disc (Como, 1925; Brongers, 1969), rather like Victorian trephining instruments of steel with ebony handles; clearly the practice was a popular one. A final piece of evidence is the nineteenth-century observation of *trépaneurs* of the Chaouias group in North Africa, who used both saw and drill in their operations, and who practised on human skulls (Fig. 79a). All of these finds suggest that trepannation was a widespread practice, carried out in varying ways, and with general success. The patients sometimes had the benefit of delicate instruments, but sometimes had to accept rougher treatment. That many survived is a tribute both to their physicians and their own strength.

Inhumations provide the bulk of measurable evidence for reconstructing ancient populations, but much recent work has suggested that cremations too can add to the data. Many societies of the past, as today, cremated their dead, and without these studies there would be immense gaps in our knowledge. Yet this is a relatively recent development. In 1930 a celebrated Swedish anthropologist and anatomist stated:

I would straight away place on record my considered opinion, based on experience, that cremated remains of human bones in burial urns are almost devoid of any anthropological interest, especially in cases of such in a mass cemetery. From an anthropological view, therefore, these bones are of no scientific value, and I consider that nothing is lost if they are neither submitted to nor preserved in the Museum.

Quoted in Gejvall, 1969

It is a matter for rejoicing that Swedish archaeologists disregarded these remarks and continued to recover and preserve cremated remains for future scientific developments. Among the pioneers of techniques for studying cremations, the work of N–J. Gejvall is eminent. His early work involved detailed examination of modern cremations, of known physical character, and experiments with re-burning of bone samples from prehistoric cremations in order to test firing techniques (Gejvall, 1969). Ancient pyres were in the open air, where oxygen was plentiful, fuel of wood was probably abundant, and bones could be moved from time to time with sticks to ensure burning. Modern cremations in gas ovens take less than one hour, and the control of fuel and heat makes for effective reduction of the body to burnt bone and ashes. Ancient cremations were less regimented, some entirely successful, and others very poorly reduced. The less successful cremations provide the better guides to physical anthropologists in their studies, and today many anthropologists can age and sex cremated remains, as well as provide specialized information about physical disabilities and disease. Population studies, based upon some of the enormous cremation cemeteries, are also a regular contribution.

Recent experiments have, however, cast some doubt about the ability of excavators to recognize funeral pyres. Archaeologists in Europe have

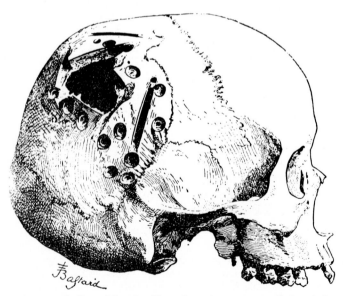

Fig. 79a. A human skull used by the Chaouias *trépaneurs*, a professional class of men employed to carry out the operation of trephining. This skull was one used for practice and training; marks of saw and drill can be seen. (After Malbot and Verneau, *L'Anthropologie* 8 1897; see Brongers, 1969.)

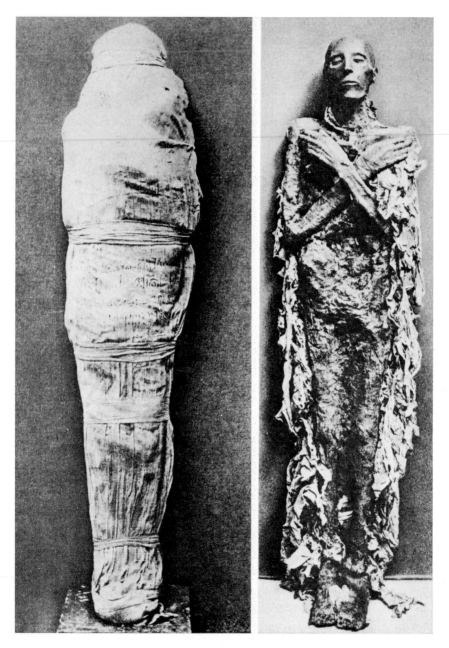

FIG. 79b. Egyptian mummies. *Left*, mummy of Ramses the Great, 1301–1234 B.C.; *right*, unwrapped mummy of Sethos I, 1320–1301 B.C. (Photos: Emil Brugsch, 1881; courtesy Trustees of the British Museum.)

always considered that in some regions and at some times in the prehistoric past, funeral pyres were placed away from the actual cemeteries; in other times and places, the pyres themselves were incorporated in the burial. A recent experiment in Sweden set out to determine if a pyre would leave sufficient traces in the ground to allow its recognition by archaeologists (Gräslund, 1975–77). An oak and ashwood pyre was constructed, 2·5 m long, part lying on a sandy subsoil and part directly on the grassy turf; in a light breeze, the fire soon reached an estimated 800°C, and the wood was consumed, as well as a few bits of meat and bone, within $2\frac{1}{2}$ hours; the bone was well burned and crackled by the heat. After excavation, the exposed sand was found to be burned white to a depth of 10 cm at the centre of the pyre; where the sand had been protected by the turf, it was stained grey only to a depth of 2–3 cm. Beside the pyre the sand was burned red where the flames had scorched freely in an oxidizing atmosphere. As a result of this experiment, the archaeologists could point to a number of thin grey sandy patches found during the excavation of a Viking cemetery, and could suggest that these, lying between the cremations and the unstained subsoil, were the remains of actual pyres set upon the original turf. No pyres had been built on sands cleared of turf by the Vikings. The obvious point can be made that without both experiment and careful excavation, such slight traces could be missed or ignored or misunderstood.

Other experiments with cremated remains have suggested that there are perhaps more uncertainties than anthropologists suspect. It is well known that burial of burnt bone may create conditions for shrinkage, cracking and distortion; and frost, water, heat and burrowing animals can all cause problems and alterations in the bone. Experimental cremation of an Alsatian dog's paw and femur showed large alteration in size from the original, and also variations in shrinkage between bones with marrow, or medullary cavity, and bones with spongy interiors (Iregren and Jonsson, 1973). Bones also shrank more in width than in length, in ratios of approximately 3:1 for the femur, and from 3:2 to 5:3 for metatarsals. Other experiments used human skeletons and monkey bodies on wood pyres. It was discovered that the soft tissues of the monkey body dried, charred and then burned before the bones began to burn, so that the tissues had little effect on the resulting bone changes. In a wood pyre, high temperatures of 700–1000°C were reached, leading to calcination of organic materials, and deformation and contraction of the bones (Strzalko and Pimtek, 1974); the contraction was of the order 6–13 per cent, and suggested that estimates of stature would be affected. The experimental burning of human remains opened sutures, sometimes completely; and this supports the current views that suture closure is no true guide to ageing of human remains (McKern, 1970; Strzalko *et al.*, 1974). These and other experiments are an excellent example of the normal, often non-experimental archaeological process: a new theory is created, procedures are devised, results emerge and are accepted; then reaction sets in, further tests of the theory are made, difficulties discovered, and warnings publicized. The process is entirely and absolutely to be welcomed, as only in these ways can modification of techniques be suggested, tested and take their place in the overall development of archaeology as a scientific discipline.

In a few areas of the world, mummification of the dead was practised. "Mummy" is a term generally applied to an animal body preserved by bitumen, gum, spices or natron (Budge, 1972). Mummy is in fact a word derived from bitumen, and within the last few centuries bitumen has been used on the bodies of animals and others, followed by binding and exposure to the sun, to produce "Mummies" suitable for sale to passing traffic. The traffic in mummies in the sixteenth century was extraordinary, and only halted by imposition of exorbitant taxes in Egypt. Millennia before this time, however, important persons were mummified in order to ensure their everlasting life. It was believed that the soul would return after death to revive the body, and elaborate preparations were taken to ensure that the body was ready to receive its soul and regain its lifetime's functions (Fig. 79b).

The methods used by ancient Egyptians to mummify the dead are known by analysis of the bodies, by experiment, and by accounts of Greek historians. Herodotus recorded that the embalmers of the dead operated at three levels: expensive with nothing spared, less expensive, and cheap. For those who truly believed in the importance of mummification, the choice must have been a desperate one. Herodotus described the method as follows:

First they draw out the brains through the nostrils with an iron hook, taking part of it out in this manner, the rest by infusion of drugs. Then with a sharp Ethiopian stone they make an incision in the side, and take out all the bowels; and having cleansed the abdomen and rinsed it with palm-wine, they next sprinkle with pounded perfumes. Then having filled the belly with pure myrrh pounded, and cassia and other perfumes, frankincense excepted, they sew it up again; and when they have done this, they steep it in natrum, leaving it under for 70 days; for a longer time than this it is not lawful to steep it. At the expiration of the 70 days, they wash the corpse, and wrap the whole body in bandages of flaxen cloth, smearing it with gum which the Egyptians commonly used instead of glue. After this the relations, having taken the body back again, make a wooden case in the shape of a man, and having made it, they enclose the body; and thus, having fastened it up, they store it in a sepulchral chamber, setting it upright against the wall. In this manner they prepare the bodies that are embalmed in the most expensive way.

Those who, avoiding great expense, desire the middle way, they prepare in the following manner. When they have charged their syringes with oil made from cedar, they fill the abdomen of the corpse without making any incision or taking out the bowels, but inject it at the fundament; and having prevented the injection from escaping, they steep the body in natrum for the prescribed number of days, and on the last day they let out from the abdomen the oil of cedar which they had before injected, and it has such power that it brings away the intestines and vitals in a state of dissolution; the natrum dissolves the flesh, and nothing of the body remains but the skin and bones. When they have done this they return the body without any further operation.

The third method of embalming is this, which is used only for the poorer sort. Having thoroughly rinsed the abdomen in syrmae, they steep it with natrum for 70 days, and then deliver it to be carried away.

Other accounts are in general agreement with Herodotus's description, and yet insufficiently specific to prevent much discussion about precise methods, in particular the character of the "steep" and the need to stuff the body in order to prevent its collapse and shrinkage. Experiments carried out by A. Lucas attempted to show that the steeping was not necessarily a wet soak, but could be dry, and that the introduction of materials into the body was not necessary (Lucas, 1962). By experimenting with chickens and pigeons, it was determined that desiccation of the body was the main essential, and could be obtained by an 8 per cent natron solution for 40 days, or a dry natron packing for 40 days. (Natron or natrum is a sodium carbonate found in desertic regions.) Ancient Egyptian methods doubtless varied, and the experiments did not produce a single solution to the problem.

Bodies require burial and arguably the most famous burial chambers in the world lie within and beneath the pyramids of Egypt. Archaeologists and many others have studied the ways by which these immense monuments were built (Edwards, 1961). Of course, no real full-scale experimental work has been done, although some models have been made to demonstrate possible methods. The three Pyramids at Giza, built for Cheops, Chephren and Mycerinus, constitute the most celebrated group. The Great Pyramid of Cheops is by far the largest of any. Its construction of local and Tura limestone involved 2·3 million separate blocks, averaging 2·5 tonnes each. The four sides of the pyramid at its base measure 230·25–230·45 m, almost perfectly identical. The size of this pyramid is difficult to grasp without comparisons of known buildings. The Houses of Parliament and St Paul's Cathedral would fit easily inside the area of the base which is 5·3 ha; Napoleon calculated that the three pyramids of Giza contained enough stone to build a wall, 3 m high and 0.3 m thick, around the whole of France. The Great Pyramid was originally 146.7 m high, and its sides are inclined at 51° 52′ to the ground; removal of the facing blocks, the apex and other quarrying have severely damaged the monument. Nonetheless it stands today as not only the most famous structure in the world but as a challenge to engineers and archaeologists in deducing how it was originally built.

According to Herodotus, Cheops pyramid took 20 years to build, with teams of 100 000 men working for three months at a time, i.e. an annual work force of 400 000 men. It is now argued that perhaps only 100 000 were employed, bringing blocks to the site during the season of inundation of the land by Nile floodwaters from August to the end of October each year when water transport could deliver them to within 500 m of the site. The blocks weigh on average 2·5 tonnes, and each could probably have been manipulated by a team of 8–10 men, with an estimated delivery and positioning of 10 blocks per team in 3 months; 2·3 million blocks in 20 years would therefore involve about 115 000 men per year. The sequence of construction seems relatively clear:

1. The site was cleared of sand to expose the rock base, which was levelled by water and smoothed down; it deviated by barely 1 cm across the whole 5·3 ha.
2. The sides were surveyed and marked out, with ground measurements and star orientation; the sides deviate in length by only 20 cm in 230 m.
3. The causeway approaching the site was made to allow delivery of stone.
4. The Tura limestone facing blocks were quarried by separate gangs and brought to the site for storage; the names of some of the gangs were painted on the blocks of another pyramid and perpetuate the Boat Gang, Vigorous Gang, Enduring Gang, Sceptre Gang etc. Quarrying of limestone was easily achieved by copper saws and chisels, and wooden wedges; the granite blocks for parts of the pyramid were more difficult, but dolerite ball pounding, and the use of heat, would allow detachment of blocks and surface dressing (Engelbach, 1923).
5. The transport of the blocks, maximum weight 50 tonnes, but almost all much lighter, by water, sledge and roller, would have presented little problem; Egyptian reliefs depict the movement of 60-tonne statues with huge work forces hauling on ropes, the statues seated on sledges with rollers beneath. The largest stones at Giza are the 200-tonne slabs in the Mycerinus temple.
6. The pyramid and its burial chambers were built; the rock core was built up at the centre, then extended sideways to form the bulk of the monument before the facing blocks were put on the sides at a slope of c. 52°. The jointing of the facing stones was carefully done, with average joint openings of less than 1 mm.

The problems of course must have been enormous, particularly in the lifting of the blocks up the sides of the pyramids. Herodotus states that wooden machines lifted them, level by level, up the pyramid, but the precise character of the machines is unknown. Several other monuments have remains of earth and stone ramps up which the blocks were dragged, and this is probably the method used for the pyramids, as Herodotus also notes. Various types of ramp have been suggested, a single ramp covering all or part of one face, augmented as the monument rose, or a continuous ramp on all four faces, spiralling its way up. A single ramp covering all of one face would take 17·5 million m³ of earth and stone—a staggering amount. If it stopped at 80 m, 90 per cent of the blocks could be delivered, leaving only 10 per cent to be raised by other means to the top, and the earth fill would be reduced to only 2·6 million m³ (Garde-Hansen, 1974). If the ramp tapered to the top, less than 1 million m³ would be needed (Lauer, 1974), but the blocks still had to be moved sideways and around the corners to the other three faces. A scale model of the Mycerinus pyramid suggests that ascending spiral ramps would have allowed the blocks to be dragged upwards, and if four such ramps were made, clinging to the sides of the pyramid, three could be used to haul upwards, and one for the return journey of the men (Dunham, 1956). The ramps rose at 1:8 slope and were three metres wide, and the scale model suggested that they could accommodate only 2500 men at any one time. In the absence of full-scale experiments, all of these conjectures are possible, but not one is proved. One further point should be made, that the largest stones in the Great Pyramid are all in the lower courses, and that above the seventh course only four out of 191 courses are over one metre high, and most are only 0·5–0·75 m high; many of these small blocks could have been carried, lifted and hauled by teams of men, either by roping the blocks or hauling them on skids, or by simple levering. Hence even the earthen ramp, certainly used elsewhere, need not have been the only method used here.

The transport and erection of huge stones have always fascinated archaeologists, not only because of the engineering principles involved, but because any massive project must infer some organization of the society. The decisions taken about large-scale projects require some firm direction and guidance, and these reflect upon the whole cultural setting of the community, providing ample data for admittedly conjectural but exciting hypotheses about social structures. Practical experiments cannot provide any immediately applicable data for such hypotheses, except to demonstrate the organization of manpower and control over supplies, and these should perhaps be taken rather more into account than they have up to the present (Heizer, 1966). Even in recent times, the desecration of ancient sites by collectors has involved huge manual expenses (Fig. 80); the removal of the bull and lion sculptures from Nimrud to the Tigris River was comparable to the depictions at Nineveh of Assyrians moving a 30-tonne statue in the eighth century, with containing crib, sledge, rollers, levers and lines of men pulling ropes. The removal of an Egyptian obelisk from Luxor to the Place de la Concorde, Paris, took 6 years (1830–36), with sea transport in a ship with removable bow (Gorringe, 1882).

FIG. 80. Lowering the colossal bull at Nimrud. The problems encountered by nineteenth-century dismantlers of ancient structures in the Near East and Egypt provide some indication of the capabilities of the original builders, who had to quarry, carve, transport, and erect hundreds of statues and megaliths. (From Layard, 1873.)

The greatest stone of all, a granite obelisk at Aswan, 42 m high and 1168 tonnes, still lies in its quarry. The largest Mycenaean blocks (120 tonnes), megalithic tomb slabs of western Europe (100 tonnes), Stonehenge sarsens (30 tonnes), Maya and Aztec statues (20–60 tonnes), Easter Island statues (60 tonnes) and the largest New World stone, at Teotihuacan in Mexico (217 tonnes), all are impressive but nowhere approaching the Near Eastern and Egyptian totals. The two Colossi of Memnon at Thebes weigh 1000 tonnes each. A few experiments have been carried out on the quarrying, shaping, transport and erection of monuments such as these. The use of dolerite balls hurled down upon the granite at Aswan reduced the level of stone by 5 mm in one hour over a small area worked by one man (Engelbach, 1923); from this, the Aswan obelisk would have occupied 400 men for 15 months, 260 hurling the hammers down and 140 clearing away the dust. The problem here is that the scale of experiment is so small, and the monument so large that to extrapolate is very dangerous. Smaller stones could doubtless be quarried and shaped in relatively short periods of time (McFarland, 1977), particularly by experienced workers, as experiments on Easter Island showed (Skjolsvold, 1961), and as the high quality exhibited on many statues suggest: "[Olmec sculptures] can have been carved only by professional sculptors relieved from all other work, and maintained by the community" (Kubler, 1962, p. 71).

The movement of stones to make the chambers of burial monuments was another massive task, as the pyramids have demonstrated. Water transport would probably have been employed wherever possible, but on land the only way seems to have been dragging with ropes, sledges and rollers unless the stone could be lifted and carried. An experiment in Colombia showed that 35 men could actually carry a 1-tonne statue, and managed about 1 km per day through heavy jungle; in Mexico, a 2-tonne column was lifted by shoulder poles and rope slings by 35 men (Drucker et al., 1959). A stone of the same weight and copying one of the bluestones from Stonehenge was hauled about on a sledge with and without rollers by a team of 24 to 32 (Atkinson, 1956), and a 10–12-tonne statue on Easter Island was moved on a sledge by 180 men (Heyerdahl, 1952). A similar weight required over 500 men in Sumba, but the terrain was more difficult and the distance travelled much greater (Heizer, 1966). All of these experiments suggest the use of many men to transport megaliths, and comparable effort was needed to lift, erect or position the stones once they had arrived at the site.

That the country of Denmark was once cultivated and worked by giants is affirmed by the enormous stones which are in the barrows of the ancients. Should any man question that this was accomplished by superhuman force, let him look to the top of certain mountains and say, if he knows how, what man has carried such immense boulders up to their summits.

(translation, Saxo Grammaticus, c. A.D. 1200)

We do not now accept this view, and not only because our belief in giants is less strong than it was 700 years ago. Experiments on Easter Island, where the stones were indeed considered to have been moved and positioned by miraculous powers, demonstrated a method of raising the stone statues: a platform was built of stones, and the statue raised horizontally upon this by levers, with a gradual raising end by end (Fig. 81). At an appropriate height, the statue was allowed to slip and slide down on to its stone base, then was pulled upright by ropes (Heyerdahl, 1958; Skjolsvold, 1961).

Megalithic tombs, built of upright slabs supporting capstones, were probably built in the same way, with ramps or platforms, although no full-scale
experiments have been completed on these monuments, other than on

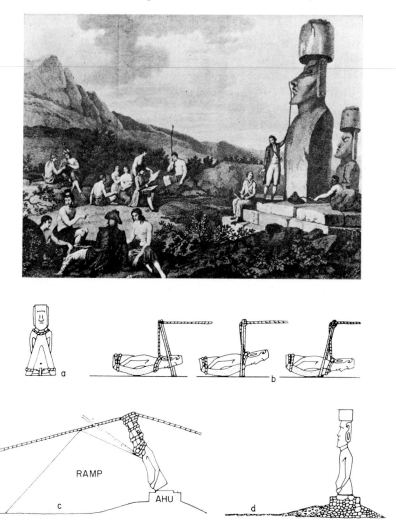

Fig. 81. *Upper.* Statues on Easter Island, drawn by La Pérouse in 1786 when they
were still in place on their stone *ahu* platforms, and still carried the reddish topknot
stones; soon afterwards most of the statues were overthrown.

Lower. Transport and erection of the stone statues on Easter Island according to
one theory which conforms to the tradition that the stones walked themselves to their
places. a, Forked sled attached; b, transport by means of a bipod or cradle; c,
erection upon a stone ramp before leverage down on to the *ahu*, with topknot
attached; d, final result. (From Bellwood, 1978.)

quite small cists (McAdam and Watkins, 1974). More attention has been paid to Stonehenge because of its unique character, and here the use of earthen ramps or wooden platforms, shearlegs and levers would have allowed the monument's uprights and lintels to be positioned with relatively little difficulty (Atkinson, 1956). The scale model (1:12) experiments of an engineer, E. H. Stone, provide a scientific and charming picture of how it could have been done (Stone, 1924), although the reliability of very small scales such as this for enormously heavy or large monuments is a question still to be resolved and accepted. It might be felt that imponderables, such as irregularities of rock surfaces, sticking and jamming, slipping and the exhaustion of men over long periods of work, would pose problems not encountered in small models carefully manipulated by scaled efforts.

Many prehistoric and early historic burials were not placed in stone chambers, whether small stone cists or massive pyramids. Instead, they were placed beneath mounds or heaps of earth or small stones, and these barrows line ancient routes and cluster in cemeteries in various parts of the world. Because they were visible, and because they contained no, or few, heavy stones, they were exclusively plundered, even within days of burial. Just as tomb robbers in Egypt were not deterred by huge stone blocks, neither were their contemporaries in northern Europe or eastern America hindered by heaps of earth. Their knowledge of the wealth of grave goods put with some burials must have encouraged "exploration". Many other burials, however, survived, to be desecrated today when little interest is shown in preserving traditional monuments of the past. Within such mounds of earth, inhumations and cremations lie in varying stages of decay, associated with their richer or poorer artifacts. The investigation of these monuments has sometimes included assessments of the time and effort needed to build them, the processes of their weathering and erosion, and the rates of decay of material buried with them.

A number of earthen monuments, round mounds or linear earthworks, have been constructed to test the ancient methods of digging and carrying earth. At Overton Down, Wiltshire, a turf and chalk earthwork 21 m long, 7 m wide and 2 m high, was built in 1960 with material from a ditch beside the mound (Jewell, 1963). Part of the work was done with antler picks, ox and horse scapulae shovels, and wicker baskets, and overall these were shown to be only slightly less effective than modern picks and shovels and buckets, with the greatest contrast between the shovels. As a result of this experimental work, some much-needed estimates could be made of the time required to build ordinary burial mounds of chalk; an average size of barrow, 12 m in diameter, might represent 6–8 workers for 15 days. Huge earthen mounds such as Silbury Hill in England, the largest artificial

FIG. 82. The experimental earthwork at Wareham, Dorset, England.

Upper. The earthwork, made of turf and sand, after 9 months; slight erosion has already occurred, and the first silting has sealed the ditch floor edges.

Lower. The earthwork after 9 years; the bank has slumped considerably (note vertical markers), the ditch floor has been completely covered. One of the first sections has been cut for recording and analysis.

(Photos: British Association for the Advancement of Science, Experimental Earthwork Committee.)

mound in Europe (40 m high), or the Viking burial mounds of Scandinavia, are less suitable for extrapolation although Silbury contains 50 million "basketfuls" of earth, a formidable task even now and certainly 4000 years ago.

In 1963 another experimental earthwork at Wareham, Dorset, was built of turf and sand (Fig. 82) (Evans and Limbrey, 1974) and periodically both Wareham and Overton Down have had sections cut through both bank and ditch silts to observe rates of erosion and weathering, and to test the decay of materials such as wood, bone, flint, pottery, hide, textiles, coins, and glass, placed at strategic points within and outside the bank. The examinations were planned to take place at intervals of 1, 2, 4, 8, 16 etc. years, but some variation has been introduced to observe the rapid alterations in silting, slumping and weathering (Jewell and Dimbleby, 1966). It has of course been argued that short-term alterations are of little relevance to archaeologists investigating remains many hundreds and thousands of years old, but this is an erroneous view. The single observation concerning the preservation of ditch corners by the first silts to fall has allowed excavators to look for, and find, the original ditch edges on ancient sites, just as the experiments on weathering of wattle-and-daub walls have shown the likely preservation of original wall thicknesses (p. 152). There are numerous other aspects of the earthwork experiments both here and elsewhere (e.g. Lüning, 1972, 1974; Ascher, 1970) which also shed light on excavator's observations, or suggest new ways to approach old sites; and it is to be hoped that the many specialists, including archaeologists, involved in these experiments will not neglect their responsibilities in the future work of examination, analysis and publication.

7 Conclusions

Theory without practice is empty; practice without theory is blind.
                                                    Immanuel Kant

IN THE PRECEDING CHAPTERS we have seen something of the character of
investigation into long-distance voyages by sea, the production of food and
the building of houses, the manufacture and use of tools and weapons,
achievements in arts and music, the erection of monumental structures
designed for the dead, and finally modern attempts to experience "life in
the past". Many of these experiments have provided unique information
for the archaeologist in his attempts to understand the evidence he has
obtained from the earth, and it has been stressed that those who fail to
exploit the experimental approach do so in the knowledge that they neglect
one of the very few mechanisms which can transform hypothesis into
legitimate inference (p. 42; Ascher, 1961, p. 812). Experimental testing,
if honestly done, can create conditions of understanding that come as close
as any other approach to the original human problems of settlement,
subsistence, shelter and a variety of arts and crafts. It must be realized that
these problems do not include all aspects of cultural behaviour; social and
political organization, and religious beliefs, are vital and important human
elements which cannot be recreated or tested by hardware experiments.
Other forms of model-building, of theoretical character, are often used to
attempt such reconstructions, and they provide a stimulating source of
exercise and argument, but they do not, and cannot, claim to be infallible.
Nor can experiments, of course, and the point has repeatedly been made in
this book that we cannot expect to achieve absolute proof of any particular
event, no matter what approach we adopt.
    Experimental archaeology has the virtue that it deals with the basic
sources of archaeological data, the material remains of stone, bone, wood
and metal. This is the traditional stuff of archaeology, the inspiration for
the development of the subject, and still the major source of evidence about

human societies. Current opinion is sharply divided over the importance
of these tangible remains, and their value to archaeologists seeking to
comprehend human behaviour in all its aspects. What has survived
represents only a fraction, and a sample, of the original equipment. This
sample may be entirely fair and adequate, or it may be totally biased and
misleading, and we often do not know which; yet in the absence of other
surviving cultural evidence, we must use what has survived. Archaeological
studies involving the morphology of artifacts, distributions, environmental
reconstructions, ethnographic analogies, and other forms of models are all
designed to attempt to comprehend the patterns of human behaviour
represented by such remains. The only criticism should be directed at those
archaeologists who stop short at one or another stage of the enquiry,
ignoring the character of the material evidence, or its associated biological
or environmental data, or its functional significance, or the theoretical
models suggested by the tangible expressions. All should be included in any
honest attempt to get through the barriers thrown up by time, namely the
alteration and erosion of evidence. Experimental archaeology, then, is not
the complete answer; there is no complete answer, and only by trying all
the avenues will a direction close to the truth be discovered.

The achievements of experimental archaeology are not restricted to
increased understanding of technological processes and the function of
implements. Within long-term projects, opportunities for education are
very great, and these have hardly been realized except at the Historical–
Archaeological Research Centre, at Lejre in Denmark; some of the individual experiments and series of tests at Lejre have been discussed in this
book. The projects at Lejre have been underway since 1964, when
it was created with major financial support by the Carlsberg Foundation. In 1968 financial undertaking for the Centre was assumed
by the government. Originally designed to function only during the
summer months, the development of the Centre coincided with the evolution of new ideas about the teaching of history in the schools, the role of
museums, and ecological concepts. The result was that the Centre not only
could initiate a series of long-term experiments in house-building and
primitive technologies, but also could serve as a focus for education of
young and old alike in the early history of Denmark, and in the relationships between man and his environment (West and Hansen, n.d.). The
unsuspected attraction of open-air museum displays, reconstructions and
visible experiments actually underway created opportunities both for
financial viability, and for correction of many erroneous "reconstructions"
and ideas about ancient life, perpetuated in books, broadcasting and,
sadly, some museums. The delicate balance required by the Lejre Centre

for research, display and education has not always been possible to maintain over the past decade, but the success of the project owes much to personal initiative and determination by its leaders and staff.

> The center, encouraged to explore many different areas, had its fumbling trials, first in one direction, then in another. But this, in one respect, was an advantage. As it went in all different directions, the center was able to more fully map those possibilities which the project should and could exploit in its role as a research center and museum.
>
> Hansen, 1974

In the ten years or so of the Centre's existence, over half a million visitors have toured the fields, village, workshops and displays; over 1000 teachers have attended courses of instruction in primitive technologies, and over 10 000 children have lived for a short time under unfamiliar conditions in order to experience and appreciate other types of existence. Thousands of children have been trained each year in spinning and weaving, whereas prior to 1969 such instruction had been almost non-existent in Denmark.

The Historical–Archaeological Research Centre now contains a wide variety of structures, livestock, workshops and demonstration areas within its 50 ha. Its public face shows ongoing experiments in pottery, weaving, ironwork, and housebuilding and maintenance. Other experiments are mounted from time to time, and regular demonstrations, lectures and exhibits dealing with the Iron Age and medieval periods also occur. Behind all this activity, however, is another role, in the compilation of details about all of the scientific work, individual or seasonal experiments, and particularly those comprising series tests of pottery-manufacture, weaving and house maintenance and erosion. These data are not necessarily intended for publication, but form a huge body of information available for future projects and research. In this aspect alone, the Centre serves as a standard for all other projects, although we might hope that in due time some indication of the types and quantities of information available will be publicized. Perhaps only in this way will the real contribution of the Centre to archaeology, and not just experimental archaeology, be realized.

There are other research and demonstration centres, more recently established, and some of their experiments have already been described in this book. The open-air museum at Asparn-an-der-Zaya in Austria is important as a demonstration area of prehistoric and early historic houses (p. 140). Two others, Little Butser and West Stow, both in England, are restricted to single chronological episodes—Butser to the Iron Age (p. 114), West Stow to the Anglo-Saxon period (p. 146). Both are attempting to

I

combine research with public education; at Butser, a separate demonstration plot has been established, well apart from the scientific research area, but at West Stow, both aspects are to be linked in the one complex. The advantage of both these projects over most others is in the avowed aim to relate a whole series of experiments to one particular episode. In this way the functioning unit of an Iron Age farm, or a small Anglo-Saxon settlement, will be able to demonstrate the close relationships in the cycle of annual activities of such communities, rather than to treat each relic or set of relics as objects for individual study. In such circumstances, the whole must surely be greater than the sum of its separate parts. For projects such as these, it is probably important to publish periodic reports, detailing the evolution of the settlement and its land as both become established within the routine of an agricultural cycle. This is the point where the Centre at Lejre cannot itself contribute because of its far wider and more generalized scope. All these centres, and others not noted here, hardly overlap in their interests and all can therefore make original contributions to the subject.

We have already noted that scientific laws, immutable and constant, do not yet exist in archaeology; in other sciences, theorems are based on explicit and observable laws, tested repeatedly and never failing. Archaeology has no such laws, but the publication of experimental data from recognized centres such as those noted here could begin to establish a series of facts (laws) dealing with technological matters, which could then be absorbed into archaeological doctrine without the need for recurring demonstration. As examples, the structural qualities of traditional house framing, the functional capabilities of standard stone and bone tools, the performance of early cultivating implements in certain soils, the procedures for making varieties of prehistoric and early historic pottery and metal objects, all could be readily quantified by persistent experiment followed by adequate publication. The result would be a body of data available to all, not requiring further testing, and able to support or deny more theoretical work about the place of such technologies in early and primitive societies. As facts, such experimental data would be a powerful agent in augmenting and helping to control these imaginative and interesting hypotheses (see Ascher, 1961; Clarke, 1972; Knudson, 1978).

The achievements of modern experimental archaeology are not restricted to established long-term projects: far from it. The bulk of experiments described in this book were individual one-off efforts, and there are many others which are not considered here for reasons of space, and duplication of approach. Of single experiments, it is unfair to compare rather ordinary humdrum work, such as pottery-making or stone-chipping, with the spectacular and dangerous exploits in untested boats, and with more visually or audibly attractive projects such as painting (Fig. 83) or testing musical instruments. Yet to a very great extent it is the ordinary experiments which will contribute most to archaeology as a discipline for recovering and understanding the evidence about past behaviour. The vast bulk of artifacts recovered from excavations over the past century consist of these basic substances of stone and clay, more rarely wood, and these are the materials which we must fully understand if we are to make any attempt to manipulate them in formulation of hypotheses and models of all kinds. It would therefore seem crucial for experimental archaeology to develop some mechanism whereby these experiments, and there are many, could be assimilated into a single or a series of projects, readily available to the large number of specialists and others interested in the work. The appearance of *Lithic Technology* is an important step in this direction, as it should bring together a wide range of specialist information, provide a forum for discussion and argument, and publish new insights as well as new problems concerning stone technologies. No such vehicle for information exists for other aspects of experimental work, although the Centre at Lejre had originally hoped to serve as a repository for work done in Denmark and elsewhere in Europe.

Some of the experiments described in this book were devised out of curiosity, and we have seen this as the major impetus to the subject in the nineteenth century. Since these early days, more experiments have had

FIG. 83. Painting with natural pigments on a rock face in Arizona (photo: E. Callahan).

their origins in projects, and full examination of a site and all its finds, or the testing of alternative methods of manufacture or use. Many of these have been carried out by professional archaeologists, with the full range of specialist scientific facilities associated with their university, museum or governmental departments. Many other experiments have been completed by amateurs (part-time specialists seems a better description), and these have been of standards equal to any others, although the absence of analytical equipment, for example, has sometimes proved to be a handicap. Nonetheless the role of the amateur has been considerable, and experiments are one of the all-too-few aspects of serious archaeology still open to such people.

The growth of archaeology as a professional discipline, with regional or national support and a hierarchy of positions, has tended to push the amateur away from the traditional excavation or field-work roles. Costs of such operations are now so great that few unpaid archaeologists can devise and operate significant projects. Experimental archaeology, however, has not yet reached the stage where major finance is available, or where financially viable operating units can exist. Here is where the amateur can, and does, find a place in which significant contributions can be made to the understanding of ancient technologies and practices. The scope for work and the need for it is very considerable, whether single pieces of research or longer-term projects.

Where professional or amateur participation is not required, and never really was, is in the well-publicized attempts to "live in the past". We have singled out only two experiments concerned with human behaviour under simulated ancient conditions, the Pamunkey project and the Dutch family experiment. Neither of these ever claimed that it represented, in any precise way at all, life as it was before written history. Both were concerned, particularly the Pamunkey project, with series tests of experiments related to one ancient episode, in the same way as the Butser and West Stow projects are restricted to their own place and time. The Dutch experiment was, in a way, a philosophical exercise, testing not for archaeology but for participants themselves, although adhering to the rules of the game; as such, it has been a refreshing and wholly amateur exercise, involving the members' own time and energies, and claiming no more than survival, education and enjoyment—surely an excellent combination.

The Pamunkey project is unique in that it attempts to relate a series of technological experiments with the human problems occurring on the contemporary site. It seems legitimate to attempt this, insofar as stone tool production was never the sole pursuit of ancient people, but was only one of a series of activities all designed to fit into an acquired or desired life patern. To experiment with stone tools is a laboratory exercise; to try to see how this fitted into the behaviour of a community involves work with food production, the provision of shelter and environmental and social commitments. Some of these are problems capable of an answer through experiment, but others are certainly not; the Pamunkey project can claim its fair share of achievement in several technological spheres, and would not assert more. There are some aspects of past human behaviour that are beyond recall, by experiment or any other known scientific facility; to pretend that modern people, wrenched from their environment and placed in a totally alien situation, can thereupon fall into a way of life extinct for centuries and millennia is a fallacy. The controlled demonstrations, exhibits and lectures at centres such as Lejre are designed to provide authentic views of what archaeology knows about the past, and not to exceed the bounds of understanding without clear statements of the un-certainties. Experimental reconstructions of past human behaviour need not be exaggerated, and authentic and well-researched attempts would show that the truth can be equally as strange as fiction, and far more rewarding for children, adults, amateurs, professionals, and even pro-gramme directors.

The experiments described in this book are varied and extensive, yet there still remains scope for much work. It may be appropriate here to indicate just a few of the subjects requiring investigation, although almost every aspect of ancient life that survives could be profitably examined by experiment, at least until some acceptable and documented series becomes available. We have briefly touched upon the pressing need for experi-mental examination of excavation techniques in order to expand the possi-bilities for recovery of new and more data, but this subject would require a manual in itself. In small-scale work, the quarrying and shaping of rock into axes, beads and other artifacts has lapsed since the nineteenth-century interest (p. 19); the variety of ancient quarries now known, yielding flint, obsidian and many different rocks, suggest that a rewarding project could examine their exploitation, relative ease of working, and functional capa-bilities. Travel and transport over land, so vital for communities at all times, has hardly been touched upon; there are many studies of wagons, carts and sledges, but few involve experiment. Related to these two subjects of rocks and transport is an ever-present problem for experiment, in the shaping, movement and erection of megalithic monuments, abundant in many parts of the world and hardly tested by full-scale work. Further investigation into water transport is also needed, not the long-distance voyages of discovery but the cross-channel, estuarine and riverine traffic by punt, dugout, raft, skin boat or planked boat; hardly any work has been done on this important aspect of human colonization and settlement. A last type of experiment urgently needed concerns the disposal of the dead by cremation; the multitude of cremated remains in prehistoric and early historic burials requires some investigation by experiment in order to assist the physical anthropologists in his analyses of the remains, and the archaeologist in deducing the nature of the ritual practices. What is required is a whole series of bodies cremated in different ways, in pits, on pyres or platforms, wth different quantities and types of fuel, and under varied environmental conditions of sun, wind and rain. All that is needed for this work are volunteers, a statement that applies to other projected experiments as well, although in a rather different way. These suggestions for future work merely give some idea of the scope and variety of experiments in the future. In almost all fields of enquiry into past human behaviour, experimental archaeology can contribute to those seeking the evidence and experience of life.

References

Adovasio, J., Fry, G., Zabucia, J. and Gunn, J. (1974). The Boarts site: a lithic workshop in Laurence county. *Penn. Archaeol.* **44**, 31–112.

Andersen, H. (1951). Et Landsbyhus på Gørding Hede. *Kuml*, 1951, 40–64.

Anderson, J. (1886). *Scotland in Pagan Times: The Bronze and Stone Ages.* Douglas, Edinburgh.

Arber, E. (ed.) (1910). *Travels and Works of Captain John Smith.* John Grant, Edinburgh.

Ascher, R. (1961). Experimental Archaeology. *Am. Anthrop.* **63**, 793–816.

Ascher, R. (1970). Cues I: design and construction of an experimental archaeological structure. *Am. Antiq.* **35**, 215–216.

Atkinson, R. J. C. (1956). *Stonehenge.* Hamilton, London.

Avoncroft Museum (1976). *Avoncroft Museum of Buildings.* Avoncroft Museum, Bromsgrove.

Balfour, H. (1903). On the method employed by the natives of N.W. Australia in the manufacture of glass spear heads. *Man*, **3** (35), 65.

Barbieri, J. A. (1937). Technique of the implements from Lake Mohave. In *The Archaeology of Pleistocene Lake Mohave: A Symposium. South-west Museum Papers*, **11**, 99–107.

Barrow, T. (1962). An experiment in working nephrite. *J. Polynes. Soc.* **71**, 254.

Bechtol, C. (1963). Sailing characteristics of oceanic canoes. *Polynes. Soc. Mem.* **34**, 98–101.

Becker, C. J. (1962). A Danish hoard containing Neolithic chisels. *Acta Archaeol.* **33**, 79–92.

Bellwood, P. (1978). *The Polynesians.* Thames and Hudson, London.

Berndt, R. M. (ed.) 1964. *Australian Aboriginal Art.* Macmillan, London.

Biberson, P. and Aguirre, E. (1965). Experiences de taille d'outils préhistoriques dans des os d'éléphant. *Quaternaria*, **7**, 165–183.

Bimson, M. (1956). The technique of Greek black and Terra Sigillata red. *Antiq. J.* **36**, 200–204.

Binford, S. R. and L. R. (1969). Stone tools and human behaviour. *Scient. Am.* **220** (4), 70–87.

Birley, R. (1977). *Vindolanda: a Roman Frontier Post on Hadrian's Wall.* Thames and Hudson, London.

Bjørn, A. (1969). *Exploring Fire and Clay.* Van Nostrand Reinhold, New York.

Blacking, J. (1953). Edward Simpson, alias "Flint Jack". *Antiquity*, **27**, 207–211.

BÖHNE, C. (1968). Uber die Kupferverhüttung der Bronzezeit. *Archaeol. Austriaca*, **44**, 49–60.

BONANNI, FILIPPO (1723). *Gabinetto Armonico* (edited by F. L. Harrison and J. Rimmer as *The Showcase of Musical Instruments* (1964)). Dover, New York.

BORDES, F. (1968). *The Old Stone Age*. World Univ. Library, New York.

BOSINSKI, G. and FISCHER, G. (1974). *Die Menschendarstellungen von Gonnersdorf. Der Ausgrabung von 1968*. Röm.-Germ. Komm., F. Steiner, Wiesbaden.

BRADLEY, B. (1974). Comments on the lithic technology of the Casper Site materials. In *The Casper Site: A Hell Gap Bison Kill on the High Plains* (G. C. Frison, ed.). Academic Press, New York and London.

BRAILSFORD, J. and STAPLEY, J. E. (1972). The Ipswich torcs. *Proc. prehist. Soc.* **38**, 219–34.

BRANDT, F. (1972). On the navigation of the Vikings. In *The World of the Vikings*, pp. 14–19. National Maritime Museum, Greenwich.

BRENOT, P. and RIGUET, R. (1977). La trépanation néolithique. *Archéologia* (Paris), **104**, 8–17.

BREUIL, H. (1939). Bone and antler industry of the Choukoutien Sinanthropus site. *Palaeont. Sinica*, **6**.

BRIGHTWELL, A., DEMETRIOU, G., MASSEY, M. and NEACY, N. (1972). The Horniman Museum Kiln experiment at Highgate Wood. Part I. *The London Archaeologist*, **2**, 12–17. Part 2, ibid. 53–59.

BROGGER, A. and SHETELIG, H. (1970). *The Viking Ships*. Oslo 1953, London 1970.

BROHOLM, H. C. and HALD, M. (1935). Danske Bronzealders Dragter. *Nord. Fortidsminder*, **2** (5–6), 215–347.

BROHOLM, H. C., and HALD, M. (1948). *Bronze Age Fashion*. Gyldendal, Copenhagen.

BROHOLM., H. C. LARSEN, W. P. and Skjerne, G. (1949). *The Lures of the Bronze Age*. Gyldendal, Copenhagen.

BRØNDSTED, J. (1960). *The Vikings*. Penguin Books, London.

BRONGERS, J. A. (1965–66). Evidence for trepanning practice in the Netherlands during pre- and protohistoric times. *Ber. Rijksdienst oudheidk. Bodemonderz*. **15–16**, 221–226.

BRONGERS, J. A. (1969). Ancient Old-World trepanning instruments. *Ber. Rijksdienst oudheidk. Bodemonderz*. **19**, 7–16.

BROSE, D. S. (1975). Functional use of stone tools: a cautionary note on the role of animal fats. *Am. Antiq.* **40**, 86–94.

BROTHWELL, D. (1971). Forensic aspects of the so-called neolithic skeleton from Maiden Castle, Dorset. *Wld Archaeol.* **3**, 233–241.

BRYANT, G. F. (1970). Two experimental Romano-British kiln firings at Barton-on-Humber, Lincolnshire. *J. Scunthorpe Mus. Soc.* **3** no. 1, 1–16.

BRYANT, G. F. (1971). Experimental Romano-British kiln firings at Barton-on-Humber, Lincolnshire. *Workers' Educ. Ass., Barton-on-Humber, Occ. Pap.* **1**.

BRYANT, G. F. (1977). A Romano-British pottery kiln at Claxby, Lincolnshire excavation, discussion and experimental firings. *Lincs. Hist. Archaeol.* **12**, 5–16.

BUCK, P. H. (1945). An introduction to Polynesian anthropology. *Bull. Bernice P. Bishop Museum*, Honolulu. **187**.

BUDGE, E. A. W. (1972). *The Mummy*. Collier, New York.

BURNEZ, C. and CASE, H. (1966). Les camps néolithiques des Matignons à Juillac-le-Coq. *Gallia Préhist.* **9**(1), 131–245.

CALDER, C. S. T. (1956). Stone Age house sites in Shetland. *Proc. Soc. Antiq. Scotl.* **89**, 340–397.

CALLAHAN, E. (1974). The Wagner basalt quarries: a preliminary report. *The Ape. Experimental Archaeology Papers*, vol. 3, pp. 9–128. Virginia Commonwealth University, Richmond.

CALLAHAN, E. (1976). The Pamunkey project, Phase I and II. *The Ape. Experimental Archaeology Papers*, vol. 4. Virginia Commonwealth University, Richmond.

CALLEN, E. (1967). Analysis of Tehuacan coprolites. In *The Prehistory of the Tehuacan Valley* (D. J. Byers, ed.), vol. 1, pp. 261–289. The University of Texas, Austin.

CARTER, H. (1923–1933). *The Tomb of Tut-Ankh-Amen*. Cassell, London.

CHILDE, V. G. and THORNEYCROFT, W. (1938). The experimental production of the phenomena distinctive of vitrified forts. *Proc. Soc. Antiq. Scotl.* **72**, 44–55.

CHILDE, V. G. (1954). *New Light on the Most Ancient East*. Routledge and Kegan Paul, London.

CHRISTENSEN, A. E. (1968). *Boats of the North*. Oslo.

CHRISTENSEN, A. E. and MORRISON, I. (1976). Experimental archaeology and boats. *Int. J. naut. Archaeol. underwat. Explor.* **5**, 275–284.

CLARK, J. G. D. (1963). Neolithic bows from Somerset, England, and the prehistory of archery in north-west Europe. *Proc. prehist. Soc.* **29**, 50–98.

CLARK, J. G. D. and THOMPSON, M. W. (1953). The groove and splinter technique of working antler in Upper Paleolithic and Mesolithic Europe, with special reference to the material from Star Carr. *Proc. prehist. Soc.* **19**, 148–160.

CLARK, G. (1957). *Archaeology and Society*. Methuen, London.

CLARKE, D. L. (1972). Models and paradigms in contemporary archaeology. In *Models in Archaeology* (D. L. Clarke, ed.), pp. 1–60. Methuen, London.

CLARKE, J. C. and BOSWELL, R. C. (1976). Tests on round timber fence posts. *Forest Record*, **108**.

CLEERE, H. (1971). Ironmaking in a Roman furnace. *Britannia*, **2**, 203–217.

COGHLAN, H. H. (1940). Prehistoric copper and some experiments in smelting. *Trans. Newcomen Soc.* **20**, 49–65.

COLES, J. M. (1962). European Bronze Age Shields. *Proc. prehist. Soc.* **28**, 156–190.

COLES, J. M. (1963). Irish Bronze Age horns and their relations with northern Europe. *Proc. prehist. Soc.* **29**, 326–356.

COLES, J. M. (1973). *Archaeology by Experiment*. Hutchinson, London.

COLES, J. M. (1977). Experimental archaeology—theory and principles. In *Sources and Techniques in Boat Archaeology* (Brit. Archaeol. Rep. S.29) (S. McGrail, ed.), pp. 233–244.

COLES, J. M. and DARRAH, R. J. (1977). Experimental investigations in hurdle-making. *Somerset Levels Papers*, **3**, 32–38.

COLES, J. M., HEAL, S. V. E. and ORME, B. J. (1978). The use and character of wood in prehistoric Britain and Ireland. *Proc. prehist. Soc.* **44**, 1–46.

COMO, J. (1925). Das Grab eines römischen Arztes in Bingen. *Germania*, **9**, 152–162.

CONE, P. (ed.) (1977). *Treasures of Early Irish Art* 1500 B.C. *to* 1500 A.D. Metropolitan Museum of Art, New York.

COOKE, C. K. (1953). Examination of ash-filled pits in the Magosian deposits at Khami. *Occ. Pap. Nat. Mus. South. Rhod.* **18**, 529.

COSNER, A. J. (1956). Fire hardening of wood. *Am. Antiq.* **22**, 179–80.

COUTIER, L. (1929). Experiences de taille pour rechercher les anciennes techniques paléolithiques. *Bull. Soc. préhist. Fr.* **26**, 172–174.

COWAN, H. J. K. (1974). On "Papyrus Rafts Across the Atlantic". *Curr. Anthrop.* **15**, 332–333.

CRABTREE, D. E. (1966). A stoneworker's approach to analyzing and replicating the Lindenmeier Folsom. *Tebiwa.* **9** (1), 3–39.

CRABTREE, D. E. (1970). Flaking Stone with Wooden Implements. *Science*, **169**, 146–153.

CRABTREE, D. (1972). An Introduction to Flintworking. Part I. An introduction to the technology of stone tools. *Occ. Pap. Idaho State Univ.* **28**.

CRABTREE, D. E. and DAVIS, E. L. (1968). Experimental manufacture of wooden implements with tools of flaked stone, *Science*, **159**, 426–428.

CROSS, T. P. and SLOVER, C. H. (1936). *Ancient Irish Tales*. London.

CRUMLIN-PEDERSEN, O. (1970). The Viking ships of Roskilde. In *Aspects of the History of Wooden Shipbuilding*, pp. 7–11. Maritime Monographs and Reports, vol. 1.

CRUMLIN-PEDERSEN, O. (1975). Viking seamanship questioned. *Mariners' Mirror*, **61**, 127–131.

CUMMING, W. P., SKELTON, R. A. and QUINN, D. B. (1971). *The Discovery of North America*. Elek, London.

CURWEN, E. C. (1930a). Prehistoric flint sickles. *Antiquity*, **4**, 179–186.

CURWEN, E. C. (1930b). The silting of ditches in chalk. *Antiquity*, **4**, 97–100.

CURWEN, E. C. (1935). Agriculture and the flint sickle in Palestine. *Antiquity*, **9**, 62–66.

CURWEN, E. and E. C. (1926). On the use of scapulae as shovels. *Sussex Arch. Coll.* **67**, 139–145.

CUSHING, F. H. (1894). Primitive copper working: an experimental study. *Am. Anthrop.* **7**, 93–117 (old series).

CUSHING, F. H. (1895). The Arrow. *Amer. Anthrop.* **8**, 307–349 (old series).

DANNHEIMER, H. (1976). Siedlungsgeschichtliche Beobachtungen in Osten der Münchner Schotterebene. *Bayerische Vorgeschichtsblätter*, **41**, 107–120.

DAUVOIS, M. (1974). Industrie osseuse préhistorique et expérimentations. In

L'Industrie de l'os dans la préhistoire (H. Camps-Fabrer, ed.), pp. 73–84. University Provence.

DE BUCK, A. (1948). *Egyptian Readingbook,* vol. **1**. Leiden.

DE HAAS, R. HORREÜS (1977). Leven in het stenen tijdperk. *Avenue,* Feb. 1977, 8–13.

DE HAAS, R. HORREÜS (1978). *Living a Stone Age Life.* Privately printed.

DE NAVARRO, J. M. (1955). A doctor's grave of the Middle La Tène period from Bavaria. *Proc. prehist. Soc.* **21**, 231–48.

DEWDNEY, S. and KIDD, K. E. (1962). *Indian Rock Paintings of the Great Lakes.* University of Toronto Press, Toronto.

DIECK, A. (1976). Tatauierung in vor-und frühgeschichtlicher Zeit. *Archäol. Korrespondenzbl.* **6**, 169–173.

DRACK, W. (ed.) (1969, 1971). *Ur-und frühgeschichtliche Archäologie der Schweiz.* II. *Die Jüngere Steinzeit* (1969). III. *Die Bronzezeit* (1971). Schweizerische Gesellschaft für Ur-und Frühgeschichte, Basel.

DRESCHER, H. (1958). *Der Überfangguss: ein Beitrag zur Vorgeschichtlichen Metalltechnik.* Römisch-Germanischen Zentralmuseums, Mainz.

DRUCKER, P., HEIZER, I. F. and SQUIER, R. (1959). Excavations at La Venta, Tabasco, 1955. *Bur. Am. Eth. Bull.* **170**.

DUNHAM, D. (1956). Building an Egyptian pyramid. *Archaeology,* **9**, 159–165.

EAMES, F. (1915). *The Fashioning of Flint.* 27th Ann. Arch. Rep., Min. Education, Toronto.

EDGREN, B. and HERSCHEND, F. (1979). Nya gamla hus. Rekonstruktions-arbetena i Eketorps borg 1978. *Rapport Riksantikvarieämbetet och Statens Historiska Museer* 1979 (3).

EDWARDS, C. R. (1960). Sailing rafts of Sechura: history and problems of origin. *SWest. J. Anthrop.* **16**, 368–391.

EDWARDS, I. E. S. (1961). *The Pyramids of Egypt.* Penguin Books, Harmondsworth, Middlesex.

ELKIN, A. P. (1964). *The Australian Aborigines* (4th edition). Doubleday, New York.

ENGELBACH, R. (1923). *The Problem of the Obelisks.* Fisher Unwin, London.

ERASMUS, C. (1965). Monument building: some field experiments, *SWest. J. Anthrop.* **21**, 277–301.

EVANS, J. (1897). *Ancient Stone Implements, Weapons and Ornaments of Great Britain* (2nd edition). Longmans, London.

EVANS, J. G. and LIMBREY, S. (1974). The experimental earthwork on Morden Bog, Wareham, Dorset, England: 1963 to 1972. *Proc. prehist. Soc.* **40**, 170–202.

EVANS, J. G. (1971). Habitat change on the calcareous soils of Britain: the impact of Neolithic man. In *Economy and Settlement in Neolithic and Early Bronze Age Britain and Europe* (D. D. A. Simpson, ed.), pp. 27–73. University Press, Leicester.

FINNEY, B. R. (1967). New perspectives on Polynesian voyaging. *Bernice P. Bishop Mus. Spec. Pub.* **56**, 141–66.

FINNEY, B. R. (1977). Voyaging canoes and the settlement of Polynesia. *Science*, **196**, 1277–1285.

FISCHER, A. ET AL. (1979). *Stenalder eksperimenter i Lejre*. National Museum of Denmark, Copenhagen.

Flintknappers' Exchange. Department of Anthropology, The Catholic University of America, Washington D.C. 20064.

FOX, A. LANE (1875). On early modes of navigation. *J. anthrop. Inst.* **4**, 399–437.

FOX, A. LANE (1876). Excavations in Cissbury Camp, Sussex. *J. anthrop. Inst.* **5**, 357–390.

FRANKE, P. R. and WATSON, D. (1936). An experimental cornfield in Mesa Verde National Park. In *Symposium on Prehistoric Agriculture. Univ. New Mexico Bull.* **296**, 35–41.

FREDSJÖ, Å., JANSON, S., and MOBERG, C.-A. (1969). *Hällristningar i Sverige*. Forum, Oskarshamn.

GARDE-HANSEN, P. (1974). *On the Building of the Cheops Pyramid*. Danish Technical Press, Copenhagen.

GEJVALL, N.-G. (1969). Cremations. In *Science in Archaeology* (2nd edition). (D. Brothwell and E. S. Higgs, eds), pp. 468–479. Thames and Hudson, London.

GJESSING, G. (1936). *Nordenfjeldske Ristninger og Malinger av den Arktiske Gruppe*. Oslo.

GLADWIN, T. (1977). East is a big bird. In *Man's Many Ways* (R. A. Gould, ed.), pp. 94–110. Harper and Row, New York.

GLOB, P. V. (1969). *The Bog People*. Faber and Faber, London.

GORDON, D. H. (1953). Fire and sword: the technique of destruction. *Antiquity*, **27**, 149–153.

GORRINGE, H. H. (1882). *Egyptian Obelisks*. Gorringe, New York.

GOULD, R. A. (1977). Chipping stones in the Outback. In *Man's Many Ways*, (R. A. Gould, ed.), 62–69. Harper and Row, New York.

GOWLAND, W. (1902). Recent excavations at Stonehenge. *Archaeologia*, **58**, 37–118.

GRAHAM, J. A., HEIZER, R. F. and HESTER, T. R. (1972). A bibliography of replicative experiments in archaeology. Arch. Res. Facility, Dept. of Anth., University of California.

GRANT, C. (1967). *Rock Art of the American Indian*. Crowell, New York.

GRÄSLUND, A-S. (1975–77). Bränning på platsen eller särskild bålplats? Några notiser om ett bränningsförsök. *Tor*, **17**, 363–73.

GUILLET, E. (1963). *The Pioneer Farmer and Backwoodsman*. Ontario Publishing Company, Toronto.

HAKLUYT, R. (1589). *The Principall Navigations, Voiages and Discoveries of the English Nation*. London.

HALL, B. (1833). *Fragments of Voyages and Travels*, ser. 3, vol. 2, 80ff. London.

HAMMERICH, A. (1893). *Aarbøger*, 1893.

HAMMOND, N. (1972). Classic Maya music. *Archaeology*, **25**, Part 1, 124–131; Part 2, 222–228.

HAMPL, F. (1968). Paläethnographie und das Museum für Urgeschichte in Asparn a.d. Zaya, N.O. *Archaeologia Austriaca*, **44**, 34–48.

HAMPL, F. (1970). *Das Museum für Urgeschichte des Landes Niederosterreich mit urgeschichtlichem Freilichtmuseum in Asparn an der Zaya*. Vienna.

HANSEN, H. O. (1961). Undommelige Oldtidhuse. *Kuml*, 1961, 128–45.

HANSEN, H. O. (1962). *I Built a Stone Age House*. Phoenix, London.

HANSEN, H. O. (1966). *Bognaeseksperiment*. Lejre, Denmark.

HANSEN, H. O. (1968). Report of imitative ploughing experiments with copies of a prehistoric ard with passing-through stilt (Dostrop-type) 1962–8. *Reports from Experiments in Lejre* 1968, **1**.

HANSEN, H. O. (1969). Experimental ploughing with a Dostrop and replica. *Tools and Tillage*, **1**(2), 67–92.

HANSEN, H. O. (1974). *Some main Trends in the Development of the Lejre Center*. Lejre, Denmark.

HANSEN, H. O. (1977). *The Prehistoric Village at Lejre*. Historical–Archaeological Research Centre, Lejre.

HARDING, A. and YOUNG, R. (1979). Reconstruction of the hafting methods and function of stone implements. In *Stone Age Studies* (T. Clough and W. Cummins, eds), vol. 23, pp. 102–105. Council Brit. Archaeol. Res. Rep.

HARRIOT, T. (1588). *A briefe and true report of the New Found Land of Virginia*. London.

HARRISON, F. and RIMMER, J. (1964). *European Musical Instruments*. Studio Vista, London.

HARRISSON, T. and MEDWAY, LORD (1962). The first classification of prehistoric bone and tooth artifacts. *Sarawak Mus. J.* **10**, 335–362.

HAURY, E. W. (1931). Minute beads from prehistoric pueblos. *Am. Antiq.* **33**, 80–87.

HEIZER, R. F. (1966). Ancient heavy transport, methods and achievements. *Science*, **153**, 821–30.

HENSHALL, A. S. (1950). Textiles and weaving appliances in prehistoric Britain. *Proc. prehist. Soc.* **16**, 130–162.

HESTER, J. A. (1953). Agriculture economy and population densities of the Maya. *Carnegie Inst. Washington, Year Book*, vol. 52, pp. 288–92.

HESTER, T. R. and HEIZER, R. F. (1973). *Bibliography of Archaeology 1: Experiments, Lithic Technology and Petrography*. Addison–Wesley Modules, vol. 29.

HEYERDAHL, T. (1950). *The Kon-Tiki Expedition. By Raft Across the South Seas*. Allen and Unwin, London.

HEYERDAHL, T. (1952). *American Indians in the Pacific*. Allen and Unwin, London.

HEYERDAHL, T. (1955). The balsa raft in aboriginal navigation off Peru and Ecuador. *SWest. J. Anthrop.* **11**, 251–264.

HEYERDAHL, T. (1957). Guara navigation: indigenous sailing off the Andean coast. *SWest. J. Anthrop.* **13**, 134–143.

HEYERDAHL, T. (1958). *Aku-Aku*. Rand McNally, Chicago.

HEYERDAHL, T. (1971). *The Ra Expeditions*. Allen and Unwin, London.

HEYERDAHL, T. (1978a). *Early Man and the Ocean*. Allen and Unwin, London.

HEYERDAHL, T. (1978b). Tigris sails into the past. *Natn. geogr. Mag.* **154**, 806–827.

HOBLEY, B. (1967). An experimental reconstruction of a Roman military turf rampart. 7th Congress of Roman Frontier Studies (Tel-Aviv), pp. 21–33.

HOBLEY, B. (1971). The Lunt. *Curr. Archaeol.* **24**, 16–21.

HOBLEY, B. (1973). Reconstructing the past. The Lunt Roman fort: theory and practice of experimental archaeology. *Nat. Heritage Museum News*, **3**, 4–5.

HOBLEY, B. (1974). The Lunt: reconstruction. *Curr. Archaeol.* **44**, 276–280.

HOBLEY, B. (1975). The Lunt Roman fort and training school for Roman cavalry, Baginton, Warwickshire. *Trans. Bgham Warwicks Archaeol. Soc.* **87**, 1–56.

HODGES, H. W. M. (1962). Thin sections of prehistoric pottery: an empirical study. *Bull. Univ. Lond. Inst. Arch.* **3**, 58–68.

HOLE, F. and HEIZER, R. F. (1977). *Prehistoric Archaeology. A brief introduction.* Holt, Rinehart and Winston, New York.

HOLMES, W. H. (1919). *Handbook of Aboriginal American Antiquities. I. The Lithic Industries. Bur. Am. Ethnol. Bull.* **60**.

HUTCHINSON, T. J. (1875). Anthropology of prehistoric Peru. *J. R. Anthrop. Inst.* **4**, 1875.

INGERSOLL, D., YELLEN, J. E. and MacDONALD, W. (ed.) (1977). *Experimental Archaeology*. Columbia University Press, New York.

IJZEREEF, G. F. (1974). A medieval jaw-sledge from Dordrecht. *Ber. Rijksdienst Oudheidk. Bodemonderz.* **24**, 181–184.

IREGREN, E. and JONSSON, R. (1973). Hur ben krymper vid kremering. *Fornvännen*, **68**, 97–100.

IVERSEN, J. (1956). Forest clearance in the Stone Age. *Scient. Am.* **194**, 36–41.

JASINK, J. (n.d.) *M. Radwan Museum of Ancient Metallurgy at Nowa Slupia*. Museum of Technology, Warsaw.

JENNINGS, J. D. (1957). Danger Cave. *Soc. Am. archaeol. Mem.* **14**.

JEWELL, P. A. (1963). *The Experimental Earthwork on Overtown Down, Wiltshire. 1960.* Br. Ass. Adv. Sci.

JEWELL, P. A. and DIMBLEBY, G. W. (1966). The experimental earthwork on Overtown Down, Wiltshire, England: the first four years. *Proc. prehist. Soc.* **32**, 313–42.

JEFFERYS, C. W. (1942). *The Picture Gallery of Canadian History. I. Discovery to 1763.* Ryerson, Toronto.

JOHANSSON, T. (1975–77). Experimentella studier av skifferpilspetsar. *Tor*, **17**, 107–157.

JOHNSON, D. L., MUHS, D. R. and BARNHARDT, M. L. (1977). The effects of frost heaving on objects in soils, II: laboratory experiments. *Plains Anthrop.* **22**, 133–147.

JOHNSON, L. L. (1978). A history of flint-knapping experimentation, 1838–1976. *Curr. Anthrop.* **19**, 337–372.

JOHNSON, T. (1957). An experiment with cave-painting media. *S. Afr. Archaeol. Bull.* **47**, 98–101.

JOHNSTONE, P. (1957). *Buried Treasure.* Phoenix, London.

JOHNSTONE, P. (1972). Bronze Age sea trial. *Antiquity,* **46**, 269–74.

JOHNSTONE, P. (1974). *The Archaeology of Ships.* Bodley Head, London.

JONES, GWYN (1964). *The Norse Atlantic Saga.* Oxford University Press, London.

JONES, J. and BRAY, W. (1974). *El Dorado. The Gold of Ancient Colombia.* New York Graphic Society, New York.

JUAN, G. and DE ULLOA, A. (1748). *Relacion Historica del Viaje a la America Meridional,* vol. 1. Madrid.

KEELEY, L. H. and NEWCOMER, M. H. J. (1977). Microwear analysis of experimental flint tools: a test case. *J. Archaeol. Sci.* **4**, 29–62.

KELLER, F. (1878). *The Lake Dwellings of Switzerland and other parts of Europe.* Longmans Green, London.

KENNEDY, R. F. (ed.) (1961). *Thomas Baines. Journal of Residence in Africa 1842–1853.* Van Riebeck, Cape Town.

KIRBY, P. R. (1946). The trumpets of Tut-ankh-amen and their successors. *Jl. R. Anthrop. Inst.* **77**, 33–45.

KLAR, M. (1971). Musikinstrumente der Romerzeit in Bonn. *Bonn. Jahrbuch,* **171**, 301–33.

KLEIN, R. G. (1969). *Man and Culture in the Late Pleistocene.* Chandler, San Francisco.

KLEINDIENST, M. R. and KELLER, C. M. (1976). Towards a functional analysis of handaxes and cleavers: the evidence from Eastern Africa. *Man,* **11**, 176–187.

KNOWLES, W. J. (1903). Irish flint arrow- and spear-heads. *Jl R. Anthrop. Inst.* **33**, 44–56.

KNOWLES, F. H. S. (1944). The manufacture of a Flint Arrowhead by Quartzite Hammer-stone. *Occasional Papers on Technology,* vol. 1. Pitt Rivers Museum, Oxford.

KNUDSON, S. J. (1978). *Culture in Retrospect. An Introduction to Archaeology.* Rand McNally. Chicago.

KNUTSSON, K. (1975–77). Skrapor och skrapning. *Tor,* **17**, 19–62.

KORFMANN, M. (1972). Schleuder und Bogen in Sudwestasien. Von den frühesten Belegen bis zum Beginn der historischen Stadtstaaten. *Antiquitas,* vol. 13. Habelt, Bonn.

KROEBER, T. (1961). *Ishi in Two Worlds: a Biography of the Last Wild Indian in North America.* University of California Press, Berkeley. 1976 edition (ill.)

KRZAK, Z. (1971). Najwcześniejsze statki wschodnioatlantyckie i zachodniośródziemnomorskie. Ze studiów nad rekonstrukcją. (The earliest east-Atlantic and West-Mediterranean ships. Studies in reconstruction). *Kwartalnik Historii Kultury Materialnej,* **19**, 605–625.

KRZAK, Z. (1972). The problem of reconstructing an Afro-Iberian ship from the Neolithic Age. *Almogaren,* **3**, 147–166.

KUBLER, G. (1962). *The Art and Architecture of Ancient America*. Penguin Books, Harmondsworth, Middlesex.

LAJOUX, J.-D. (1963). *The Rock Paintings of Tassili*. Thames and Hudson, London.

LAKE, F. and WRIGHT, H. (1977). *Bibliography of Archery*. Simon Archery Foundation. University of Manchester.

LANDSTRÖM, BJÖRN (1966). *Columbus. The Story of Don Cristóbal Colon, Admiral of the Ocean, and his Four Voyages Westward to the Indies According to Contemporary Sources*. Macmillan, New York.

LANDSTRÖM, B. (1970). *Ships of the Pharaohs*. Allen and Unwin, London.

LANGE, F. W. and RYDBERG, C. R. (1972). Abandonment and post-abandonment behaviour at a rural central American house-site. *Am. Antiq.* **37**, 419–432.

LAUDONNIÈRE, R. DE (1586). *L'histoire notable de la Floride.*

LAUER, J.-P. (1974). *Le Mystère des Pyramides*. Paris.

LAYARD, A. (1873). *Nineveh and its Remains*. John Murray, London.

LEAKEY, L. S. B. (1954). Working stone, bone and wood. In *A History of Technology* (C. Singer, E. J. Holmyard and A. R. Hall, eds), vol. 1, pp. 128–43. Clarendon Press, Oxford.

LEE, R. B. and DE VORE, I. (ed.) (1968). *Man the Hunter*. Aldine, Chicago.

LEE, R. B. and DE VORE, I. (ed.) (1976). *Kalahari Hunter-Gatherers: Studies of the Kung Sang and their neighbours*, Cambridge, Massachusetts.

LEECHMAN, D. (1950). Aboriginal tree-felling. *Natl. Mus. Canada, Bull.* **118**, 44–9.

LEEDS, E. T. (1926). A Saxon village at Sutton Courtenay, Berkshire. *Archaeologia*, **76**, 59–80.

LEROI–GOURHAN, A. (1968). *The Art of Prehistoric Man in Western Europe*. Thames and Hudson, London.

LEVISON, M., WARD, R. G. and WEBB, J. W. (1973). *The Settlement of Polynesia*. University of Minnesota Press, Minnesota.

LEWIS, D. (1972). *We, the Navigators. The Ancient Art of Land-finding in the Pacific*. Australian National University Press, Canberra.

Lithic Technology. Center for Archaeological Research, University of Texas, San Antonio.

LONG, S. V. (1965). Cire-perdue casting in pre-Columbian Mexico: an experimental approach. *Am. Antiq.* **30**, 189–192.

LOTHROP, S. K. (1932). Aboriginal navigation off the west coast of South America. *Jl R. Anthrop. Inst.* **62**, 229–256.

LOWERY, P. R., SAVAGE, R. D. A. and WILKINS, R. L. (1971). Scriber, graver, scorper, tracer: notes on experiments in bronzeworking technique. *Proc. prehist. Soc.* **37**(1), 167–182.

LUCAS, A. (1962). *Ancient Egyptian materials and industries*. Edward Arnold, London.

LUND, C. (1973). Oldtidens Orkester. *Skalk*, 1973 (2), 18–28.

LÜNING, J. (1972, 1974). Das Exsperiment in Michelsberger Erdwerk in Mayen. *Archäol. Korrespondenzbl.* **2**, 251–2, **4**, 125–131.

MALINA, J. (1973). Petroarchaeological notes on manufacturing technology of Neolithic polished stone industry. *Scripta Fac. Sci. Nat. Ujep Brunensis, Geologia*, **2-3**, 3, 103–107.

MALLOWAN, M. E. L. (1965). *Early Mesopotamia and Iran*. Thames and Hudson, London.

MARINATOS, S. (1960). *Crete and Mycenae*. Thames and Hudson, London.

MARSTRANDER, S. (1976). Building a hide boat. An archaeological experiment. *Int. J. naut. Archaeol. underwat. Explor.* **5**, 13–22.

McADAM, E. and WATKINS, T. (1974). Experimental reconstruction of a short cist. *J. Archaeol. Sci.* **1**, 383–386.

MACADAM, R. (1860). Ancient Irish Trumpets. *Ulster J. Arch.* **8**, 99–110.

McGRAIL, S. (1974). *The Building and Trials of the Replica of an Ancient Boat: the Gokstad Faering. 1. Building the Replica.* Maritime Monographs and Reports, vol. 11. Greenwich.

McGRAIL, S. (ed.) (1977a). *Sources and Techniques in Boat Archaeology*. Brit. Archaeol. Rep. S29.

McGRAIL, S. (1977b). Aspects of experimental boat archaeology. In McGrail 1977a, 245–258.

McGRAIL, S. (1978). *Logboats of England and Wales*. Brit. Archaeol. Rep. 51.

MACGREGOR, A. J. (1975). Problems in the interpretation of microscopic wear patterns: the evidence from bone skates. *J. Archaeol. Sci.* **2**, 385–390.

McGUIRE, J. D. (1891). The stone hammer and its various uses. *Am. Anthrop.* **4**, 301–312.

McGUIRE, J. D. (1892). Materials, apparatus and processes of the aboriginal lapidary. *Am. Anthrop.* **5**, 165–176.

McGUIRE, J. D. (1896). Study of the primitive methods of drilling. *U.S. Nat. Mus., Rep.* 1894.

McINTOSH, R. J. (1974). Archaeology and mud wall decay in a West African village. *Wld Archaeol.* **6**, 154–171.

MacIVER, R. (1921). On the manufacture of Etruscan and other ancient black wares. *Man*, **21**, 86–88.

McKEE, E. (1974). *The Building and Trials of the Replica of an Ancient Boat: The Gokstad Faering. 2. The Sea Trials.* Maritime Monographs and Reports, vol. 11. Greenwich.

McKEE, J. E. G. (1977). Hypothetical reconstructions in boat archaeology. In *Sources and Techniques in Boat Archaeology* (S. McGrail, ed.), Brit. Arch. aeol. Rep. S29, pp. 205–214.

McKERN, T. (1970). Estimation of skeletal age. In *Personal Identification in Mass Disasters* (T. D. Steward, ed.), pp. 41–56. Smithsonian Institute.

McPARLAND, P. (1977). Experiments in the firing and breaking of rocks. *The Calgary Archaeologist*, **5**, 31–33.

MEANS, P. A. (1942). Pre-Spanish navigation off the Andean coast. *Am. Neptune*, **2**, 2.

MEGAW, J. V. S. (1960). Penny whistles and prehistory. *Antiquity*, **34**, 6–13.

MEGAW, J. V. S. (1968). Problems and non-problems in paleo-organology: a musical miscellany. In *Studies in Ancient Europe* (J. Coles and D. Simpson, eds), pp. 333–358. University Press, Leicester.

MILISAUSKAS, S. (1972). An analysis of Linear Culture longhouses at Olszanica Bi, Poland. *Wld Archaeol.* **4**, 57–74.

MOIR, R. (1919). *Pre-Paleolithic Man.* Private print, London.

MOIR, R. (1926). Experiments in the shaping of wood with flint implements. *Nature*, **117** (2949), 665–6.

MORITZ, L. A. (1958). *Grain Mills and Flour in Classical Antiquity.* Clarendon Press, Oxford.

MORITZ, L. A. and JONES, C. R. (1950). Experiments in grinding wheat in a Romano-British quern. *Milling*, June 1950, 2–4.

MORRIS, E. H. and BURGH, R. F. (1954). *Basket Maker II Sites near Durango, Colorado.* Publ. 604. Carnegie Inst., Washington.

MUNRO, R. (1897). *Prehistoric Problems.* William Blackwood, London.

NASH, C. H. (1968). Residence mounds: an intermediate Middle Mississippian settlement pattern. *Memphis State Univ. Anth. Research Center, Occ. Pap.* 2.

NELSON, E. W. (1899). *The Eskimo about Bering Straits.* Bur. Am. Ethnol. 18th Ann. Rep. (1).

NELSON, N. C. (1916). Flint-working by Ishi. *Holmes Anniversary Volume*, pp. 397–402.

NELSON, R. K. (1969). *Hunters of the Northern Ice.* University of Chicago Press, Chicago.

NEWCOMER, M. H. (1970). Conjoined flakes from the lower loam, Barnfield pit, Swanscombe. *Proc. R. Anthrop. Inst.* 1970, 51–59.

NEWCOMER, M. H. (1971). Some quantative experiments in handaxe manufacture. *Wld Archaeol.* **3**, 85–94.

NEWCOMER, M. H. (1974). Study and replication of bone tools from Ksar Akil (Lebanon). *Wld Archaeol.* **6**, 138–153.

NIELSON, S. (1966). Eksperiment. *Skalk*, 1966(3), 13–23.

NISBET, H. C. (1974). A geological approach to vitrified forts: part 1, the archaeological and scientific background. *Sci. Archaeol.* **12**, 3–12.

NISBET, H. C. (1975). A geological approach to vitrified forts: part 2, bedrock and building stones. *Sci. Archaeol.* **15**, 3–16.

OATES, J., DAVIDSON, T. E., KAMILLI, D. and McKERRELL, H. (1977). Seafaring merchants of Ur? *Antiquity*, **51**, 221–234.

ODDY, W. A. (ed.) (1977). *Aspects of Early Metallurgy.* Historical Metallurgy Society and British Museum Research Laboratory.

O'KELLY, M. J. (1954). Excavation and experiments in ancient Irish cooking-places. *Jl R. Soc. Antiq. Irel.* **84**, 105–155.

OLSEN, O. and CRUMLIN-PEDERSEN, O. (1967). The Skuldelev Ships. *Acta Archaeol.* **38**, 73–174.

O'MEARA, J. (1976). *The Voyage of Saint Brendan.*

PAYNE, S. (1972). Partial recovery and sample bias: the results of some sieving experiments. In *Papers in Economic Prehistory* (E. S. Higgs, ed.), pp. 49–64. University Press, Cambridge.

PEARCE, R. J. (1979). Excavations and reconstruction of the Lawson site. *Newsletter* 1, no. 1. Museum of Indian Archaeology, University of Western Ontario, Canada.

PEI, WEN CHUNG (1936). Le rôle des phénomènes naturels dans l'éclatement et le façonnement des roches dures utilisées par l'homme préhistorique. *Revue Géogr. phys. Géol. dyn.* **9**, 349–423.

PETRIE, W. M. F. (1884). On the mechanical methods of the ancient Egyptians. *J. Anthrop. Inst.* **13**, 88–118.

PFEIFFER, J. (1969). *The Emergence of Man.* Harper and Row, New York.

PIGGOTT, S. (1940). A trepanned skull of the Beaker period from Dorset and the practice of trepanning in prehistoric Europe. *Proc. prehist. Soc.* **6**, 112–132.

PIGGOTT, S. (1959). The Carnyx in Early Iron Age Britain. *Antiq. J.* **39**, 19–32.

POND, A. (1930). Primitive methods of working stone. Based on experiments by Halvor L. Skavlem. *Logan Mus. Bull. Beloit College, Wisc.* **2**.

POPE, S. T. (1918). Yahi Archery. *Univ. Calif. Publ. Am. Archaeol. Ethnol.* **13**(3), 103–152.

POPE, S. T. (1923). A study of bows and arrows. *Univ. Calif. Publ. Am. Archaeol. Ethnol.* **13**(9), 329–414.

PULESTON, D. E. (1971). An experimental approach to the function of Classic Maya chultuns, *Am. Antiq.* **36**, 322–34.

RANDOLPH, J. R. (1973). *British Travellers among the Southern Indians, 1660–1763.* University of Oklahoma Press, Norman.

RAU, C. (1869). Drilling in stone without metal. *Smithson. Instn. Ann. Rep.* 1869, 392–400.

RAU, C. (1881). Aboriginal stone drilling. *Am. Nat.* **15**, 536–542.

RAY, P. H. (1886). Manufacture of bows and arrows among the Natano (Hupa) and Kenuck (Klamath) Indians. *Am. Nat.* **20**, 832–833.

REDDING, B. B. (1879). How our ancestors in the Stone Age made their implements. *Am. Nat.* **13**, 667–674.

REED, R. (1973). *Ancient Skins, Parchments and Leathers.* Seminar Press, London and New York.

REYNOLDS, P. J. (1974). Experimental Iron Age storage pits: an interim report. *Proc. prehist. Soc.* **40**, 118–131.

REYNOLDS, P. J. (1976). Experimental archaeology and the Butser ancient farm project. *Rescue News*, **11**, 7–8.

REYNOLDS, P. J. (1977a). Experimental archaeology and the Butser Ancient Farm Research Project. In *The Iron Age in Britain—A Review* (J. Collis, ed.), pp. 32–40. University of Sheffield.

REYNOLDS, P. J. (1977b). Slash and burn experiment. *Archaeol. J. 134*, 307–318.

REYNOLDS, P. J. (1978). Archaeology by experiment: a research tool for tomorrow. In *New Approaches to our Past. An archaeological Forum* (T. C. Darvill, M. Parker Pearson, R. W. Smith and R. M. Thomas, eds.), pp. 139–155. University of Southampton.

REYNOLDS, P. J. (1979). *Iron Age Farm—the Butser Experiment*. British Museum, London.

RIBAULD, CAPT. (1563). *The Whole and True Discoverye of Terra Florida*. London.

RIETH, A. (1958). Zur Technik des Steinbohrens im Neolithikum. *Z. Schweizerische Archäologie Kunstgeschichte*, **18**, 101–109.

RIGAUD, A. (1972). La technologie du burin appliqée au matériel osseux de la Garenne (Indre). *Bull. Soc. Préhist. F.* **69**, 104–108.

RIMMER, J. (1969). *Ancient Musical Instruments of Western Asia in the British Museum*. British Museum, London.

ROBINSON, E. (1942). Shell fishhooks of the California coast. *Occ. Pap. Bernice P. Bishop Mus.* **17**(4).

ROBINSON, H. R. (1972). Problems in reconstructing Roman armour. *Bonn. Jahrbuch*, **172**, 24–35.

ROBINSON, H. R. (1975). *The Armour of Imperial Rome*. Arms and Armour Press, London.

ROESDAHL, E. (1978). Vognen og Vikingerne. *Skalk*, 1978 (4), 9–14.

RUDENKO, S. I. (1970). *Frozen Tombs of Siberia. The Pazyryk Burials of Iron Age horsemen*. Dent, London.

RUDNER, J. and RUDNER, I. (1970). *The Hunter and his Art*. Struik, Cape Town.

RUSSELL, H. S. (1963). Pot boiling with red-hot stones. *Bull. Mass. Archaeol. Soc.* **24**, 58–60.

RYDER, M. L. (1966). Can one cook in a skin? *Antiquity*, **40**, 225–227.

RYDER, M. L. (1969). Paunch cooking, *Antiquity*, **43**, 218–220.

RYLATT, M. (1978). The Lunt Gyrus. *Curr. Archaeol.* **63**, 123–125.

SADEK-KOOROS, H. (1972). Primitive bone fracturing: a method of research. *Am. Antiq.* **37**, 369–382.

SALMEN, W. (1970). Urgeschichtliche und mittelalterliche Musikinstrumente aus Schleswig-Holstein. *Offa*, **27**, 5–19.

SARAYDAR, S. and SHIMADA, I. (1971). A quantitative comparison of efficiency between a stone axe and a steel axe. *Am. Antiq.* **36**, 216–217.

SCHLABOW, K. (1976). *Textilfunde der Eisenzeit in Norddeutschland*. Karl Wacholtz, Neumünster.

SCHMIDT, H. (1973). The Trelleborg house reconsidered. *Medieval Archaeol.* **17**, 52–77.

SCHNEIDER, R. C. (1972). *Crafts of the North American Indians. A Craftsman's Manual*. Van Nostrand Reinhold, New York.

SELMER, C. (1959). The Navigatio Sancti Brendani Abbatis. *Medieval Studies*, vol. 4. University of Notre Dame Press.

SEMENOV, S. A. (1964). *Prehistoric Technology*. Cory, Adams and Mackay, London.

SEVERIN, T. (1978). *The Brendan Voyage*. Hutchinson, London.

SHAW, C. T. (1945). Bead-making with a bow-drill in the Gold Coast. *Jl R. Anthrop. Inst.* **75**, 45–50.

SHAW, T. (1966). Experimental archaeology. *W. Afr. Archaeol. Newsletter*, **4**, 38–39.

SHAW, T. (1969. Tree-felling by fire. *Antiquity*, **43**, 52.

SHAW, T. (1970). Methods of earthwork building. *Proc. prehist. Soc.* **36**, 380–381.

SHEETS, P. D. and MUTO, G. R. (1972). Pressure blades and total cutting edge: an experiment in lithic technology. *Science*, **175**, 632–634.

SJØVOLD, T. (1959). *The Oseberg Find and other Viking Ship Finds*. Oslo.

SKJOLSVOLD, A. (1961). The stone statues and quarries of Rano Raraku. In *Archaeology of Easter Island* (T. Heyerdahl and E. Ferdon, eds), pp. 339–372. Allen and Unwin, London.

SLATER, E. A. and CHARLES, J. A. (1970). Archaeological classification by metal analysis. *Antiquity*, **44**, 207–213.

SMITH, A. L. and KIDDER, A. V. (1951). *Excavations at Nebaj, Guatemala*. Carnegie Inst. Washington Publ. 594.

SMITH, G. V. (1893). The use of flint blades to work pine wood. *Ann. Rep. Smithsonian Inst.* 1891, 601–605.

SPENCER, L. (1974). Replicative experiments in the manufacture and use of a Great Basin atlatl. In *Great Basin Atlatl Studies* (T. R. Hester, M. P. Mildner and L. Spencer, eds). Ballena Press, Ramona, California.

SPRUYTTE, J. (1977). *Etudes Expérimentales sur l'attelage. Contribution à l'histoire du cheval*. Editions Crépin-leblond, Paris.

SPURRELL, F. C. J. (1892). Notes on early sickles. *Archaeol. J.* **49**, 53–69.

STANFORD, D., BONNICHSEN, R. and MORLAN, R. (1979). Modern and prehistoric evidence of a bone-flaking technology. *Science* (in press).

STARTIN, W. (1978). Linear Pottery Culture houses: reconstruction and man power. *Proc. prehist. Soc.* **44**, 143–160.

STEELE, R. H. (1930). Experiments in Kaitahu (Ngai-Tahu) methods in drilling. *J. Polynes. Soc.* **39**, 181–188.

STEENSBERG, A. (1943). *Ancient Harvesting Implements*. National Museum, Copenhagen.

STEENSBERG, A. (1955). Mit Braggender Flamme. *Kuml*, 1955, 63–130.

STEENSBERG, A. (1973). A 6000-year-old ploughing implement from Satrup Moor. *Tools and Tillage*, **2**, 105–118.

STEGGERDA, M. (1941). *Maya Indians of Yucatan*. Carnegie Inst. Washington Publ. 531.

STELCL, J. and MALINA, J. (1970). *Anwedung der Petrographie in der Archaeologie*. Folia Fac. Sci. Nat. Univ. Purkynianae Brunensis. Geologia, vol. 11, no. 5.

STENTON, F. (ed.) (1957). *The Bayeux Tapestry*. Phaidon. London.

STEPHENSON, R. L., FERGUSON, A. L. L. and H. G. (1963). *The Accokeek Creek Site: a Middle Atlantic Seaboard Culture Sequence*. Anthrop. Pap. 20, Mus. Anthrop., Univ. Michigan.

STEWART, H. (1973). *Artifacts of the Northwest Coast Indians*. Hancock House, Saanichton, B.C.

STEWART, T. D. (1958). Stone Age skull surgery: a general review with emphasis on the New World. *Smithsonian Report 1958*, 469–491.

STONE, E. H. (1924). *The Stones of Stonehenge.* Scott, London.

STRZAŁKO, JAN and PIONTEK, JANUSZ. (1974). Wplyw Spalania w Warunkach Zblizonych do Kremacji Pradziejdwych na Morfologie Kości. (Influence of experimental cremation in conditions close to those of prehistory on the morphology of bones). *Przegl. antrop.* **40**, 315–326.

STRZAŁKO, JAN, PIONTEK, JANUSZ and MALINOWSKI, ANDRZEJ (1974). Mozliwości Identyfikacji Szczatków Ludzkich z Grobów Ciałopalnych w Świetle Wyników Badań. Eksperymentalnych. (Possibilities of burned human bones identification in the light of experimental investigations). In *Metody, Wyniki i Konsekwencje Badań Kości z Grobów Cialopalnych.* (Methods, results and consequences of investigations of bones from cremation burials), pp. 31–42. Posnan.

SWANSON, E. (ed.) (1975). *Lithic Technology: Making and using Stone Tools.* Mouton, Hague.

TAYLOR, J. J. (1968). Early Bronze Age gold neck-rings in western Europe. *Proc. prehist. Soc.* **34**, 259–265.

THOMAS, R. A. and WARREN, N. H. (1970). A middle woodland cemetery in Central Delaware: excavations at the Island Field site. *Bull. Archaeol. Soc. Delaware, n.s.* **8**.

THOMPSON, M. W. (1954). Azilian harpoons. *Proc. prehist. Soc.* **20**, 193–211.

THOMSEN, T. (1929). Egekistefundet fra Egtved, fra den aeldre Bronze-alder. *Nordiske Fortidsminder*, **2** (4), 165–214.

THOMSEN, E. G. and THOMSEN, H. H. (1970). Precolumbian obsidian ear-spools: an investigation of possible manufacturing methods. *Univ. Calif., Contrib. Arch. Res. Facility*, **8**, 41–53.

THROCKMORTON, P. (1970). *Shipwrecks and Archaeology.* Gollancz, London.

TILLEY, A. F. (1971). An experiment under oars. *Antiquity*, **45**, Pl. 10–11.

TIXIER, J. (1974). Glossary for the description of stone tools, with special reference to the Epipalaeolithic of the Maghreb. *Newsletter of Lithic Technology Spec. Publ.* 1.

TODD, M. (1975). *The Northern Barbarians.* Hutchinson, London.

TRIER, B. (1969). *Das Haus im Nordwesten der Germania Libera.* Provinzial-institut f. Westfälische Landes-und Volkskunde, vol. 4.

TURNBULL, C. (1968). *The Forest People.* Simon and Schuster, New York.

TYLECOTE, R. F. (1969). Iron smelting experiments at Varde, Denmark. *Bull. hist. Metall. Group*, **3**, 64–65.

TYLECOTE, R. F. (1973). Casting copper and bronze into stone moulds. *Bull. hist. Metall. Group*, **7**, 1–5.

TYLECOTE, R. F. (1974). Can copper be smelted in a crucible? *Bull. hist. Metall. Group*, **8**, 54.

TYLECOTE, R. F. (1977). Summary of results of experimental work on early copper smelting. In *Aspects of early metallurgy: papers presented at a symposium ... organised by the Historical Metallurgy Society and the British Museum Research Laboratory and held at the British Museum on 22nd and 23rd April 1977* (W. Oddy, ed.), pp. 5–12.

TYLECOTE, R. F. and BOYDELL, P. J. (1978). Experiments on copper smelting based on early furnaces found at Timna. Chalcolithic copper smelting. Excavations and experiments. *Archaeo-metallurgy, monog.* 1, 27–49.

TYLECOTE, R. F. and OWLES, E. (1961). A second-century iron-smelting site at Ashwicken, Norfolk. *Norfolk Archaeol.* **32**(2), 142–162.

Unité de Recherche Archéologique (1977). Reconstitution d'une maison néolithique à Cuiry-les-Chandardes. Les Fouilles Protohistoriques dans la Vallée de l'Aisne, 5. *Unité de Recherche Archéologique*, **12**, 251–261.

VAN DER LEEUW, S. E. (1976). *Studies in the Technology of Ancient Pottery.* Huisdrukkerij Universiteit von Amsterdam.

VAN DE VELDE, P. (1973). Rituals, skins and Homer: The Danubian "tan-pits". *Analecta Praehistorica Leidensia*, **6**, 50–65.

VAN MENSCH, PETER, J. A. (1974). A Roman soup-kitchen at Zwammerdam? *Ber. Rijksdienst oudheidk. Bodemonderz.* **24**, 159–165.

VAN SPILLBERGEN, J. (1619). *Speculum Orientalis Occidentalis que Indiae Naviga-tion 1614–18.* Leiden.

VOCE, E. (1951). Bronze casting in ancient moulds. *Pitt-Rivers Mus. Occ. Pap. Tech.* **4**, 112–115.

VOGT, E. (1954). Pfahlbaustudien. In *Das Pfahlbauproblem* (E. Vogt, ed.), pp. 119–219. Schweizerische Gesellschaft für Urgeschichte, Schaffhausen.

VOSS, O. (1962). Jernudvinding i Danmark i forhistorisk Tid. *Kuml*, 1962, 7–32.

WARREN, S. H. (1914). The Experimental Investigation of Flint Fracture and its Application to Problems of Human Implements. *Jl R. Anthrop. Inst.* **44**, 512–551.

WATSON, P. J. and YARNELL, R. A. (1966). Archaeological and palaeo-ethnobotanical investigation in Salts Cave, Mammoth Cave National Park, Kentucky. *Am. Antiq.* **31**, 842–849.

WEINER, J. S. (1955). *The Piltdown Forgery.* Clarendon Press, Oxford.

WELLS, C. (1964). *Bones, Bodies and Disease.* Thames and Hudson, London.

WELLS, C. (1974). Trephination of five early Saxon skulls. *Antiquity*, **48**, 298–302.

WEST, M. T. and HANSEN, H.-O. (n.d.) *The Lejre Approach to Environmental Awareness.* Historical–Archaeological Research Center, Lejre.

WEST, S. (1973). West Stow. *Curr. Archaeol.* **40**, 151–158.

West Stow Environmental Archaeology Group (1974). Experiment and the Anglo-Saxon Environment. In *Anglo-Saxon Settlement and landscape: papers presented to a symposium, Oxford 1973* (T. Rowley, ed.). Brit. Archaeol. Rep. vol. 6, pp. 78–86.

WHEELER, R. E. M. (1953). An Early Iron Age "beach head" at Lulworth, Dorset. *Antiq. J.* **33**, 1–13.

WHEELER, R. E. M. (1954). *The Stanwick Fortifications.* Rep. Res. Comm. Soc. Ant. Lond., vol. 17.

WILD, J. P. (1970). *Textile Manufacture in the Northern Roman Provinces.* University Press, Cambridge.

WILLOUGHBY, C. C. (1903). Primitive metal working. *Am. Anthrop.* **5**, 55–57.

WILSON, T. (1899). Arrowpoints, spearheads and knives of prehistoric times. *Ann. Rept., Smithsonian Inst.* (*for 1897*), 823–988.

WIMMER, F. (1930). Vier neuentdeckte la-Tène Gräber in Guntramsdorf. *Materialen Urgeschichte Osterreichs*, **5**, 127–136.

WISE, F. (1742). *Further observations upon the White Horse and other Antiquitie in Berkshire with an Account of the Whiteleaf Cross in Buckinghamshire.* University Printing House, Oxford.

WOOLLEY, L. (1934). *Ur Excavations II. The Royal Cemetery.* British Museum, London, and University Museum, Pennsylvania.

WORSAAE, J. J. (1843). *Danmarks Oldtid oplyst ved Oldsager og Gravhøie*, Copenhagen.

WOODMAN, M. (1976). *Food and Cooking in Roman Britain.* Corinium Museum, Cheltenham.

WRIGHT, J. V. (1974). *The Nodwell Site.* National Museum of Man. Mercury Series Archaeol. Survey of Canada, Paper 22. Ottawa.

WULFF, H. E., WULFF, H. S. and KOCH, L. (1968). Egyptian faience. A possible survival in Iran. *Archaeology*, **21**, 98–107.

WYNNE, E. J. and TYLECOTE, R. F. (1958). An experimental investigation with primitive iron-smelting techniques. *J. Iron Steel Inst.* **190**, 339–48.

ZEUNER, F. E. (1963). *A History of Domesticated Animals.* Hutchinson, London.

ZUROWSKI, KAZIMIERZ (1974). Zmiękczanie Poroży i Kości, Stosowane Przez Wytworców w Starozytności i we Wczesnym Średniowieczu. (Softening of antlers and bones as applied by manufacturers in antiquity and middle ages). *Acta Univers. Nicolai Copernici Archaeologia*, **4**, 3–23.

Subject Index